THE
EMBROIDERER'S HANDBOOK

INSPIRATIONS

THE EMBROIDERER'S
HANDBOOK

ISBN 0-9750920-6-5

First Printed in Australia 2004
by Inspirations

First Printed in UK 2005
by David & Charles

Reprinted by David & Charles 2005,
2006, 2007, 2008, 2009, 2010, 2011

Reprinted by Inspirations
2006 and 2017

PUBLISHER AND AUTHOR

Inspirations Studios Corporation
PO Box 10177
Adelaide Business Hub
South Australia 5000
Tel: +61 8 8293 8600

Email: info@inspirationsstudios.com
www.inspirationsstudios.com

EDITOR

Anna Scott

EDITORIAL ASSISTANTS

Marian Carpenter
Heather Moody
Susan O'Connor
Ellaine Bronsert

GRAPHIC DESIGNERS

Lynton Grandison
Jenny James

PHOTOGRAPHY

ADP

Printed and bound in China

Contents

4 Getting started
- fabrics
- threads
- needles
- transferring designs
- great beginnings, happy endings
- hoops
10 Algerian eye stitch
11 Arrowhead stitch
11 Attaching beads
11 Beads over cord
12 Back stitch
12 Beaded back stitch
13 Beaded edging
13 Beaded forget-me-not
14 Blanket stitch
- joining a new thread
- detached filling
- detached bar
- detached twisted bar
- double
- knotted
- looped
- pinwheel
- long and short
- scallops
23 Braid stitch
24 Bullions
- threads
25 Bullion knot
- long
- couched
- loop
- tapered
- bears
- rose
- rose with padded satin stitch centre
- rosebuds
- detached chain stitch combination
35 Buttonhole stitch
36 Cast-on stitch
- rose
- double-sided
39 Chain stitch
- alternating
- heavy
- interlaced
- open
- rose
- rosette
- twisted
46 Chinese knot

47 Colonial knot
48 Concertina rose
49 Coral stitch
50 Couching
- beads
- Bokhara
- puffy
- ribbon
- ribbon bow
- Roumanian
55 Cretan stitch
56 Cross stitch
- double
- long-armed
- straight stitch combination
59 Crow's foot
60 Cutwork
61 Danish knot
62 Detached back stitch
63 Detached chain
- flowers
- French knot combination flower
- twisted
65 Drizzle stitch
- flower
67 Ermine filling stitch
67 Eyelet
- flowers
- shaped
69 Faggoting
- single
71 Feather stitch
- closed
- double and triple
73 Fishbone stitch
- raised
75 Fly stitch
- twisted
- leaf
77 Folded ribbon rose
78 Folded ribbon rosebud
79 Four-legged knot stitch
79 Four sided stitch
80 French knot
80 French knot
- colonial knot berry
- ribbon flower
82 Gathered ribbon blossom
83 Gathered ribbon rose
84 Ghiordes knot
85 Glove stitch
85 Grab stitch

86 Gobelin stitch
 - straight
88 Granitos
 - blossom
 - bud
91 Hem stitch
 - antique
 - serpentine
93 Herringbone stitch
 - double
 - detached
 - shadow work
95 Holbein stitch
96 Kloster blocks
 - cutting away threads
97 Laid work
98 Lattice couching
99 Long and short stitch
100 Lacing embroidery
101 Lazy stitch
101 Loop stitch
 - bow
 - flower 1
 - flower 2
103 Moss stitch
104 Needlelace - woven bar
104 Needleweaving
 - bar
 - closed base picot
 - open base picot
 - heartsease
108 Net stitch
109 Outline stitch
109 Overlapping sequins
109 Oyster stitch
110 Palestrina stitch
111 Pekinese stitch
112 Pin stitching
113 Pistil stitching
113 Plaiting
114 Pompom
115 Raised cup stitch
116 Rhodes stitch
 - circular
117 Ribbon stitch
 - folded
 - looped
 - side
119 Rolled ribbon rose
120 Rope stitch
120 Rosette stitch
121 Roumanian stitch

122 Running stitch
 - whipped
 - double whipped
 - colonial knot combination rose
124 Satin stitch
 - bow
 - leaf
 - padded
 - padded spot
127 Scottish stitch
128 Scroll stitch
128 Seed stitch
129 Shadow work
 - double back stitch
 - closed herringbone stitch
130 Shadow trapunto
132 Sheaf filling stitch
132 Shisha stitch
134 Smocker's knot
134 Soft shading
135 Spider's web rose
136 Split back stitch
137 Split stitch
137 Star stitch
138 Stem stitch
 - encroaching
 - Portuguese knotted
 - raised
 - padded raised
 - whipped
 - ribbon rose
143 Straight overcast stitch
144 Straight stitch
 - flower
145 Tassel
145 Tent stitch
 - basket weave
 - continental
147 Tête de Boeuf stitch
147 Thread painting
148 Trellis couching
149 Twirled ribbon rose
150 Vandyke stitch
150 Wheatear stitch
 - detached
151 Whipping stitch
152 Whipped straight stitch rose
153 Wool rose
155 Woven filling stitch
156 Zigzag stitch

For alternative stitch names
see index pages 157 to 159

HINTS

13 Beading
23 Perlé cotton
28 Creating perfect bullion knots
28 Bullion knot problem solving
37 Cast-on stitch roses
38 Rayon embroidery threads
40 Colour
45 Hoops
46 Embroidering a three
 dimensional object
47 Knot stitches
48 Satin ribbon
50 Using stranded metallic thread
55 Crewel embroidery
56 Canvas work
57 Starting canvas work
58 Stitching and finishing
 canvas work
59 Scissors
60 Cutwork embroidery
62 Detached chain
64 Threading needles
65 Threading ribbon onto a needle
66 Embroidery on clothing
68 Signing your work
84 Ghiordes knots
87 Needlepoint
90 Why wool shrinks
95 Holbein stitch
96 Hardanger embroidery
97 Lacing and framing embroidery
100 Stitch direction
101 Loop stitch
103 Cleaning and pressing
105 Picots
114 Woollen threads
117 Ribbon
118 Ribbon
119 Ribbon
120 Embroidery on clothing
124 Satin stitch
131 Shadow work
135 Thread painting
138 Turning sharp corners
142 Cleaning ribbon embroidery
144 Left handed embroiderers
146 Tent stitch
149 Ribbon – beginning and
 ending off
154 Caring for wool embroidery
156 Wool embroidery

Getting Started

Fabrics

Almost any type of fabric is suitable for embroidery. Fabrics with patterns or woven textures offer background interest that can add extra dimension to your work. It is important to keep in mind that in most cases the fabric will show through the stitches.

When choosing your fabric consider it in relation to the threads you intend to use. The weight and weave of the fabric will need to be able to support the weight of the stitches. Lightweight fabrics usually combine well with finer threads. Heavier threads are more suitable for thicker fabrics.

If using a stretch fabric, you may need to apply a fusible interfacing to the wrong side of the fabric to stabilise it before beginning the embroidery.

Some embroidery techniques such as counted cross stitch, pulled thread, drawn thread and canvas work, require a certain type of fabric.

It is always a good idea to work a small sample on a spare piece of fabric to ensure the fabric, threads and stitches you are about to use will give you the result you are looking for.

Fabrics suitable for surface embroidery

CALICO

Calico is a plain, firm, unbleached cotton fabric. It is an excellent surface for embroidery and can also be used as a backing fabric. Calico can be easily dyed or painted to add extra interest, or create a background image.

COTTON

Cotton is one of the most durable of fabrics. It is available in a large range of colours and patterns. It comes in a variety of weights, from fine lawns to the heavier poplins and twills.

LINEN

Linen is elegant, strong and durable. It has a natural lustre and the creamy white and light tan fabrics are easily dyed. Linen is available in a wide variety of weights from fine handkerchief linen to heavy twill and damask.

SILK

Silk is a luxurious and sensuous fabric available in a comprehensive range of colours. It comes in a wide variety of both weights and finishes from fine transparent chiffon and organza to textured silk dupion, heavy twill and brocade.

FURNISHING FABRIC

Furnishing fabrics offer some wonderful choices of plain colours or self-patterns, such as damask. You can sometimes obtain small pieces that are suitable for embroidery from upholsterers. Sample books are another excellent source of small pieces of fabric.

FELT

Felt is a non-woven fabric that will not fray when cut. Traditionally made from wool, today many felts are made from synthetic fibres.

WOOL

Woollen fabrics come in a large variety of weights and finishes, from fine flannel, ideal for baby wraps, to thick and cosy blanketing.

Backing fabric and interfacing

Some lightweight fabrics may require a backing fabric or interfacing to stabilise and give extra body. Ensure the grain of the backing fabric is aligned with that of your fabric.

top bright cotton prints appliquéd onto cashmere velour blanketing **above** natural coloured linen embroidered with stranded cotton **below** damask forms a rich background for embroidery **bottom** needlepoint on mono canvas

Fabrics suitable for counted thread embroidery

Counted thread embroidery is worked on evenweave fabrics or canvas. The count of these fabrics is the number of threads per square inch (2.5cm) and this determines the size of the stitches as well as the size of the finished embroidery. The higher the count, the finer the canvas.

EVENWEAVE LINEN AND COTTON

These are single-thread fabrics available in a large variety of colours and counts. Most stitches are worked over more than one pair of fabric threads, so as not to distort the fabric.

AIDA CLOTH

The threads in Aida cloth are woven in distinctive blocks making the holes very easy to see. The fabric is very popular for cross stitch but is less suitable for designs with half stitches. The count of the fabric refers to the number of blocks.

CANVAS

Canvas is a very firm fabric that can support dense stitching.

Today canvas comes in two basic types - mono or single evenweave canvas and double or Penelope canvas. All canvas is available in different counts.

Preparing the fabric for embroidery

Pre-wash fabrics according to the specified care instructions to test for shrinkage and colourfastness.

To prevent the raw edges from fraying while stitching, neaten all edges with a machine zigzag or overlock stitch.

Avoid using tape to seal the edges as the glue may permanently discolour the fabric and will attract dirt.

Ensure you allow enough fabric around the design for the intended purpose of the finished piece.

Threads

Some threads are more easily handled than others and it is possible to use the very finest of threads right through to lightweight string.

All threads can be adversely affected by direct light, especially sunlight. The colour can fade quickly so store your threads in light resistant containers.

The dyes in some threads can be very unstable, so they are an unsuitable choice for items that will require laundering. Bright and dark coloured threads and overdyed threads are the most likely to cause problems. To ensure the threads you wish to use are colourfast, work a few stitches on a scrap of your selected fabric and launder this in the same way that you intend to launder the finished project.

STRANDED COTTON

These low sheen threads come in an amazing variety of colours and are easy to work with. You can vary the thickness by altering the number of strands used - fewer strands create finer stitches.

When using more than one strand at a time, it is important to separate the strands and then put them back together. This is known as 'stripping' the thread.

Use short lengths of thread, as long threads eventually become tired and worn as the fabric abrades them.

If the thread untwists or overtwists, let the needle hang freely. The thread will spin back to the correct amount of twist.

top crewel wool on linen twill **above** ribbon embroidery on ivory taffeta **below** stranded silk embroidery **bottom** purple daisies worked in rayon threads

PERLÉ COTTON

This thread is generally available in four different weights or thicknesses, the larger the number, the finer the thread. For hints on perlé cotton see page 23.

SILK THREAD

A wide range of silk threads from flat, untwisted filament silks to stranded threads and heavy button-hole threads are available.

Many silk threads are not washable because of their inability to hold dyed colour. You therefore need to decide whether silk is an appropriate thread for your project. If the silk is not labelled 'colourfast' wash the thread first to test.

Silk is an incredibly strong fibre and unlike cotton does not wear easily and break suddenly.

Silk embroidery is enhanced by being ironed lightly on the back. Steam increases the thread sheen.

WOOL

Fine crewel wool is easy to work with and is available in many colours. For heavier stitches, tapestry wool can be used. To avoid the yarn becoming worn, use short lengths. For hints on wool see page 114.

RAYON THREAD

Rayon threads have a spectacular sheen, favoured by many embroiderers. However, they have a mind of their own and can be difficult to use.

Dampening the thread can make it more manageable. Moisten your fingertips and slowly pull the thread between them. Place the thread in the freezer for a few hours. This reduces static electricity.

Use short lengths of thread to minimise twisting and tangling.

METALLIC THREAD

Metallic thread can be difficult to work with and often wears easily. Use short lengths of thread to make it more manageable.

The section of thread in the eye of the needle wears quickly. Adjust the thread frequently or tie the tail of thread to the eye of the needle.

VARIEGATED THREADS

Undo the skein of thread and lay it out so you can clearly see the range of colours. Lay sections of the same colour side by side. To obtain the exact colour you want to use, cut selected sections from the thread.

Create your own 'variegated' thread by blending strands from different skeins and threading them into your needle together.

EMBROIDERY RIBBON

Ribbons are available in widths ranging from 2mm (⅛") through to 50mm (2"). When working on large scale designs, it is best to use the wider ribbons. Combinations of different widths and textures in ribbons can be most effective, so choose the ribbons for the particular effect you wish to achieve and buy the best quality you can afford.

Needles

Needles come in a variety of types and sizes. The size of a needle is given as a number. The higher the number, the finer the needle. Ideally, the shaft of the needle should be of a similar thickness to the thread being used. The thread should fill the hole left by the needle when it passes through the fabric.

For hints on threading needles see pages 64 and 65.

No.24 Chenille
No.18 Chenille
No.7 Crewel
No.3 Crewel
No.12 Sharp
No.8 Sharp
No.9 Milliner's (Straw)
No.5 Milliner's (Straw)
No.24 Tapestry
No.18 Tapestry

Never leave a needle in your work as it may rust and leave a mark on the fabric.

If you prick your finger and get blood on the fabric, chew a piece of sewing thread and use this to dab off the blood. Your saliva removes your own blood stains.

Transferring Designs

There are many ways to transfer a design. The method depends on the type of fabric or the particular embroidery technique to be used.

IRON-ON TRANSFERS

Transfers leave permanent marks that must be covered by embroidery. They are suitable for fabrics with smooth surfaces, such as cotton, polycotton and doctor's flannel.

Cover a smooth flat object (eg. a wooden board) with aluminium foil, shiny side up. Place the fabric over the board, right side up.

Needle Chart

NEEDLE	SIZE	SUITABLE FOR
Chenille A thick needle with a large eye. Similar to a tapestry needle but with a sharp tip. This needle was originally used for tufted chenille yarns.	18–24	Suitable for thick threads such as tapestry wool, crewel wool, six strands of stranded cotton, no. 3 and no. 5 perlé cotton, thick silk and heavy metallic thread. Ideal for ribbon embroidery and wool embroidery.
Crewel (Embroidery) A finer needle with a large, long eye. The large eye makes the needle easy to thread. Sizes 7-9 are ideal for smocking.	9–10	Suitable for fine embroidery using one or two strands of cotton, silk or rayon.
	3–8	Excellent general purpose needles. Use with three to six strands of stranded cotton, silk or rayon and coton á broder, fine wool thread, no. 8 and no. 12 perlé cotton and fine metallic thread.
Sharp A good general purpose needle. The small, round eye provides strength for the needle and prevents excess wear on the thread.	10–12	Suitable for fine embroidery including bullion knots. Use with one or two strands of stranded cotton, silk or rayon. The no. 12 is sometimes known as a hand appliqué needle.
	7–9	Use with two or three strands of stranded cotton, silk or rayon. Also suitable for bullion knots.
Milliner's (Straw) These are fabulous for bullions. A straw needle has a tiny eye and a long, fine shaft. Because the eye is no wider than the shaft, they are invaluable for beading and for pulling through the wraps when stitching bullion knots. Traditionally used for work on bonnets and hats.	9–11	Use with one or two strands of stranded cotton, silk or rayon.
	5–8	Use with three or four strands of stranded cotton, silk or rayon.
	1–4	Use with four to six strands of stranded cotton, silk or rayon, no. 8 and no. 12 perlé cotton, coton á broder and metallic threads. Also suitable for Brazilian embroidery using thick, twisted threads.
Tapestry A medium length needle with a thick shaft, a blunt tip and a long eye. The blunt tip parts the fabric threads rather than splitting them.	26–28	Suitable for decorative hem stitching on fine linens, fine counted cross stitch and petit point.
	18–24	Suitable for counted thread embroidery such as cross stitch, blackwork, pulled and drawn thread work and Hardanger. Also suitable for wool embroidery, needleweaving and shadow work.

Pin the transfer face down onto the fabric ensuring it is correctly positioned. Press firmly with a medium to hot iron, taking care not to move the transfer. Carefully lift a corner to check the design has been transferred. If not, continue pressing. Care must be taken not to scorch the fabric.

FABRIC MARKING PENS

Marking pens are non-permanent and are suitable for fabric with a smooth surface. They are not suit-able for framed pieces as the ink may reappear. The lines made with spirit based markers fade and disappear quickly. Lines made with water-soluble markers are removed using cold water before applying heat. Read the manufacturer's instructions carefully.

TRANSFER PENCILS

Heat-sensitive pencils leave per-manent lines which need to be completely covered. Draw or trace a mirror image of the design onto tracing paper. Iron the design onto the fabric in the same manner as an iron-on transfer.

Chalk based fabric pencils brush or wash off. They are excellent for dark fabrics. Trace or draw the design onto the right side of the fabric. As the chalk tends to brush off quickly as you work, tack over the design lines.

TULLE

This is particularly suitable for heavy-weight coarse fabrics, such as wool blanketing. Avoid using this method for designs that are very intricate. Trace the design onto the tulle with a black permanent marker. Allow to dry thoroughly. Pin the tracing to the right side of the fabric and trace the design with a suitable fabric marker.

DIRECT TRACING

Direct tracing is suitable for fabrics that are light in colour. Using a black pen, trace the design onto tracing paper. Tape the tracing to a lightbox or window. With the right side facing up, centre the fabric over the tracing and tape it in place. The light shining through will make the design visible through the fabric. Using a pencil or fabric marker, carefully trace the design onto the fabric.

TEMPLATES

This method is useful for trans-ferring simple shapes that are to be repeated several times. First draw or trace the shape onto tracing paper and cut out. Pin the shape to the fabric. Using small stitches and contrasting sewing thread, tack around the shape close to the edge. Remove the paper. Alternatively, the shape can be cut out in thin card or plastic. Draw around the shape using a chalk pencil or a sharp lead pencil.

TACKING

Tacking is time consuming but gives the most satisfactory result as it leaves no permanent marks. Designs can be altered as the work progresses. This method is excellent for wool blanketing or other fabrics with a rough surface.

Using a fine tipped pen, trace the design onto tissue paper. Pin the tracing onto the right side of the fabric. With contrasting sewing thread, tack along the design lines with small, even running stitches. Lightly moisten the tissue paper with a damp sponge, wait a few seconds, then carefully remove the paper. Remove the tacking as you work the design.

DRESSMAKER'S CARBON

Carbon paper comes in several colours and is suitable for fabrics with a smooth surface. The chosen colour will need to show on the background fabric and blend with the embroidery as the lines may be permanent.

Place the carbon onto the fabric,

coloured side down. Place the design over the carbon. Hold in place with tape. Draw the design lines using a sharp lead pencil or empty biro.

Great Beginnings, Happy Endings

It is important to secure the thread so that your embroidery stitches don't come undone. This needs to be done when starting a thread and finishing it off. Try to avoid unsightly lumps and large knots on the back of your work.

Extra care should be taken with embroideries that require frequent washing, as this can loosen threads. Avoid carrying your thread for long distances on the back of the work, as this may show through on the front, especially if the thread colour is dark. It is better to end off and start again.

Choose your method of beginning and ending according to the type of embroidery you are working.

BACK STITCHING

This method is suitable for most emb-roidery. Before beginning to stitch, bring the thread to the front in an area to be covered with embroidery. Anchor the thread with two tiny back stitches. Split the first stitch with the second to make the thread very secure. Give it a good tug to test. Work several stitches, then trim away any excess thread on the back.

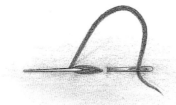

Work two tiny back stitches on the wrong side of the fabric in the same manner to end off.

WASTE KNOT

Using a waste knot involves leaving the knot on the surface, a short distance from the start of the embroidery. This method is particularly suited to techniques where there is nowhere to conceal the starting point. These include shadow work, canvas work and petit point. This method can be used with or without a hoop.

Knot the end of the thread. Position the knot on the front approximately 5cm (2") away from where the first stitch will be placed. Bring the thread to the front at the start of the embroidery and begin stitching. To end off the waste knot, separate it from the fabric surface and cut it off. On the wrong side, re-thread the tail into the needle and secure by weaving it under the stitching, and cut off any excess thread.

WEAVING

Weaving or taking a tail of thread under the stitching on the back of the work is only suitable for framed embroideries or pieces that do not need washing. Weaving should be used in combination with back stitches to make the tail secure enough for repeated handling.

Leave a 10cm (4") tail of thread hanging on the back of the fabric. After working a small part of the embroidery, re-thread the tail and take two tiny back stitches through the stitching on the back as before.

Trim away any excess thread. Working threads can be ended off in the same manner.

KNOTS

These can be used where you have a textured surface, as the small lump caused by the knot won't be noticeable. A knot combined with back stitches is very secure - great for embroidered clothing, table linen or anything that needs to be washed.

For hints on beginning and ending ribbon see page 149.

Hoops

Whether to use a hoop or not is very much a personal choice, however the best results are often achieved when the background fabric is held under tension.

Some stitches can be either 'sewn' or 'stabbed' (eg satin stitch). Always stab the needle through the fabric when working in a hoop as skimming the needle may distort the grain.

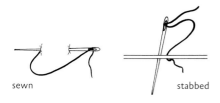

sewn   stabbed

Choose a hoop large enough to encompass the entire design to avoid flattening finished sections of the embroidery. Free standing hoops are also useful as both hands are free to manipulate the threads.

If choosing to use a slate frame or stretcher bars, ensure it is large enough to cover the entire area of the design.

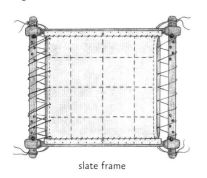

slate frame

See page 45 for hints on hoops.

PLACING FABRIC IN A HOOP

To place a piece of fabric in a hoop, adjust the tensioning screw so that the two rings just slip apart. Place the inner ring onto a flat surface, then position the fabric over the ring. Keep the grain of the fabric straight, press down the outer hoop and tighten the screw.

If you need to tighten the fabric further, make sure that you only pull with the straight of the grain. If you pull the fabric on the bias it will stretch and become distorted.

Pieces of fabric that are too small to fit in a hoop can be enlarged by adding a calico border.

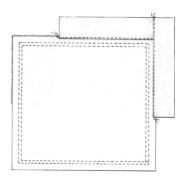

Binding a Hoop

Binding helps to prevent the fabric from slipping while you are stitching and also enables you to achieve a firmer tension on the mounted fabric. It is necessary to bind only the inner ring. The most suitable materials for this task are woven cotton tape, bias binding ironed flat or strips of plain fabric cut on the bias.

1 Separate the two pieces of the hoop.

2 Hold the end of the binding and wrap it around the inner ring of the hoop.

3 Secure the binding with small back stitches at the edge of the binding.

4 Wrap the binding around the hoop, ensuring there are no creases and the layers of binding overlap.

5 When reaching the starting point, cut off the excess binding and secure the end with small back stitches.

6 Fabric mounted in the hoop.

Algerian Eye Stitch

Also known as star eyelet stitch, Algerian eye is a counted thread stitch often used in canvas work. It consists of eight straight stitches which form a star shape.

1 Bring the thread to the front at A, two fabric threads above the centre hole. Take it to the back through the centre.

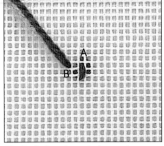

2 Pull the thread through tightly to open up the centre hole. Count two fabric threads to the left of A. Bring the thread to the front in the next hole (B).

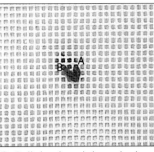

3 Pull the thread through, then take it through the centre hole to form a diagonal stitch.

4 Count two fabric threads to the left of the centre hole. Re-emerge in the next hole (C). Take the thread to the back through the centre hole and pull through.

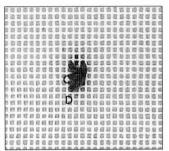

5 Count down two fabric threads from C. Bring the thread to the front in the next hole (D) and take it to the back through the centre. Pull the thread through.

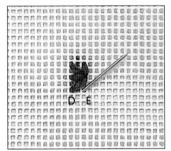

6 Count two fabric threads to the right of D. Bring the thread to the front through the next hole (E). This is directly below the centre hole.

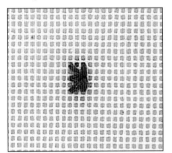

7 Pull the thread through. Take it to the back through the centre hole and pull through.

8 Count two fabric threads to the right of E and bring the thread to the front through the next hole (F). Take it to the back through the centre hole and pull through.

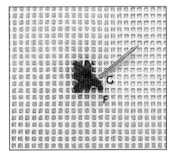

9 Count two fabric threads to the right of the centre and bring the thread to the front in the next hole (G). This is directly above F.

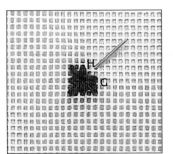

10 Take the thread to the back through the centre hole and pull through. Count two fabric threads above G and bring the thread to the front in the next hole (H).

11 Pull the thread through. Take the needle to the back through the centre hole.

12 Pull the thread through and end off on the back of the fabric. **Completed Algerian eye stitch.**

Arrowhead Stitch

Arrowhead stitch is often worked as a filling stitch in counted thread and surface embroidery. The arrowhead is made by using two straight stitches at right angles to each other. Here it is worked in a vertical line.

Mark three lines on the fabric to help position the stitches accurately.

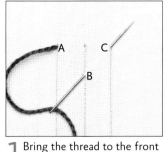

1 Bring the thread to the front at A. Insert the needle at B, below and to the right of A. Re-emerge at C.

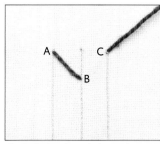

2 Pull the thread through to form the first half of the arrow-head stitch.

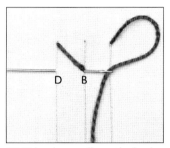

3 Take the needle to the back at B and re-emerge at D.

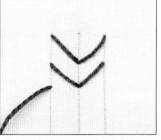

4 Pull the thread through to complete the first arrowhead stitch. The thread is in position to start the second stitch.

5 Work the second stitch in exactly the same manner, keeping the stitches even in length and at right angles to each other.

6 Continue working stitches. To end off, take the thread to the back at the tip. Secure the thread on the back. **Completed arrowhead stitches.**

Attaching Beads Beads can be attached singly, in rows, as a string or in combinations of beads.

ATTACHING WITH A SECOND BEAD

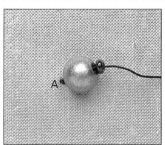

1 Bring the needle up at A. Thread a large bead. Thread a smaller bead and slide it down onto the first bead.

2 Take the needle back through the first bead, then to the back of the work close to A. Secure with a back stitch.

INDIVIDUALLY SEWN BEAD

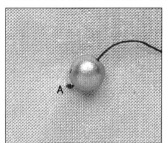

1 Bring the needle up at A. Place the bead onto the needle. Slide the bead down the thread and settle it in place.

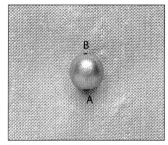

2 Leaving a space the same size as the bead, take the needle to the back at B and secure with a back stitch.

Beads Over Cord Attaching rows of beads over a cord adds dimension to bead embroidery.

1 Lay the cord onto the fabric and couch in place.

2 Bring the thread to the front at A, just beside the edge of the cord. Thread beads and lay diagonally over the cord.

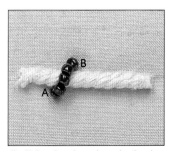

3 Take the thread to the back at B and settle the beads into place.

4 Secure on the back with a back stitch. Continue attaching beads in repeating rows over the cord.

Back Stitch

Back stitch can be worked by either skimming the needle through the fabric while holding it freely in your hand as shown here, or by stabbing the needle up and down with the fabric held taut in a hoop or frame.

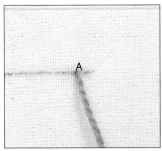

1 Mark a line on the fabric. Bring the thread to the front at A, a short distance from the right hand end of the marked line.

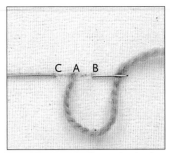

2 Take the needle to the back at B, at the beginning of the marked line. Re-emerge at C. The distance from A to C should be the same as the distance from A to B.

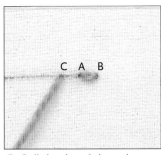

3 Pull the thread through.

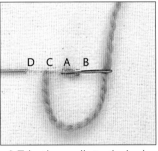

4 Take the needle to the back at A, through the same hole in the fabric. Re-emerge at D. The distance from C to D is the same as from A to C.

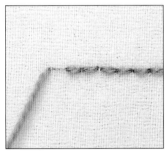

5 Continue working stitches in the same manner, keeping them all the same length.

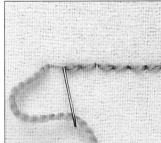

6 To finish, take the needle to the back of the fabric through the hole at the beginning of the previous stitch. Pull the thread through and end off.

Beaded Back Stitch

Beaded back stitch is used to cover smooth curves and long lines.

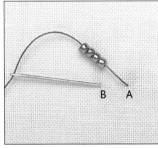

1 Bring the needle to the front at A. Thread four beads onto the needle and insert it at B.

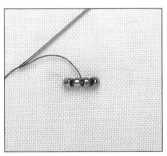

2 Bring the needle to the front between the second and third bead.

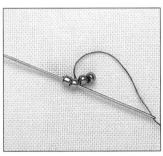

3 Take the needle through beads 3 and 4.

4 Thread two beads onto the needle and insert it at C.

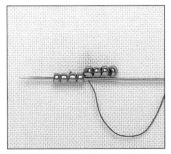

5 Repeat steps 2–4 until the row is complete.

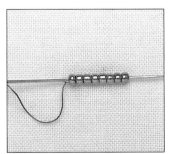

6 Bring the needle to the front at the end of the row. Thread back through the entire row. Take the needle to the back and secure.

Beaded Edging

This is an attractive edging for bags, needlecases and other small items.

Hold the work so the front is facing you and work from left to right.

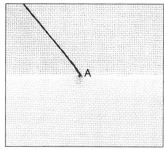

1 Bring the thread to the front at A and take a small stitch to secure the thread.

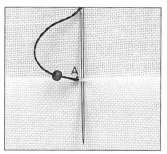

2 **First bead.** Slide one bead onto the needle. Insert the needle one bead length from A. Emerge 1mm (¹⁄₁₆") in from the edge.

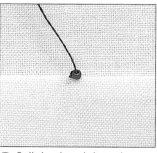

3 Pull the thread through. Insert the needle through the bead. Standing the bead on its side, pull through firmly.

4 **Second bead.** Thread the bead onto the needle. Insert the needle one bead length from the first bead. Emerge 1mm (¹⁄₁₆") down from the edge.

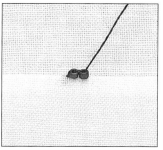

5 Pull the thread through. Insert the needle through the bead, pull through firmly. The second bead just touches the first.

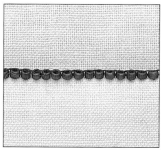

6 Continue in the same manner. Finish the last bead and secure on the back. **Completed beaded edging.**

HINTS

BEADING

Suitable threads to use are Nymo, which is a specialty beading thread and Drima or Gütermann, which are fine, strong synthetic sewing threads.

If using sewing thread, passing the thread through a block of beeswax adds strength and makes the thread more manageable. It also protects it from moisture over time.

Beads are best stored away from the light in glass bottles or jars, plastic tubes or pill bottles.

Use an even tension. If the stitching is too tight the fabric will pucker. If too loose, the beads will droop and the stitches will show.

If using a hoop or frame, assemble it upside down, as the rim provides an edge that can stop beads falling off the work.

Beaded Forget-me-not

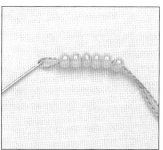

1 Using a 30cm (12") length of beading thread and a milliner's needle, thread on six beads.

2 Pass the needle and thread through the first three beads to form a circle.

3 Thread on a contrasting bead. Take the needle and thread through the sixth bead of the circle.

4 Pull firmly so the centre bead sits in the middle, slightly higher than the circle of beads.

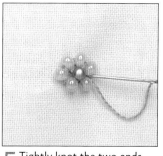

5 Tightly knot the two ends of thread. Finish off one tail and use the remaining tail to couch the circlet of beads to the fabric. **Completed forget-me-not.**

Blanket Stitch

Traditionally used for edging blankets and rugs, blanket stitch can be worked as a surface embroidery stitch as well as an edging stitch.

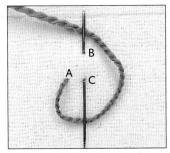

1 Bring the thread to the front at A. Take the needle to the back at B and re-emerge at C. Ensure the thread is under the needle tip.

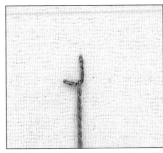

2 Pull the thread through until it lies snugly against the emerging thread but does not distort the fabric.

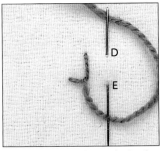

3 Take the needle to the back at D and re-emerge at E. Ensure the thread lies under the tip of the needle.

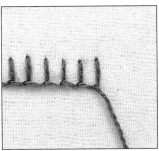

4 Pull the thread through as before. Continue working stitches in the same manner.

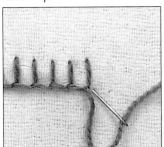

5 To finish, take the needle to the back of the fabric just over the last loop.

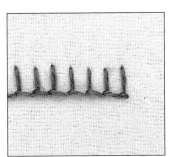

6 Pull the thread through to form a small straight stitch. Secure the thread on the back.

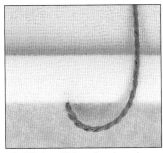

1 **Edging.** Bring the thread through the fold at A.

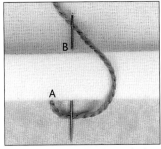

2 Take the needle through the fabric at B. Push it through until the tip appears beyond the fabric edge. Ensure the thread lies under the tip of the needle.

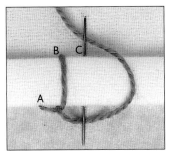

3 Pull the thread through. Take the needle through the fabric at C. Push through as before. Ensure the thread lies under the tip of the needle.

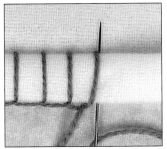

4 Pull the thread through. Continue working stitches as before. After the last stitch, take the needle over the loop and through the fold. Pull through and end off.

Blanket Stitch – Joining a new thread

Invisibly joining in a new thread can be readily achieved.

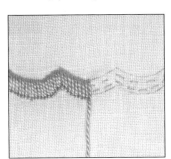

1 When ending off the old thread, unthread the needle and leave the old thread dangling on the front of the work.

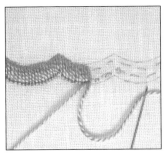

2 Bring the needle and new thread up just inside the last stitch and work the next stitch, keeping the old thread out of the way.

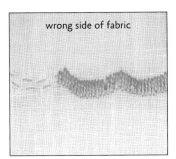

wrong side of fabric

3 Pull the old thread through to the back of the work and weave it through the previous stitches. Trim any excess thread.

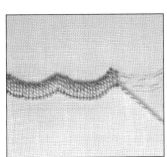

4 Continue working the blanket stitching with the new thread.

Blanket Stitch – Detached Filling

Detached blanket stitch is often used for raised embroidery and can also be used to cover the heads of tassels.

Only the first row of stitches is worked into the fabric. Take the needle through the fabric only at the beginning and end of all subsequent rows.

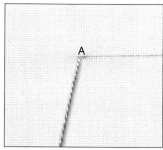

1 **First row.** Bring the thread to the front at A, on the left hand side of the first row.

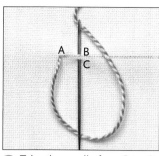

2 Take the needle from B to C, a short distance away to the right. Ensure the thread lies under the needle tip.

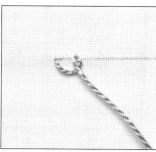

3 Gently pull the thread through until a tiny loop is formed. Do not pull the stitch tight.

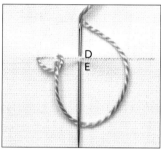

4 Take the needle from D to E, a short distance away to the right. Ensure the thread is under the tip of the needle.

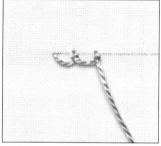

5 Keeping the tension even, pull the thread through as before to form the second stitch.

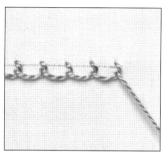

6 Continue working evenly spaced stitches in the same manner to the end of the row.

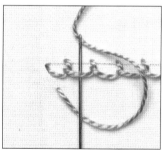

7 **Second row.** Take the needle from top to bottom under the second horizontal thread in the first row. Do not go through the fabric.

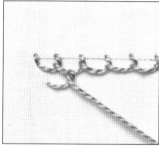

8 Ensure the thread is under the tip of the needle. Gently pull the thread through until it rests against the horizontal thread.

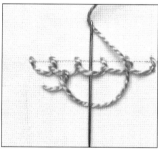

9 Place the needle under the next horizontal thread in the same manner as before. Gently pull the thread through. Continue to the end of the row.

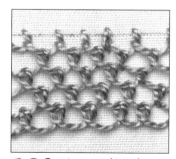

10 Continue working the required number of rows catching fabric only at the beginning and end of rows. **Completed detached blanket stitch filling.**

Detached blanket stitch filling worked over padding for the thistle base.

Blanket Stitch – Detached Bar

This variation of blanket stitch is useful for creating loops and for adding texture to dimensional embroidery. It is worked from left to right on a foundation of straight stitches. The blanket stitches do not go through the fabric.

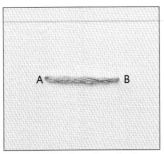

1 Bring the thread to the front at A. Take the needle to the back the required distance away (B). Pull the thread through, forming a straight stitch.

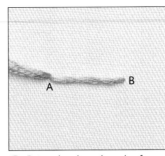

2 Bring the thread to the front in exactly the same position, or as close as possible to A.

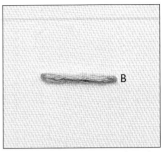

3 Pull the thread through and take it to the back in the same position as the first stitch (B). **Completed foundation.**

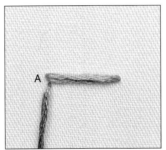

4 **Detached blanket stitch.** Bring the needle to the front, just below A. Pull the thread through.

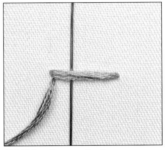

5 Take the needle from top to bottom behind the straight stitches. Do not pierce the fabric.

6 Position the thread under the tip of the needle and begin to pull the thread through.

7 Continue pulling the thread through, pulling it towards you until the stitch wraps snugly around the foundation. **Completed first stitch.**

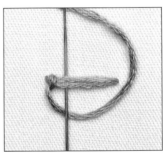

8 Again, take the needle from top to bottom behind the straight stitches without piercing the fabric. Ensure the thread is under the tip of the needle.

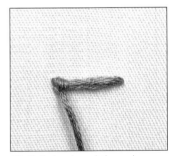

9 Pull the thread through ensuring the stitch lies snugly against the first stitch but does not overlap it. **Completed second stitch.**

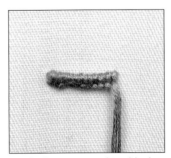

10 Continue working blanket stitches in the same manner until the straight stitches are com-pletely covered.

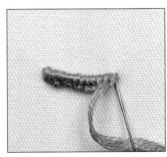

11 Take the needle to the back of the fabric just below the end of the straight stitches.

12 Pull the thread through and end off on the back of the fabric. **Completed detached blanket stitch bar.**

Blanket Stitch– Detached Twisted Bar

This stitch can be used for raised effects in embroidery. It is stitched in a similar manner to a detached blanket stitch bar.

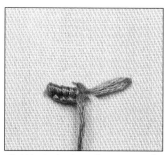

1 Work the foundation straight stitches and detached blanket stitches following the instructions on page 16. Stop halfway along the foundation.

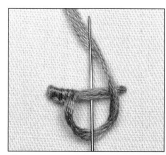

2 **First twisted stitch.** Take the needle from the top to the bottom behind the foundation, ensuring it does not pierce the fabric. The thread is under the needle tip.

3 Start to pull the thread towards you until the loop begins to close around the foundation.

4 Take the thread up and away from you.

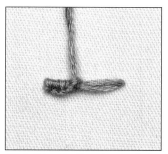

5 Pull in this direction until the stitch wraps snugly around the foundation. The loop will sit higher than the previous stitches.

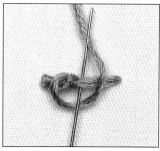

6 **Second twisted stitch.** Pull the end of the thread towards you and place the needle under the foundation in the same manner as before.

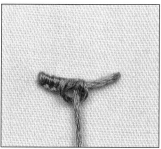

7 Ensuring the thread is under the tip of the needle begin pulling it towards you.

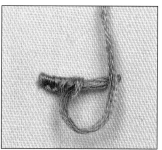

8 When the loop begins to close around the foundation, take the thread up and away from you as before.

9 Continue pulling up and away from you until the stitch sits snugly around the foundation next to the first twisted stitch.

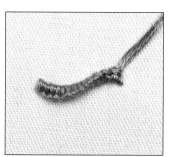

10 Continue working stitches following steps 6–9, until the foundation has been completely covered.

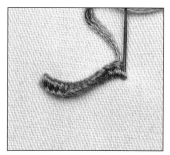

11 Take the needle to the back of the fabric next to the last loop formed.

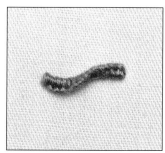

12 Pull the thread through and end off on the back of the fabric. **Completed twisted detached blanket stitch bar.**

Blanket Stitch – Double

This variation of blanket stitch can be worked in one or more thread colours and in curved or straight lines to create distinctive borders. It can also be worked as a filling stitch, adding colour or texture to a shape.

After a row of blanket stitches is worked, the fabric is turned 180 degrees. A second row is then stitched, with the vertical sections of the stitches being placed between those of the first row. Both rows should be of the same height and overlap at the centre. Drawing two parallel lines will help keep the stitches even.

The arrow indicates the top of the fabric.

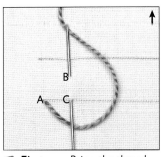

1 **First row.** Bring the thread to the front at A. Take the needle from B to C, ensuring the thread lies under the tip of the needle.

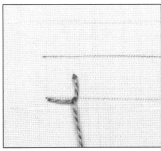

2 Pull the thread towards you until the loop rests gently on the emerging thread.

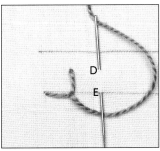

3 Take the needle from D to E. This is the same height as the previous stitch and parallel to it. Ensure the thread is under the tip of the needle.

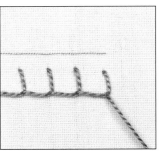

4 Pull the thread through as before. Continue to the end of the row in the same manner.

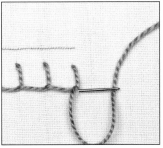

5 To end off, take the thread to the back just over the last loop.

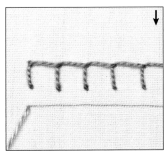

6 **Second row.** Turn the fabric 180 degrees. Bring the thread to the front directly below the end of the stitch in the previous row.

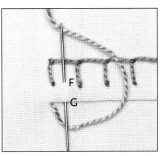

7 Take the needle from F to G in between the vertical stitches of the first row. Ensure the thread is under the tip of the needle.

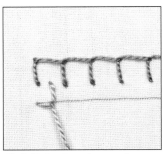

8 Pull the thread towards you until the loop rests gently on the emerging thread.

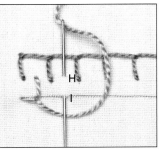

9 Take the needle from H to I between the second and third vertical stitches of the first row.

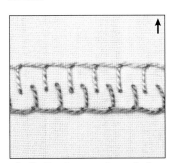

10 Continue to the end of the row, ensuring the stitches are evenly spaced. End off as before. **Completed double blanket stitch.**

Blanket Stitch – Knotted

In this variation of blanket stitch, a knot is worked at the tip of each vertical stitch, adding texture to the stitches. Some practice is required to keep the knots even and the same size.

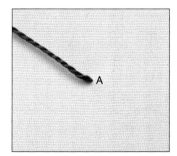

1 **First stitch.** Bring the thread to the front at A, on the lower left hand side of the area to be worked.

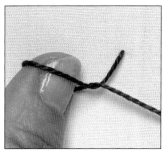

2 Wrap the thread once around your left thumb in a clockwise direction.

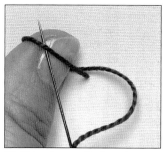

3 Take the needle from bottom to top under the loop.

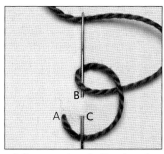

4 Remove thumb. Keeping the loop on the needle, take the needle from B to C. Ensure the emerging thread is under the needle tip.

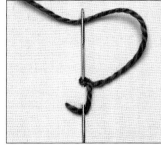

5 Pull the thread firmly so the emerging thread is taut and the loop tightens around the needle.

6 Keeping your left thumb over the loop (thumb not shown), pull the needle and thread through.

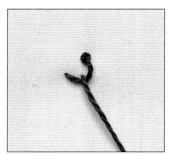

7 **Completed first stitch.**

8 **Second stitch.** Wrap the thread around your left thumb as for step 2.

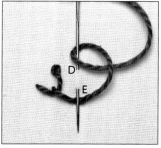

9 Slip the needle from bottom to top through the loop. Keeping the loop on the needle, take the needle to the back at D and re-emerge at E.

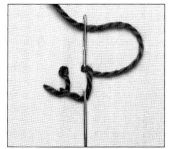

10 Tighten the thread, ensuring the emerging thread is under the tip of the needle.

11 Pull the thread through. **Completed second stitch.**

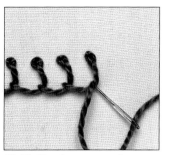

12 Continue across the row. To anchor the last stitch, take the needle to the back over the last loop.

13 Pull the thread through and end off. **Completed row of knotted blanket stitch.**

Blanket Stitch – Looped

Looped blanket stitch can be worked in a circle to form a blanket stitch rose. Loops need to be kept even and consistent in size. We used two different colours of thread for photographic purposes only.

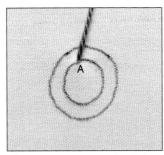

1 Draw two concentric circles on the fabric. Bring the needle to the front at A on the inner circle.

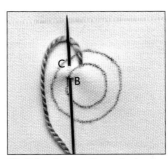

2 Take the needle to the back at B and re-emerge at C. Ensure the thread is under the tip of the needle.

3 Gently pull the thread through, leaving enough thread to make a loop that just touches the outer circle.

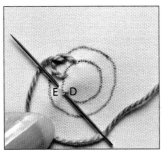

4 Hold the thread to the left with the thumb. Take the needle to the back at D and re-emerge at E. Make a second loop the same size as the first.

5 Continue working around the circle. Make the stitches as close as possible and keep the loops even in size. Turn the work as necessary.

6 To complete the circle, take the needle to the back behind the first loop.

7 **Completed first circle.**

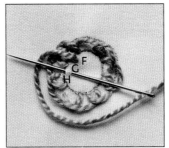

8 Bring the needle to the front at F, just inside the previous circle of stitches. Take the needle to the back at G and re-emerge at H.

9 Continue working a second circle inside the first circle of loops in the same manner.

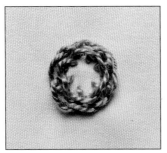

10 **Completed second circle.**

11 Work a third circle inside the second circle of loops in the same manner. **Completed third circle.**

12 Continue working smaller and smaller circles until the fabric is covered. Place a French knot in the centre. **Completed looped blanket stitch rose.**

Blanket Stitch – Pinwheel

Blanket stitch pinwheels and partial pinwheels are an effective way to create flowers.

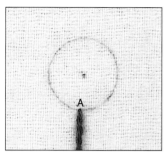

1 Draw a circle and mark the centre. Bring the thread to the front at A.

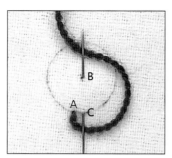

2 Take the needle to the back at B. Re-emerge at C on the edge of the circle. Ensure the thread is under the needle tip.

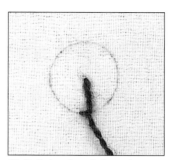

3 Pull the thread through until it lies snugly against the emerging thread but does not distort the fabric.

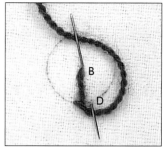

4 Take the needle from B to D. Ensure the thread is under the tip of the needle.

5 Complete the stitch as before.

6 Continue working stitches around the circle in the same manner, turning the fabric as you go.

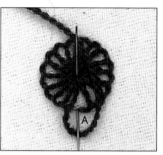

7 For the last stitch, take the needle from the centre to A. Ensure the thread is under the tip of the needle.

8 Pull the thread through as before. Take the needle to the back just over the loop.

9 Pull the thread through to form a small straight stitch. End off on the back of the fabric. **Completed pinwheel.**

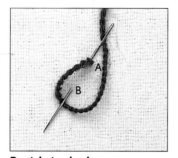

Partial pinwheel
1 Bring the thread to the front at A. Take the needle from A to B. Loop the thread under the tip of the needle.

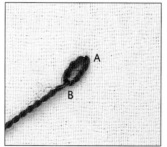

2 Pull the thread through until it lies snugly against the emerging thread but does not distort the fabric.

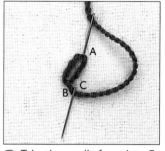

3 Take the needle from A to C. Ensure the thread is under the tip of the needle.

4 Pull the thread through as before.

5 Continue working stitches in the same manner, beginning each one at A and fanning them at the outer edge.

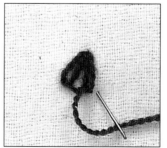

6 To finish, take the needle to the back of the fabric just over the last loop.

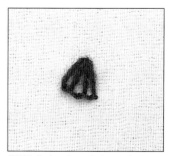

7 Pull the thread through to form a small straight stitch. End off on the back of the fabric. **Completed partial pinwheel.**

Blanket Stitch—Long and Short

This variation of blanket stitch is worked in a similar manner to blanket stitch, except the length of the stitches varies. This stitch can be incorporated as an edging stitch when working long and short stitch.

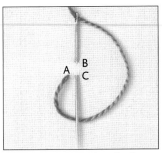

1 Bring the thread to the front at A. Take the needle from B to C ensuring the thread is under the tip of the needle.

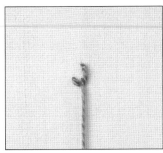

2 Pull the thread through until the loop rests gently against the emerging thread.

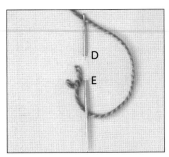

3 Take the needle from D to E, ensuring the thread is under the tip of the needle. This stitch is longer than the previous stitch.

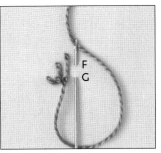

4 Pull the thread through as before. Take the needle from F to G. This stitch is shorter than the previous stitch.

5 Ensure the thread is under the tip of needle and pull through. Continue working stitches in the same manner, alternating the lengths.

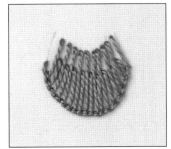

6 To fill petals, angle the stitches towards the centre of the flower. **Completed long and short blanket stitch.**

Blanket Stitch—Scallops

Blanket stitch is a versatile stitch used in many types of embroidery. Here it not only forms a decorative finish, but also neatens the raw edge of the fabric to prevent fraying. Work the stitches close together so no background fabric shows through. Mark double lines onto the right side of the fabric for the scallops. Use these lines as a guide for the length of the stitches but not for the direction in which the stitches lie.

If working on fine fabrics, tack fabric stabiliser behind the scallops for stability.

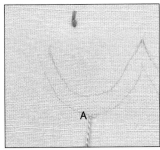

1 Using a waste knot, bring the thread to the front at A on the outside line of the deepest point of one scallop.

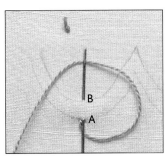

2 Take the needle from B to A, keeping the stitch at a right angle to the outer line.

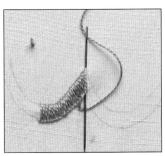

3 Continue stitching in the same manner. Ensure that only one stitch sits at the very peak of each scallop and remains at a right angle to the outer line.

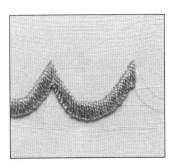

4 Finish off by taking the thread to the back just over the last loop. Cut off the waste knot and secure the tail under the threads on the back.

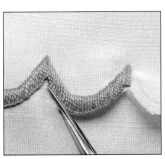

5 **Cutting scallops.** Cut away the excess fabric along the outer edge of the scallops. Take care not to cut the stitching.

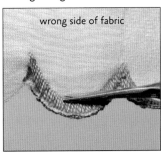

wrong side of fabric

6 After cutting the scallops, carefully trim away the excess stabiliser along the inner edge of the scallops. **Completed scallops.**

Braid Stitch

Braid stitch is worked from right to left and gives a textured border with a braided appearance. This stitch is suitable for curves or straight lines. Marking parallel lines will help to keep your stitches even.

To achieve a textured look, twisted threads such as perlé cottons should be used, rather than stranded cottons. The stitches are best worked small and close together.

Our stitches are spaced out for photographic purposes only.

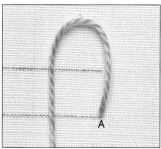

1 Bring the thread to the front at A on the lower line. Loop the thread to the left of A.

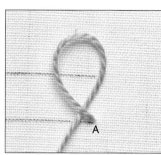

2 Fold the loop over so the working thread crosses behind the emerging thread.

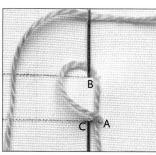

3 Holding the loop with your thumb, insert the needle through the loop at B on the upper line (thumb not shown). Re-emerge at C, directly below on the lower line.

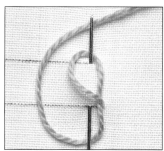

4 Loop the working thread from right to left, taking it under the tip of the needle.

5 Pull the loop tightly around the needle.

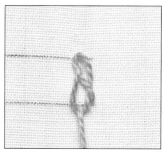

6 Pull the thread through in a downward motion.

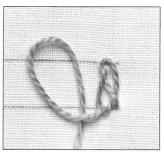

7 Make a second loop following steps 1 and 2.

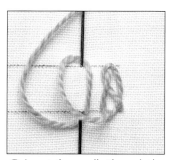

8 Insert the needle through the loop and into the fabric on the upper line. Re-emerge on the lower line. Loop the thread to the left under the needle as before.

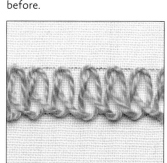

9 Pull the thread through to complete the second stitch.

10 Continue working stitches in the same manner.
Completed braid stitch.

HINTS

PERLÉ COTTON

Perlé cotton is a tightly twisted pure cotton thread with a lustrous finish. It is available in four weights.

It cannot be divided and so is best used as a single thread.

Because of the cylindrical nature of the thread, it is wonderful for creating textured effects.

Check the twist of the thread often. If it has become under-twisted or over-twisted, allow the needle to hang free. The thread will return to its normal twist.

Care instructions for the thread are the same as for cotton fabrics so it is particularly suitable for working on cottons.

Never press the embroidery on a hard surface as the thread easily crushes under the weight and heat of the iron. If necessary, place the embroidery face down on a well-padded surface to press. A folded flannelette nappy or a towel makes a suitable surface.

Bullions

Bullion or grub stitch – hardly names which are poetic or enticing. But this little stitch, shaped into rosy clusters and sprinkled on anything from baby clothes to gardening gloves, has lured thousands into picking up a needle and rediscovering the gentle art of embroidery.

THREADS

Some threads are more easily handled than others. Threads and yarns which have a tendency to break easily, or do not have a smooth surface such as chenille, will cause the most frustrations for the bullion embroiderer.

All threads have a twist. Wrapping in a clockwise direction tends to untwist the thread and results in smoother bullions. Wrapping in an anti-clockwise direction puts extra twist into the thread and makes the bullion knots tighter and sometimes rougher in appearance.

EMBROIDERY HOOPS

It is not advisable to use a hoop when working bullion knots. Because the needle is positioned in the fabric when working the wraps, it is easier to manipulate the thread, needle and fabric without the constraints of a hoop.

For hints on creating perfect bullions see pages 28 and 32.

THESE IDENTICALLY WORKED BULLION ROSES WERE STITCHED WITH DIFFERENT TYPES OF THREAD.

| *Tapestry wool* | *Persian yarn* | *Crewel wool* | *Stranded cotton* | *Stranded silk* | *Stranded rayon* | *No. 5 perlé cotton* | *Stranded metallic* |

Starting Bullions

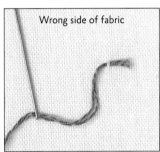
Wrong side of fabric

1 On the back, pick up approx. two fabric threads, taking a tiny 'scoop' stitch. Pull the thread through, leaving a 4mm (³/₁₆") tail.

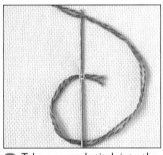

2 Take a second stitch into the same position but at a right angle to the first stitch. Keep the thread under the tip of the needle.

3 Pull the thread through, pulling it towards you.

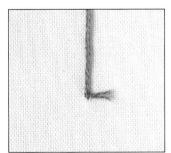

4 Pull the thread away from you to tighten.

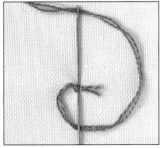

5 Work a third stitch into the same position on the fabric and in the same direction as the second stitch.

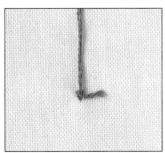

6 Pull the thread towards you and then away from you to tighten. You are now ready to begin your embroidery.

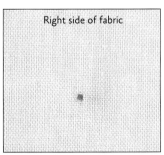
Right side of fabric

7 Secured thread on the right side of the fabric.

Bullion Knot

Bullion knots have been used in many forms of embroidery through the ages and have been known by various names. These include grub stitch, caterpillar stitch, coil stitch, knot stitch, post stitch, roll stitch, worm stitch and Porto Rico rose.

The distance from A to B is the length of the finished bullion knot. To form a straight knot the number of wraps must cover this distance plus an extra 1–2 wraps.

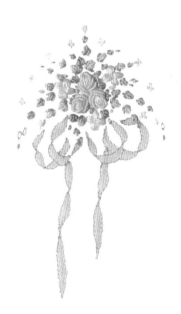

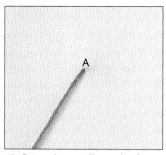

1 Bring the needle to the front at A. Pull the thread through.

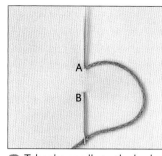

2 Take the needle to the back at B. Re-emerge at A, taking care not to split the thread. The thread is to the right of the needle.

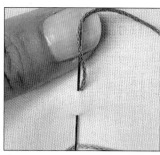

3 Raise the point of the needle away from the fabric. Wrap the thread clockwise around the needle.

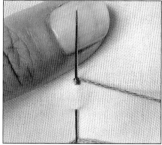

4 Keeping the point of the needle raised, pull the wrap firmly down onto the fabric.

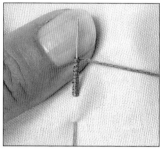

5 Work the required number of wraps around the needle. Pack them down evenly as you wrap.

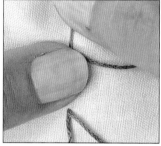

6 Keeping tension on the wraps with the left thumb, begin to ease the needle through the fabric and wraps.

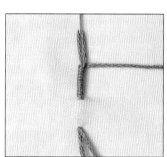

7 Continuing to keep tension on the wraps, pull the needle and thread through the wraps (thumb not shown).

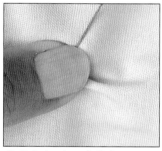

8 Pull the thread all the way through, tugging it away from you until a small pleat forms in the fabric. This helps to ensure a tight even knot.

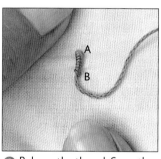

9 Release the thread. Smooth out the fabric and the knot will lie back towards B.

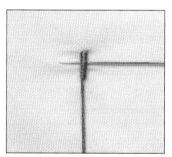

10 To ensure all the wraps are even, gently stroke and manipulate them with the needle while maintaining tension on the thread.

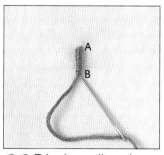

11 Take the needle to the back at B to anchor the knot.

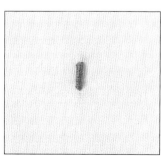

12 Pull the thread through and end off. **Completed bullion knot.**

Bullion Knot – Long

When working very long bullion knots, use the longest needle you can find, such as a milliner's (straw) needle, a long yarn darner or a doll needle.

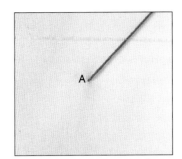

1 Bring the needle to the front at A. Pull the thread through.

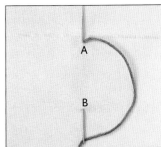

2 Take the needle through the fabric from B to A, taking care not to split the thread. The thread is to the right of the needle.

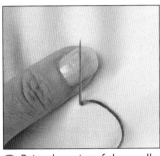

3 Raise the point of the needle away from the fabric.

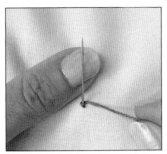

4 Wrap the thread around the needle in a clockwise direction.

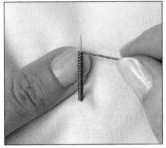

5 Continue wrapping until the needle is almost full. Take care to keep the wraps even, and not to wrap too tightly.

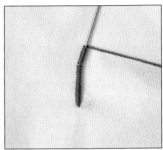

6 Holding the wraps at the tip of the needle, begin to pull the thread through (fingers not shown). Stop when only a few wraps remain on the needle.

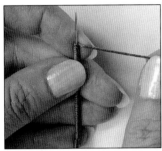

7 Continue wrapping the thread around the needle in the same manner as before. Repeat steps 5 - 6 until the required number of wraps is achieved.

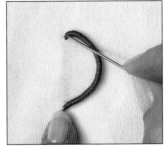

8 Firmly pull the needle and thread through the wraps. Pull the thread and manipulate the wraps until you are satisfied with the bullion knot's appearance.

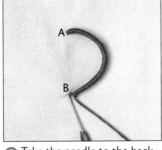

9 Take the needle to the back at B to anchor the knot.

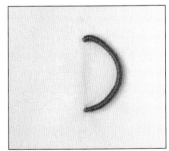

10 Pull the thread through. **Completed long bullion knot.**

Bullion Knot – Long Couched

Couching is used to hold long bullion knots in place, or to anchor a knot or loop into a particular shape. Use one strand of matching thread to ensure the stitches are invisible. Although we have shown a curved bullion knot here, the same method is used when couching a straight bullion knot.

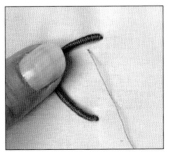

1 Work the bullion knot. Roll it to the left hand side with your thumb. Bring the thread to the front beside the bullion knot.

2 Using the tip of the needle, separate the wraps of the knot next to where the couching thread emerged.

3 Take the couching thread over the knot. Insert the needle into the fabric very close to where it emerged.

4 Pull the thread through, manipulating it so it lies between the separated wraps.

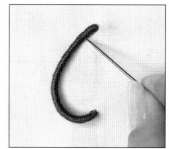

5 Run your fingernail or needle over the wraps to hide the couching thread and ensure the wraps are even again.

6 Continue working couching stitches until the knot is anchored. **Completed couched bullion knot.**

AN ALTERNATIVE METHOD FOR COUCHING

An alternative method for couching, which is particularly useful when only 1 - 2 couching stitches are required, is to use the same thread you used for working the bullion knot. Place each couching stitch carefully so it appears as an extra wrap.

Bullion Loop

A bullion loop is a variation of a bullion knot. It is formed in a similar manner, except that the distance between A and B is very short and the number of wraps is often large. Before anchoring the loop, take time to stroke and manipulate the wraps.

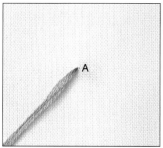

1 Bring the needle to the front at A. Pull the thread through.

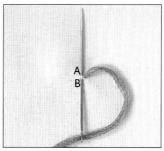

2 Take the needle through the fabric from B to A, taking care not to split the thread. The thread is to the right of the needle.

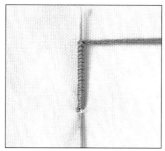

3 Raise the point of the needle and wrap the thread around it following steps 3–5 for the bullion knot.

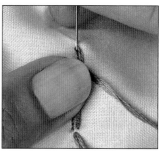

4 Holding the wraps firmly with your left thumb, begin to pull the needle and thread through the wraps.

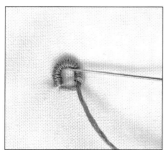

5 Pull the thread all the way through. Using the needle, separate the wraps from the adjacent thread.

6 Hold the wraps in place with your thumb (thumb not shown). Pull the thread towards you to tighten the wraps and curl them into a loop.

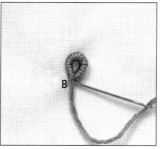

7 Take the needle to the back at B to anchor the loop.

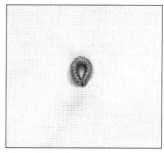

8 Pull the thread through. **Completed bullion loop.**

CREATING PERFECT BULLION KNOTS

Type of Needle

There are several advantages to using a milliner's (straw) needle for bullions. Unlike most other needles, the diameter of the shaft is the same from the top of the needle to where it starts tapering to a point. The wraps will therefore maintain an even tension when the needle and thread are pulled through.

The milliner's needle has a longer shaft than most other needles. This length is necessary to hold the varying number of wraps required.

Number of Strands

The number of strands is determined by the thickness of the stitch required – the greater number of strands used, the thicker the stitch.

Size of Bullion

The distance between A and B is the length of the bullion. You will need enough wraps to cover this distance.

For a curved bullion stitch, more wraps will be added. If 5 wraps make a straight bullion, you will need at least 3 – 4 more for a curved bullion, depending on the curve required.

Bullion Knot –Tapered

To form a straight bullion knot, the number of wraps must cover the distance from A to B.

When forming a tapered bullion knot, the number of wraps is reduced.

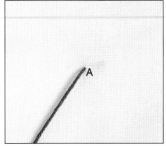

1 Bring the needle to the front at A (this will be the 'blunt' end of the knot). Pull the thread through.

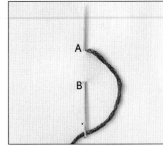

2 Take the needle to the back at B. Re-emerge at A, taking care not to split the thread. The thread is to the right of the needle.

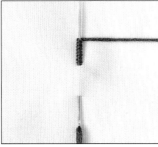

3 Raise the point of the needle. Wrap the thread clockwise around the needle for the required number of wraps.

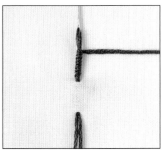

4 Keeping tension on the wraps with the left thumb, begin to ease the needle through the fabric and wraps (thumb not shown).

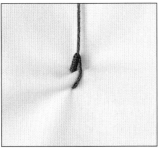

5 Continuing to keep tension on the wraps, pull the needle and thread through the wraps until a pleat forms in the fabric.

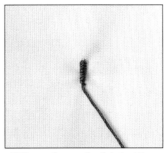

6 Smooth out the fabric. Give the knot an extra tug and let the wraps wind down at the end.

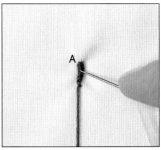

7 Using the point of your needle, push some of the wraps back towards A.

8 Hold the pushed back wraps and continue tugging to tighten the wraps on the lower segment to form a point (thumb not shown).

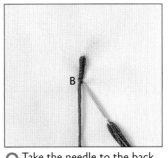

9 Take the needle to the back at B to anchor the knot.

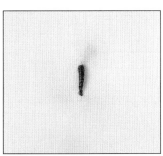

10 Pull the thread through. **Completed tapered bullion knot.**

Bullion Knot –Bears

The versatile bullion knot can be used to create whimsical motifs.

These little bears are created using four strands of silk thread. Draw a small circle for the head and an oval for the body. Mark the ends of the arms and legs with a dot.

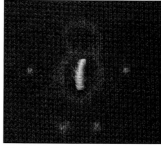

1 Body. Bring the thread to the front at the top of the bear's body. Work a 10 wrap bullion knot to form the centre of the body.

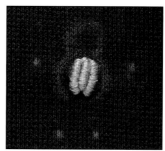

2 Work two 11 wrap bullion knots, one on each side of the first bullion.

3 Work two 7 wrap bullions, one on each side, to complete the body. These stitches are worked from the top of the body to two-thirds of the length.

4 Head. Work a 6 wrap bullion knot across the top of the body.

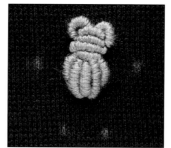

5 Work two 7 wrap bullion knots and then a 6 wrap bullion knot to complete the head. Add an 8 wrap bullion loop on each side of the head for the ears.

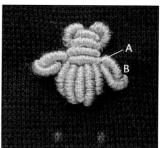

6 Arms. Work a 10 wrap bullion for the upper arm. Bring the needle to the front at A. Stitch an 11 wrap knot from B to A directly under the first. Repeat for the second arm.

7 Legs. Work a 10 wrap bullion knot for the outer leg. This knot extends from the lower end of the body's outer bullion knot.

8 Stitch an 11 wrap bullion for the inner leg. A 7 wrap bullion forms each foot. This knot curls around the ends of the two bullion knots in the leg.

9 Face. Using 1 strand of black, work 3 straight stitches vertically over the third bullion knot for the nose. Starting just under the nose, work a diagonal stitch to the left into the lower bullion.

10 From the same point at the base of the nose, work a second diagonal stitch to the right. Work 2 French knots for the eyes on the second bullion knot from the top.

11 Bow tie (boy). Using 1 strand, take the thread to the back, leaving a 15cm (6") tail on front. Bring to the front close to the entry point. Tie threads into a bow. Trim tails to 5mm (¼"). Stitch to secure bow.

12 Bow (girl). The bow on the girl bear's head is worked in the same manner as the boy bear's bow tie.

Bullion Rose

This classic rose, worked in three shades of pink, is created from two rounds of bullion knot petals surrounding a pair of bullion knots. The fabric is rotated as each petal is worked.

The arrow indicates the top of the fabric.

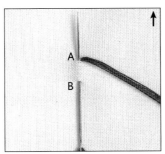

1 **Centre.** Using the darkest shade of thread, bring it to the front at A. Take the needle from B to A, taking care not to split the thread.

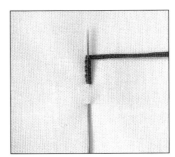

2 Raise the tip of the needle and wrap the thread clockwise around the needle six times.

3 Keeping tension on the wraps with the left thumb, pull the thread through.

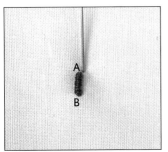

4 Anchor the bullion knot at B. Bring the needle to the front again, very close to A.

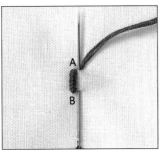

5 Pull the thread through. Take the needle from B to A, keeping the thread to the right of the needle.

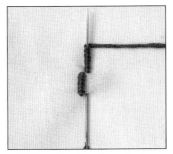

6 Wrap the thread clockwise around the needle six times, holding the thread taut.

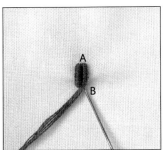

7 Take the needle to the back at B to anchor the second bullion knot.

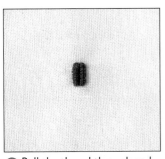

8 Pull the thread through and end off on the back of the fabric. **Completed centre.**

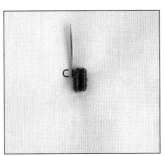

9 **Inner petals.** Change to a lighter shade of thread. Bring the needle to the front at C.

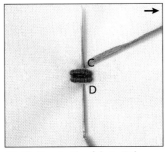

10 Rotate the fabric. Take the needle from D to C, keeping the thread to the right of the needle.

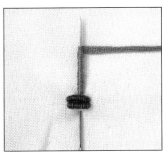

11 Wrap the thread around the needle nine times. Pack the wraps evenly down the needle.

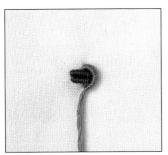

12 Pull the thread through, keeping it taut and settling the knot in position around the centre.

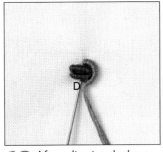

13 After adjusting the knot to your satisfaction, take the needle to the back at D to anchor the knot.

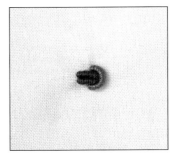

14 **Completed first petal.**

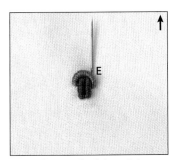

15 Rotate the fabric. Bring the needle to the front at E.

Bullion Rose CONTINUED

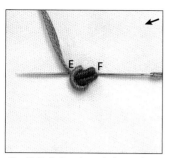

16 Pull the thread through. Rotate the fabric slightly. Take the needle from F to E.

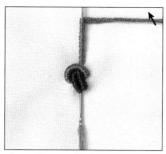

17 Rotate the fabric. Wrap the thread clockwise around the needle nine times, holding it taut to maintain tension on the wraps.

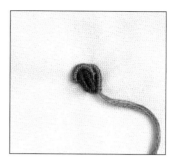

18 Pull the thread through. Settle the knot in position and adjust the wraps if necessary.

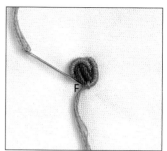

19 Take the needle to the back at F to anchor the knot.

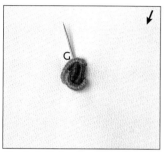

20 Pull the thread through. Rotate the fabric. Bring the needle to the front at G outside the previous petal.

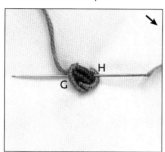

21 Pull the thread through. Rotate the fabric. Take the needle from H, inside the first petal, to G.

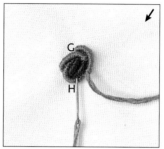

22 Rotate the fabric and wrap nine times. Pull the thread through. Adjust the stitch. Take the needle to the back at H, inside the first inner petal.

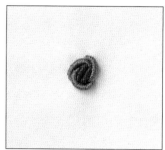

23 Pull the thread through and end off on the back. **Completed inner petals.**

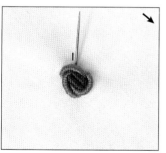

24 **Outer petals.** Rotate the fabric. Change to the lightest shade of thread. Bring the needle to the front at I.

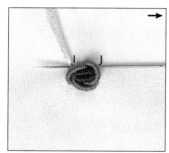

25 Pull the thread through. Rotate the fabric. Take the needle from J to I.

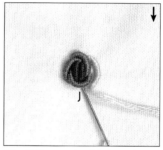

26 Rotate the fabric and wrap the thread ten times. Form the stitch in the same manner as before. Take the needle to the back at J.

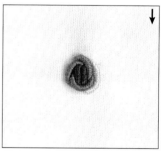

27 Pull the thread through. **Completed first outer petal.**

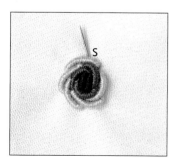

28 Work four overlapping bullions in the same manner, rotating the fabric for each petal. To complete the outer petals bring the needle to the front at S.

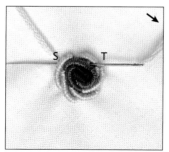

29 Rotate the fabric. Take the needle to the back at T, tucked inside the first outer petal. Re-emerge at S.

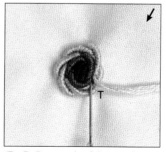

30 Rotate the fabric and wrap the thread ten times. Form the stitch in the same manner as before. Take the needle to the back at T.

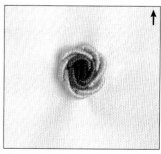

31 Pull the thread through and end off on the back of the fabric. **Completed bullion rose.**

Bullion Rose with Padded Satin Stitch Centre

A square of padded satin stitch forms the centre of this rose. It looks particularly beautiful when stitched with 1–2 strands of silk thread. The fabric is rotated as each petal is worked.

The arrow indicates the top of the fabric.

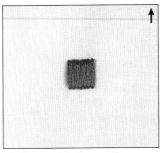

1 **Centre.** Mark a small square with sides measuring approx. 6mm (¼") onto the fabric. Fill the square with vertical satin stitches.

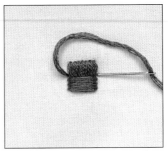

2 Work a layer of horizontal satin stitches over the first layer.

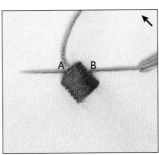

3 **Petals.** Bring the needle to the front at A, midway across the top of the square. Rotate the fabric. Take the needle from B to A.

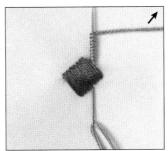

4 Rotate fabric. Wrap the thread around the needle in a clockwise direction 8–10 times.

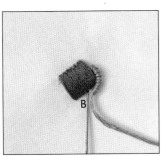

5 Pull the thread through the wraps. Take the needle to the back at B.

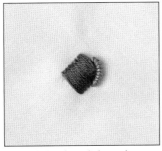

6 Pull the thread through. **Completed first petal.**

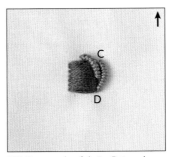

7 Rotate the fabric. Bring the needle to the front at C approx. halfway along the first knot. Rotate fabric. Take the needle from D to C. Rotate and work a second bullion knot.

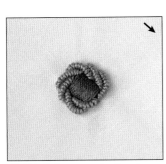

8 Work five more bullion knots in the same manner, rotating the fabric slightly before working each one.

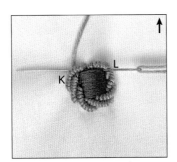

9 To work the last petal, rotate fabric and bring the needle to the front at K. Rotate and take it to the back at L, in between the first petal and the centre. Re-emerge at K.

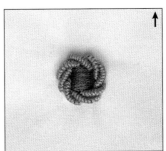

10 Complete the bullion knot in the same manner as before. **Completed rose with padded satin stitch centre.**

Bullion Knot – Rosebuds

Different types of rosebuds may be formed by varying the thread colours
and differing the number of knots and wraps.

SMALL ROSEBUD

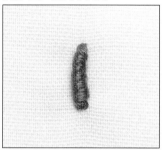  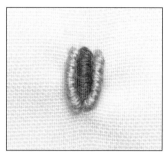 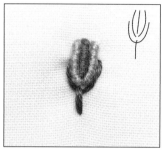

1 **Centre.** To form the centre, stitch a 6 wrap bullion knot using the darker thread.

2 **Outer petals.** Change to a lighter thread. Starting at the base of the centre knot, work a second 6 wrap bullion just to the right of the centre knot.

3 Again, starting at the base, work a third 6 wrap knot on the opposite side.

4 **Calyx.** Add a green fly stitch for the calyx. Place the tips of the fly stitch halfway along, and very close to, the outer petals. Use a long anchoring stitch.

MEDIUM ROSEBUD

1 **Centre.** Work a 6 wrap bullion knot in the darkest shade. Stitch a second knot alongside, but slightly higher than the first.

2 **Outer petals.** Change colour. Starting at the base of the right hand centre petal, work a 10 wrap bullion knot next to the left petal.

3 Change colour. Starting just below and to the left of the previous petal, work a second 10 wrap bullion on the right hand side of the centre knots.

4 **Calyx.** Change to green thread. Stitch a 6 wrap bullion on each side of the petals, starting in the same hole. Add a third bullion knot for the stem.

LARGE ROSEBUD

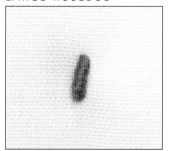   

1 **Centre.** Work a single 6 wrap bullion knot for the centre in the darkest shade of thread.

2 **Inner petals.** Change colour. Add a bullion on the right hand side, starting level with the base of the centre knot. Stitch a second bullion, starting just below the previous knot on a curve around the left side.

3 **Outer petals.** Change colour. Work 3 bullion knots, starting at the base. Place the first knot to the right. The next two knots alternate from left to right, starting each just below the previous one.

4 **Calyx.** Change to green thread. Stitch the calyx in a similar manner to the medium rosebud. The centre knot finishes at the base of the third petal.

Bullion Knot – Detached Chain Combination

This combination stitch is ideal for creating flowers. It is worked by beginning a detached chain stitch from the centre and anchoring it with a bullion knot.

To stitch a flower, draw two circles on the fabric to use as a guide.

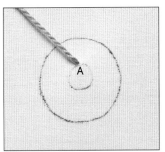

1 Bring the thread to the front at A on the inner circle.

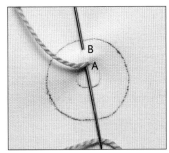

2 Take the needle to the back just next to A and emerge at B, approximately halfway between the two circles. The thread is to the left of the needle.

3 Take the thread from left to right under the tip of the needle, pulling it firmly to the right.

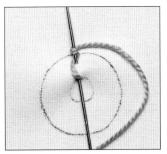

4 Wrap the thread clockwise around the needle.

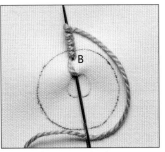

5 Pull firmly, so the first wrap lies snugly against the fabric at B. Wrap the thread around needle the required number of times, keeping wraps close together.

6 Place the left thumb over the wraps to hold firmly. Begin to ease the eye of the needle through the wraps.

7 Keeping the thumb and forefinger on the wraps, pull the thread through (fingers not shown).

8 Pull the thread firmly all the way through, until a tight bullion is formed at the end of the detached chain.

9 Take the needle to the back at C, just past the outer circle, to anchor the stitch.

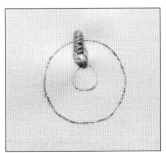

10 **Completed first petal.**

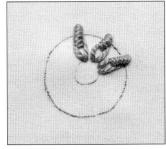

11 Stitch the required number of petals, working from the inner to the outer circle.

12 **Completed bullion knot-detached chain combination flowers.**

Buttonhole Stitch

True buttonhole stitch forms a row of 'purls' (knots) along the cut edge.

When worked as a buttonhole (as shown) or in cutwork, this adds strength to the cut edge. Mark the buttonhole on the fabric. Cut the opening.

The arrow indicates the top of the fabric.

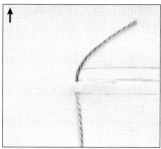

1 Take the needle through the opening and re-emerge on the lower line. Pull through leaving a 2cm (¾") tail.

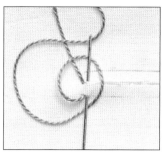

2 Take the needle through the opening and re-emerge on the lower line next to the first stitch. Wrap the thread clockwise behind the eye and then the tip of the needle.

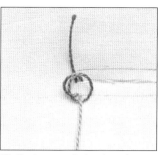

3 Begin to pull the thread through, pulling towards you and then upwards away from the opening.

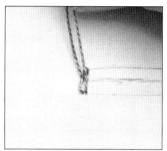

4 Continue to pull the thread upwards so the loop slips along the stitch towards the opening. A 'purl' forms on the cut edge of the opening.

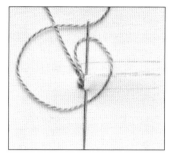

5 Take the needle through the opening and re-emerge next to the previous stitch. Wrap the thread clockwise around the needle as before.

6 Pull through until the 'purl' sits at the cut edge. Continue until you reach the end of the opening. Keep the stitches as close as possible.

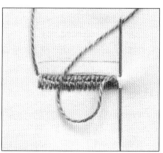

7 **Bar-tack.** Take the needle through the opening and re-emerge next to the previous stitch. Do not wrap the thread around the needle.

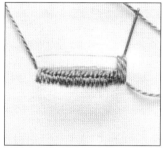

8 Pull through. Work three 4mm (³⁄₁₆") long stitches across the end. Take the needle to the back at the upper edge, next to the last stitch.

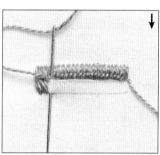

9 Rotate the fabric. Bring the thread to the front through the opening. Take the needle back through the opening and re-emerge on the lower line.

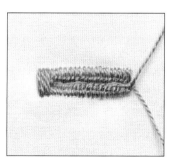

10 Wrap the thread around the needle as before. Pull through. Continue working stitches to the end.

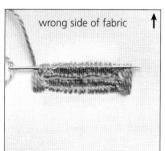

wrong side of fabric

11 Make a bar-tack as in step 8. Finish with the needle at the back. Turn the fabric to the wrong side. Take the needle behind the stitches only. Do not go through the fabric.

12 Pull through and trim the thread. Secure the tail at the beginning in the same manner. **Completed buttonhole.**

Cast-on Stitch – Rose

Cast-on stitch is used in Brazilian embroidery, which makes extensive use of raised stitches. Each cast-on stitch consists of a number of loops cast onto the needle and then anchored to the fabric.

In this rose, the centre is one cast-on stitch. Five cast-on stitches form the first round of petals and seven cast-on stitches form the second round. The fabric is rotated as each stitch is worked.

The arrow indicates the top of the fabric.

We recommend using a milliner's (straw) needle.

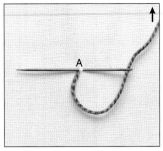

1 **Centre.** Using the darkest shade, bring the thread to the front at A. Take a tiny stitch close to A and leave the needle in the fabric.

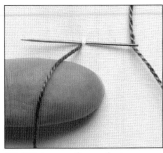

2 With your finger facing you, place the emerging thread over your left index finger.

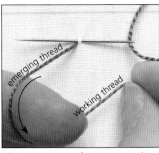

3 Rotate your finger towards you. Keep the thread taut and looped over your index finger.

4 Take the tip of your finger under the working thread and then under the emerging thread, wrapping a loop around your finger.

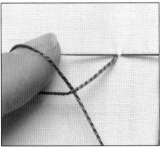

5 Keeping the tension on the thread, place your finger tip on the point of the needle.

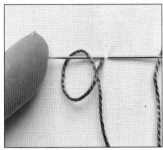

6 Slip the loop off your finger and onto the needle.

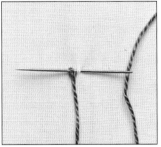

7 Pull the thread tight and slip the loop down the needle onto the fabric. First cast-on.

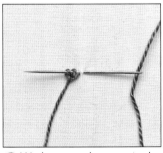

8 Work a second cast-on in the same manner, positioning it on the needle alongside the first.

9 Work 10 more cast-ons onto the needle.

10 Hold the cast-ons in your left hand. With your right hand, pull the needle and thread through the stitches.

11 To anchor the stitch, take the needle to the back at B, close to where the needle last emerged.

12 Pull the thread through. Pull firmly but do not let the fabric pucker. End off the thread. **Completed centre.**

Cast-on
Stitch–Rose

CONTINUED

CAST-ON STITCH ROSE

Ensure that the thread being used is long enough to complete each petal.

As with knitting, keep the tension even as you cast-on. Turn the work as you go, in the same manner as bullion roses.

The frilled effect of the petals is achieved by pulling the thread tight when the petal is complete.

To achieve a really plump, full rose, work extra rounds of petals.

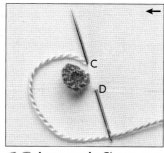

13 **Inner petals.** Change to a lighter shade. Bring the needle to the front at C. Insert the needle at D, approximately 6mm (¼") from C. Re-emerge at C. Do not pull through.

14 Follow steps 2–8 and then work 14 more cast-ons.

15 Holding the cast-ons with your left hand, pull the needle and thread through them with your right hand.

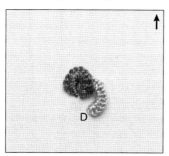

16 Anchor the stitch at D in the same manner as before.

17 Bring the needle to the front at E. Take it from F to E and leave the needle in the fabric.

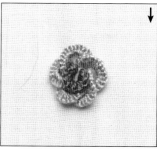

18 Work a second stitch with 16 cast-ons in the same manner as before. Work three more stitches, each with 16 cast-ons, to complete the inner round.

19 **Outer petals.** Change to a lighter shade. Bring the needle to the front just underneath one petal of the inner round.

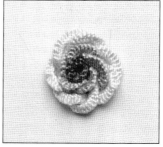

20 Work 7 overlapping stitches in the same manner, with 19 cast-ons in each stitch, to complete the outer round of petals. **Completed cast-on stitch rose.**

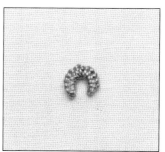

21 **Leaves.** Stitch the outer leaf first, using 14 cast-ons. The two points where the needle pierces the fabric are placed approx 4mm (³⁄₁₆") apart.

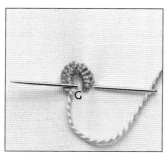

22 Bring the thread to the front, between the ends of the previous stitch. Take the needle through the fabric just beyond the first leaf and re-emerge at G.

23 Stitch the inner leaf using 12 cast-ons.

24 Work two sets of leaves alongside the rose.

Cast-on Stitch – Double Sided

This semi-detached stitch is worked with two threads, creating a neat edge on each side.
The arrow indicates the top of the fabric.

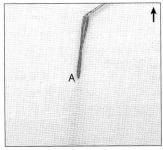

1 Bring the needle and thread to the front at A.

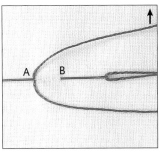

2 Take a stitch from B to A ensuring that there is a strand of thread positioned each side of the needle.

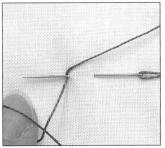

3 Wind the lower thread around your index finger and twist to create a loop.

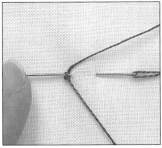

4 Place your finger on tip of needle and slip the loop onto the needle. Pull the thread tight. **Completed first stitch.**

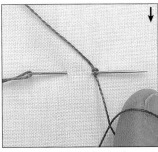

5 Rotate the work 180 degrees and repeat with the second thread.

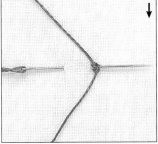

6 Slip the loop onto the needle as before. Pull the thread tight. **Completed second stitch.**

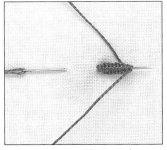

7 Continue working in this manner until the required number of cast-ons have been worked.

8 Pull the needle through and secure on the back. **Completed double sided cast-on stitch.**

Chain Stitch

This very versatile stitch can be used as an outline or in close rows as a filling stitch.

Take care not to pull the loops too tight as they will lose their rounded shape.

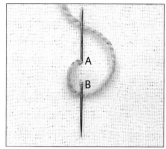

1 Bring the thread to the front at A. Take the needle from A to B, using the same hole in the fabric at A. Loop the thread under the tip of the needle.

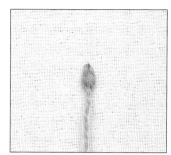

2 Pull the thread through until the loop lies snugly around the emerging thread.

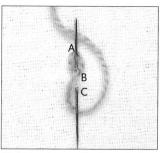

3 Take the needle through the same hole in the fabric at B and re-emerge at C. Ensure the thread is under the tip of the needle.

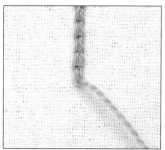

4 Pull the thread through as before. Continue working stitches in the same manner for the required distance.

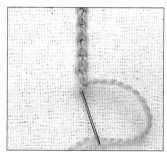

5 To finish, work the last stitch and take the needle to the back of the fabric just over the loop.

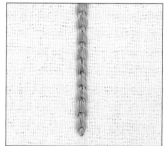

6 Pull the thread through to form a short straight stitch. End off the thread on the back of the fabric. **Completed chain stitch.**

Chain Stitch – Alternating

Also known as magic chain or chequered chain stitch, this ingenious stitch is worked with two different coloured threads, in the needle at the same time. Work the stitches downwards along a line.

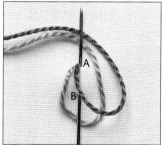

1 Bring the threads to the front at A. Insert the needle into the fabric from A to B. Ensure one thread is under the needle tip and the other is over the needle.

2 Pull the threads through, pulling downwards.

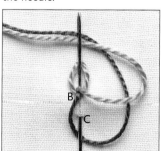

3 Insert the needle into the fabric from B to C. Swap thread colours. Ensure that the second thread is under the needle tip and the first is over the needle.

4 Pull the thread through. Continue working stitches, alternating the thread colour under the tip of the needle. **Completed alternating chain stitch.**

Chain Stitch – Heavy

This stitch produces a thick line.
The thickness is achieved by taking the needle under
two chain stitch loops for each stitch.

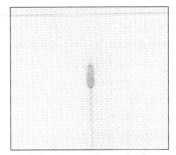

1 Bring the needle to the front at the top of the line and work a small straight stitch.

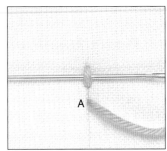

2 Bring the needle to the front at A and slide it back under the running stitch. Do not pierce the fabric.

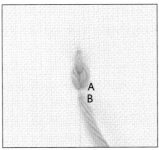

3 Insert the needle at A and emerge at B, forming a chain stitch.

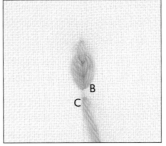

4 Slide the needle under the running stitch again, taking it to the back at B.

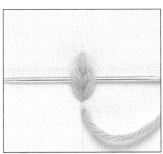

5 Bring the needle to the front at C and pass it under the two chain stitches.

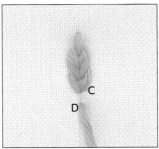

6 Take the needle to the back at C. Emerge at D.

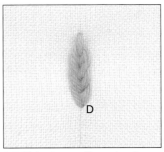

7 Slide the needle under the previous two chain stitches and take it to the back at D.

8 Continue in this manner, sliding the needle behind the previous two chain stitches each time. **Completed heavy chain stitch.**

HINTS

COLOUR

Study your environment as nature provides many examples of wonderful colour schemes.

When purchasing threads, always place your selection on a piece of the fabric you will be stitching on.

Different coloured grounds can alter the appearance of the thread colours.

Colours change depending on the strength and type of light they are viewed in.

If possible, select your colours in light similar to that in the final surroundings for the project.

Heavy chain stitch in a colourful crewelwork piece

Chain Stitch –Interlaced

This stitch can be worked with contrasting threads to give it a braid-like appearance. The lacing thread hugs the foundation stitches but does not go through the fabric except at the beginning and end. Work stitches downwards.

Use a tapestry needle for the interlacing to avoid splitting the chain stitches.

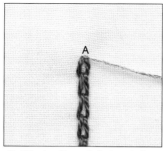

1 Work a line of chain stitch as a foundation. Interlacing the first side. Using a new thread, bring it to the front at the top of the line of chain stitch, A.

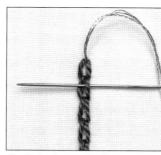

2 Slide the needle from the right to the left under the right hand side only of the second chain stitch.

3 Pull the thread through. Slide the needle from left to right under the right hand side of the first chain stitch and the adjacent lacing thread.

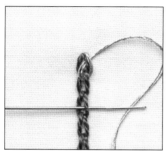

4 Pull the thread through. Slide the needle from right to left under the right hand side of the third chain stitch.

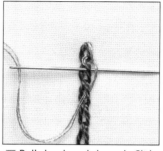

5 Pull the thread through. Slide the needle from left to right under the previous chain stitch and lacing thread.

6 Continue to the end of the line following steps 4–5. To end off, take the needle to the back at the end of the last chain stitch.

7 Secure the thread on the back. **Completed first side of interlacing.**

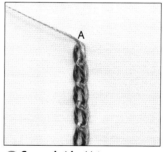

8 **Second side.** Using a new thread, bring the thread to the front at A.

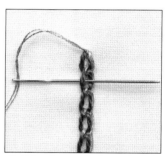

9 Take the needle from the left to the right under the left hand side of the second chain stitch.

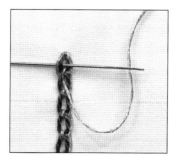

10 Pull the thread through. Take the needle from right to left under the first chain stitch and the adjacent lacing thread.

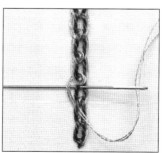

11 Pull the thread through. Continue in this manner, working a mirror image of the first side of interlacing.

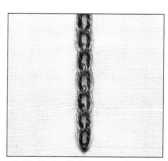

12 End off the second side in the same manner as the first. **Completed interlaced chain stitch.**

Chain Stitch–Open

This chain stitch variation gives a ladder-like effect. It is also known as Roman chain or square chain stitch. Work the stitches downwards.

Mark two parallel lines on the fabric to help keep the stitches even.

The arrow indicates the top of the fabric.

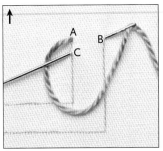

1 Bring the thread to the front at A. Take it to the back at, B level with A, on the right hand line. Re-emerge at C and loop the thread under the needle tip.

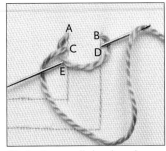

2 Begin to pull the thread through. As the loop tightens, take the needle to the back at D and re-emerge at E. The thread is under the needle tip.

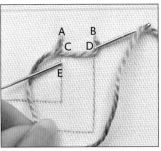

3 Pick up the working thread. Gently pull towards you until the looped stitch sits snugly around the thread and needle. **Completed first stitch.**

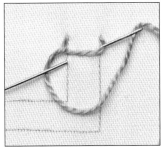

4 **Second stitch.** Loop the thread under the needle.

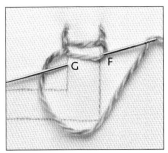

5 Pull the thread through. As the loop becomes smaller, insert the needle from F to G in the same manner as before.

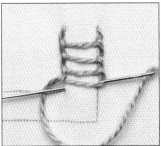

6 Complete the stitch following step 4. Continue working stitches in the same manner for the required distance.

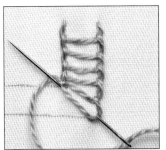

7 **Turning a corner.** On the inside corner, work the stitches very close together. The cross piece of a stitch will be diagonal at the corner.

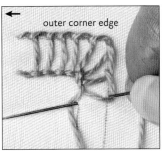

8 Rotate the fabric on reaching outer edge of the corner. Work the stitches very close together on the inside edge until the cross piece becomes horizontal again.

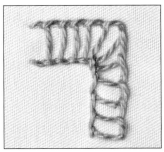

9 **Ending off a line.** Work two tiny straight stitches over the last loop, one on each marked line.

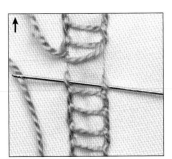

10 **To complete a border.** Work the second to last stitch. Pull through. Take the needle under the ends of the first stitch.

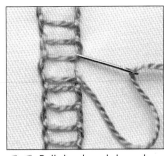

11 Pull the thread through. Take the needle to the back of the fabric inside the loop of the previous stitch.

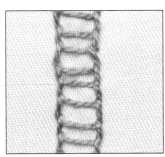

12 Pull the thread through. **Completed open chain stitch.**

Chain Stitch – Rose

Chain stitch roses may be stitched in either silk ribbon or thread. To work the chain stitches downwards, turn the fabric as you go.

Three shades of 4mm (3/16") silk ribbon and a no. 26 tapestry needle are used for this rose.

The arrow indicates the top of the fabric.

1 **Centre.** Using the darkest shade of ribbon, work a 2 wrap French knot for the centre.

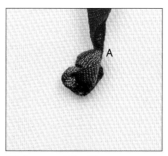

2 **Inner petals.** Change to a lighter shade of ribbon. Bring it to the front at A, approximately 2mm (1/16") away from the French knot.

3 Insert the needle at A and re-emerge at B. Keeping the ribbon flat, loop it under the needle tip.

4 Pull through until the loop gently wraps around the ribbon. Do not pull too tightly as the stitch will become thin.

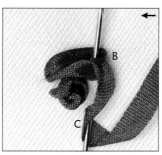

5 Rotate the fabric. Take the needle from B to C. Loop the ribbon under the needle tip.

6 Gently pull the ribbon through. The second stitch anchors the first stitch.

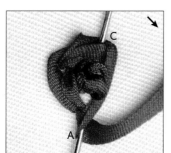

7 Rotate the fabric. Insert the needle at C and re-emerge very close to A.

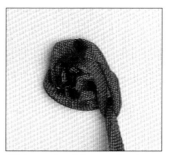

8 Loop the ribbon under the tip of the needle and gently pull through.

9 Take the needle to the back just over the loop.

10 Pull the ribbon through, forming a tiny straight stitch to anchor the last chain stitch. **Completed inner petals.**

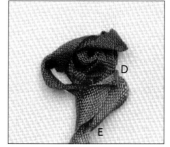

11 **Outer petals.** Using the lightest shade, bring the needle to the front at D, just outside the first round. Work a chain stitch from D to E keeping the tension loose.

12 Following the diagram, work four more chain stitches. Anchor the last chain stitch at D with a short straight stitch over the loop. **Completed chain stitch rose.**

Chain Stitch –Rosette

This variation of twisted chain stitch produces a pretty, braided line. It is a useful outline stitch and equally effective in straight lines or curves. It can also be used in small circles to make floral motifs.

Mark two parallel lines on the fabric to help keep the stitches even.

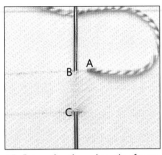

1 Bring the thread to the front at A on the right hand side of the upper line. Insert the needle into the fabric from B to C.

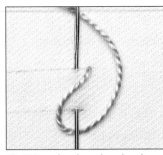

2 Wrap the thread under the tip of the needle in a counter-clockwise direction.

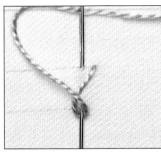

3 Continue wrapping until the thread crosses over itself. Pull the loop taut and hold in place with your left thumb (thumb not shown).

4 Keeping your thumb over the loop, pull the thread through in a downwards motion (thumb not shown).

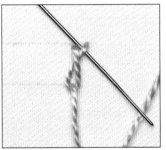

5 Slide the needle from right to left under the right hand section of thread. Do not go through the fabric.

6 Begin to pull the thread through.

7 Pull the thread through. **Completed first stitch.**

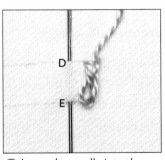

8 Insert the needle into the fabric from D to E.

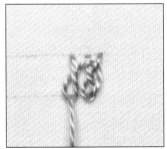

9 Loop the thread in a counter-clockwise direction around the needle as before. Pull the thread through in a downward motion.

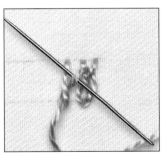

10 Slide the needle from right to left under the section of thread between the stitches. Do not go through the fabric.

11 Pull the thread through to complete the second stitch.

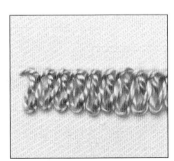

12 Continue working stitches in the same manner keeping them close together. **Completed line of rosette chain stitches.**

Chain Stitch – Twisted

This is a simple variation of basic chain stitch.

The added twist gives the stitch a textured, rope-like effect. Each stitch can vary in length and will achieve a different look depending on the thread used.

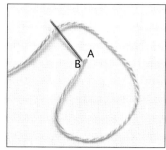

1 Bring the needle to the front at A. Take it to the back at B. Form a loop to the left with the emerging thread.

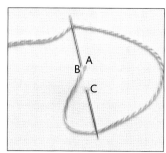

2 Bring the needle to the front at C, below A. The needle is slightly angled towards the right and the thread is positioned under the needle tip.

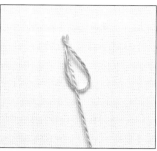

3 Begin to pull the thread through gently until the loop begins to tighten.

4 Continue pulling the thread through until the loop rests on the emerging thread. **Completed first twisted chain stitch.**

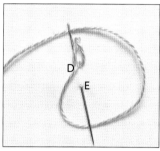

5 To begin the second stitch, take the needle from D, just to the left of the previous loop, to E. Position the thread under the needle tip.

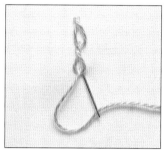

6 Continue for the required distance. To end off, take the needle to the back just below the last loop.

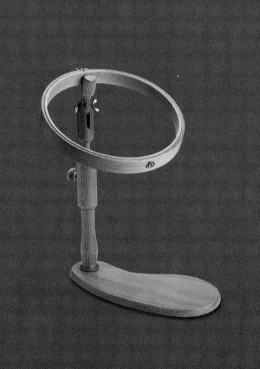

HINTS

USING HOOPS

Hoops are designed to hold the fabric taut while stitching, thus preventing unsightly puckering in your work.

When using a hoop, stab the needle through the fabric for a better result.

Always use a good quality hoop. Hoops that can be tightened with a screwdriver are best as they can hold the fabric more firmly than other hoops.

Bind the inner ring of wooden hoops with cotton tape (see page 9). This helps the hoop to hold the fabric firmly and is gentler on the fabric.

To avoid altering the tension of the fabric, hold the hoop rather than the fabric.

Whenever you are not working on your embroidery, remove the fabric from the hoop. This helps to prevent the hoop from permanently marking the fabric.

A freestanding hoop is ideal as you can stitch freely without having to hold the hoop. This is particularly useful when working stitches that require two hands (eg knots). Clamps and stands are available to attach the hoop to a table and to hold the hoop.

EMBROIDERING ON A THREE DIMENSIONAL OBJECT

To secure the thread when beginning, work two or three tiny back stitches where they will be covered by subsequent embroidery.

To move from one stitch to the next, skim the needle beneath the fabric and emerge at the start of the next stitch.

To end off a thread, secure the stitch and bring the thread to the front a short distance away from the last stitch. Pull taut and cut very close to the fabric. The thread will spring back inside.

Chinese Knot

Chinese knot is also known as blind knot, forbidden knot or Peking knot. Chinese knots were used extensively in old Chinese embroideries. Often they were the only stitches used and, when colour shading was a feature, the effect was truly sumptuous. The Chinese love of silk gave this work an even greater richness and lustre. Chinese knot may be used alone or as a filling stitch. The texture can be varied by leaving loops on the surface of the fabric.

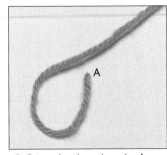

1 Bring the thread to the front at A. Loop the thread to the left.

2 Hold the loop onto the fabric with the left thumb and forefinger. The thread is trailed above.

3 Pick up the loop and fold the loop over so the working thread crosses behind the emerging thread.

4 Lay the loop on the fabric.

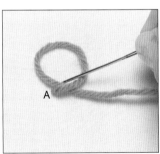

5 Insert the needle inside the loop as close as possible to A, but not in the same hole.

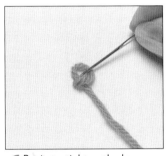

6 Begin to tighten the loop onto the needle by pulling the working thread.

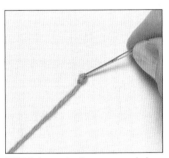

7 Tighten the loop around the needle and begin to push the needle through to the back. Keep the thread tension taut.

8 Pull the needle through to the back. Place your thumb over the loop and continue to pull the thread through to the back (thumb not shown).

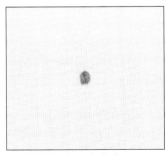

9 Pull the thread all the way through until the knot sits snugly on the surface of the fabric. **Completed Chinese knot.**

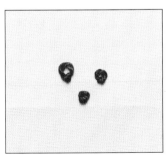

10 **Chinese knot with a loop.** Work steps 1–5. Hold the loop on the fabric at the required length with thumb. Pull the thread through (steps 6–9). Loop sits above knot.

Colonial Knot

Also known as a candlewicking knot, the colonial knot is similar in appearance, but slightly larger and higher than the more formal French knot.

Colonial knots can be worked alone or to fill a shape. They are more commonly stitched close together to form the lines within a candlewicking design.

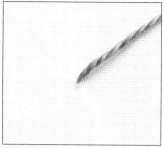

1 Bring the thread to the front at the desired position for the knot.

2 Hold the thread loosely to the left. With the right hand, take the needle tip over the thread.

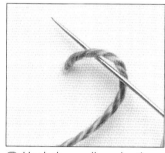

3 Hook the needle under the thread where it emerges from the fabric.

4 With your left hand, take the thread over the tip of the needle. Shorten the loop around the needle.

5 Take the thread under the tip of the needle. The thread now forms a figure eight around the needle.

6 Take the tip of the needle to the back, approximately one or two fabric threads away from where it emerged.

7 Pull the wraps firmly against the fabric and begin to take the needle to the back.

8 Keeping the working thread taut, continue to push the needle through the knot to the back of the fabric.

9 Holding the knot and loop on the fabric with your thumb, continue to pull the thread through (thumb not shown).

10 **Completed colonial knot.**

Concertina Rose

This rose is particularly effective when worked in double-sided satin ribbon.

It has lots of body and as the ribbon is folded back and forth, both sides show.

Prepare a needle threaded with matching sewing thread before you start.

Use a 30cm (11¾") length of 7mm (5/16) wide satin ribbon for this rose.

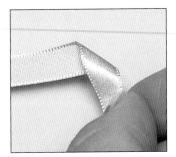

1 Fold the ribbon at a right angle at the centre. Hold the fold in place.

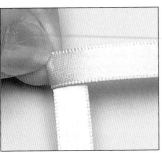

2 Fold the upper half of the ribbon over, keeping it at a right angle to the lower half.

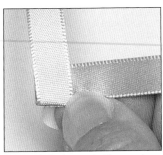

3 Fold the lower half over the upper half, ensuring the fold sits at the edge of the ribbon. Hold in place.

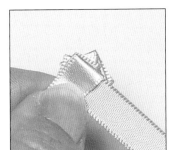

4 Repeat steps 2 and 3 the desired number of times (we repeated the steps seven times, ie folded the ribbon over fourteen times).

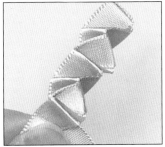

5 Hold the two ends of ribbon firmly in one hand and release the folds.

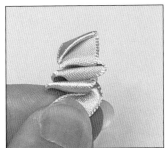

6 Still holding the ends in one hand, begin to pull one end with the other hand.

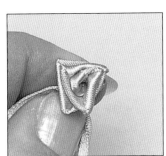

7 Continue pulling the same end until the rose forms and the folds sit close to your fingers.

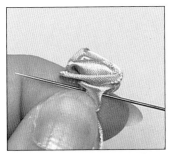

8 Hold the two ends together. Using the sewing thread, take the needle through both pieces of ribbon close to base of the rose.

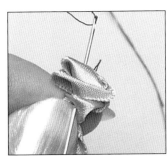

9 Pull the thread through. Take the needle from the base up through the centre of the rose and back down.

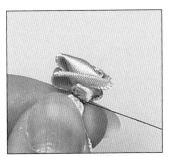

10 Wrap the thread around the base approximately three times.

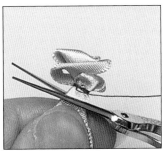

11 Take the thread through the base and end off. Trim excess ribbon, leaving a small stump.

12 Press the stump flat with your thumb. Attach the rose to the fabric by taking tiny stitches through the base and stump. **Completed concertina rose.**

Coral Stitch

Coral stitch can be used as an outline stitch or worked in rows close together to fill a shape.

It is also known as beaded stitch, German knot stitch, knotted stitch and snail trail. Changing the angle of the needle when working the knots will alter the appearance of the stitch.

We used contrasting threads for photographic purposes.

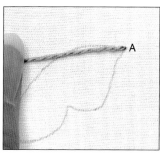

1 Bring the thread to the front at A, at the right hand side. Lay the thread along the outline for a short distance and hold in place with your thumb.

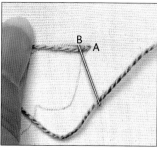

2 Still holding the thread, take the needle to the back at B, just above the thread and to the left of A. A loop forms below the held thread.

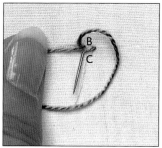

3 Still holding the thread, re-emerge at C, just below B and the held thread. Ensure the tip of the needle is inside the loop.

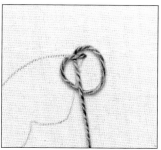

4 Keeping the thread taut, begin to gently pull it through.

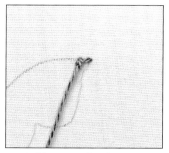

5 Still keeping the thread taut, pull until a knot forms.

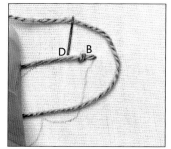

6 Lay the thread along the outline again and hold in place. Take the needle to the back at D, to the left of B.

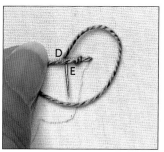

7 Still holding the thread, re-emerge at E, directly below D and the held thread. Ensure the tip of the needle is inside the thread loop.

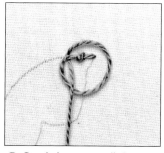

8 Gently begin to pull the thread through.

9 Continue pulling until a second knot forms.

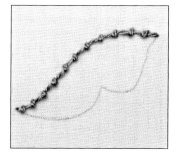

10 Continue to the end of the line. Finish with either a knot or a section of laid thread. Take the thread to the back. End off. **Completed row of coral stitch.**

11 **Filling a shape.** Beginning at the right below the previous row, work a second row of coral stitch. Position the knots between those of the previous row.

12 Continue working rows in the same manner, alternating the positions of the knots from one row to the next until the required shape is filled.

Couching

Couching can be used to work outlines or fill shapes. One or two foundation or laid threads are secured to the fabric with a second thread and tiny stitches.

These stitches hold the laid threads snugly, but do not squeeze them.

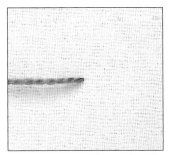

1 Bring the foundation thread to the front and lay it in the desired position on the fabric.

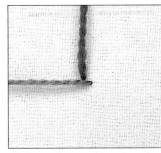

2 Bring the couching thread to the front just above the laid thread and near where it emerged from the fabric.

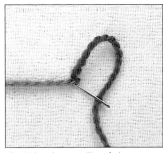

3 Take the needle of the couching thread over the laid thread and to the back of the fabric.

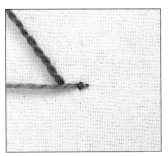

4 Pull the thread through to form the first couching stitch. Re-emerge a short distance away along the laid thread.

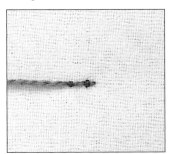

5 Take the couching thread over the laid thread and to the back of the fabric as before.

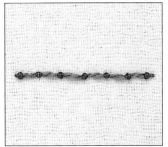

6 Continue working stitches in the same manner to the end of the laid thread. Take both threads to the back of the fabric and end off. **Completed couching.**

Couching Beads

Lengths of threaded beads can be held in place invisibly with couching stitches.

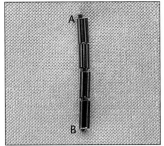

1 Take the needle to the front at A. Thread enough beads to cover the required distance and take the needle to the back at B.

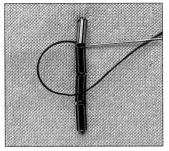

2 Bring the thread to the front between the first and second bead. Work a straight stitch over the thread between each of the beads along the row.

Couching – Bokhara

In Bokhara couching, one continuous thread is used for both the laid thread and the anchoring stitches.

Bokhara couching is similar to Roumanian couching but in Bokhara couching, the diagonal anchoring stitch is short on the surface and long on the wrong side of the fabric.

In Roumanian couching the reverse is the case. The distance between the diagonal stitches will vary according to the thread used.

Always work with the fabric in a hoop to prevent puckering. Draw the required shape onto the fabric.

1 **First laid stitch.** Bring the thread to the front on the left hand side of the shape.

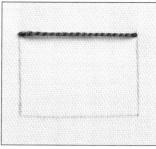

2 Take the thread to the back on the right hand side, forming a long straight stitch. Pull through until the thread lies loosely on the fabric.

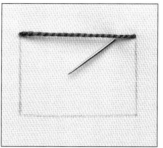

3 **First couching stitch.** Bring the needle to the front, just under the straight stitch, a short distance from the right hand edge.

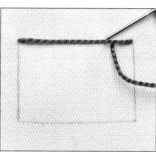

4 Pull the thread through. Take it to the back just above the straight stitch and a little to the left of where it emerged.

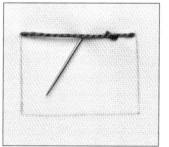

5 Pull through forming a short diagonal stitch over the straight stitch. Bring needle to front just under the straight stitch and a little further towards the left.

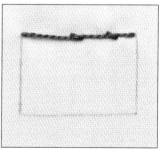

6 Pull the thread through. Take it to the back in the same manner as before to form a second short diagonal stitch.

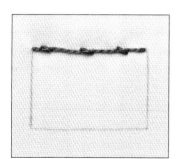

7 Continue working short diagonal stitches in the same way to the other end of the straight stitch. **Completed first row.**

8 Bring the needle to the front on the left hand side just below the first laid stitch. Work a second long straight stitch across the shape.

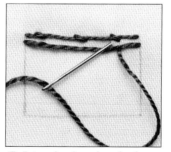

9 Bring the thread to the front just below the second laid stitch, the same distance from the edge as before. Take to the back between the two long stitches.

10 Continue working diagonal stitches along second stitch, at the same intervals as the first laid stitch. Continue working rows of couching until the shape is filled.

Couching–Ribbon

A wide variety of stitches can be used for couching ribbon or narrow braids.

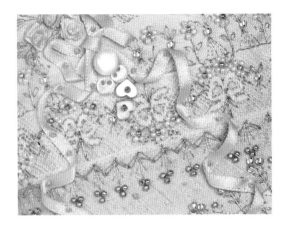

Your choice of couching stitch and thread colour will depend on whether you want the couching to be decorative or purely functional.

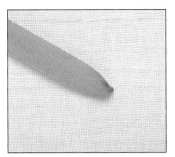

1 **Laying the ribbon.** Bring the ribbon to the front of the fabric.

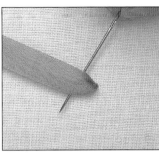

2 Smooth and spread the first section of ribbon by moving your needle behind it while applying a slight upward pressure.

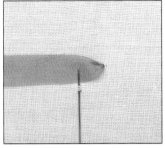

3 Lay the ribbon on the fabric in the desired position. With a pin, pick up a tiny amount of fabric on one side of the ribbon.

4 Take the pin over the ribbon and pick up a tiny amount of fabric on the opposite side.

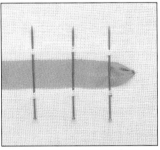

5 Continue pinning in the same manner at frequent intervals or where the ribbon changes direction.

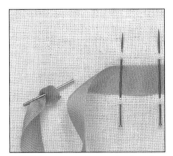

6 When near the end, take the ribbon to the back of the fabric.

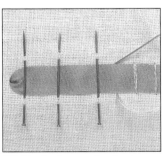

7 Pin the last section in the same manner. Couch the ribbon with the desired stitch, removing the pins as you come to them.

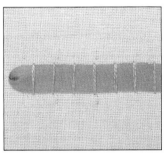

8 **Completed couching.**

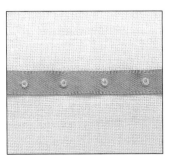

9 Ribbon couched with French knots.

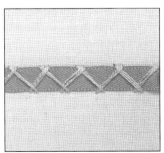

10 Ribbon couched with herringbone stitch.

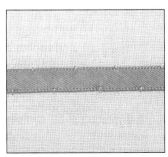

11 Ribbon couched with stab stitch.

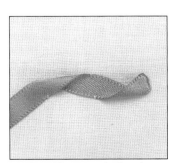

12 Ribbon couched at the folds with stab stitch.

Couching – Puffy

By manipulating the laid thread various effects can be achieved. Here a bundle of threads is puffed up between each couching stitch.

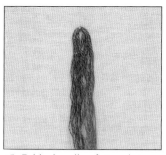

1 Fold a bundle of strands in half. Secure the fold. Carefully comb the threads to form a smooth bundle.

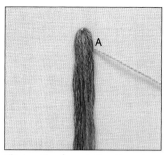

2 Lay the foundation threads along the design line. Bring the couching thread to the front at A, just under the foundation threads.

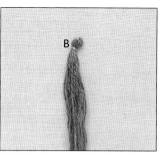

3 Take the couching thread to the back on the design line at B, forming a very short straight stitch.

4 Lift the foundation threads with a tapestry needle to puff the couching.

5 Continue couching the foundation threads, lifting each section to achieve a puffed effect.

6 To end off, sink the foundation threads to the back of the work and secure. **Completed puffy couching.**

Couching – Ribbon Bow

This stylised bow is fashioned from 45cm (17¾") of 2mm wide (¹⁄₁₆") pure silk ribbon.

Tie the bow first. Secure it in place on the fabric using French knots and two strands of thread.

This delicate design is suitable for applying to lace.

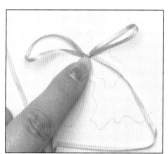

1 Tie the ribbon into a bow with ties approx 9cm (3½") long. Draw a bow design onto the fabric. Position the bow onto the traced outline.

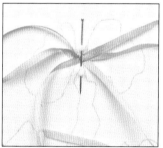

2 Place a pin across the bow knot. Catch the fabric on each side of the ribbon, taking care not to pierce the ribbon itself.

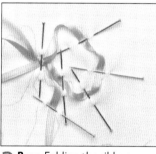

3 **Bow.** Folding the ribbon, place the bow loops to follow the design lines. Pin near each fold, picking up fabric on each side, but not piercing the ribbon.

4 **Ties.** Fold at irregular intervals, 5–20mm (¼"–¾") apart. Pin as you fold, as before, until the entire bow is anchored to the fabric. Trim excess ribbon.

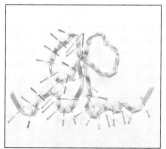

5 Work 3 wrap French knots at 4–8mm (³⁄₁₆"–⁵⁄₁₆") intervals along the centre of the ribbon. Ensure a knot is positioned near the bow knot and at each fold.

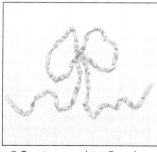

6 Continue working French knots until the entire bow is secured to the fabric. **Completed couched bow.**

Couching – Roumanian

Also known as Oriental laid stitch, figure stitch and antique couching.

Roumanian couching is worked with a continuous thread. It is effective for covering large areas where a smooth, flat surface is desired. Use a hoop to keep the work taut.

Roumanian couching is usually worked using only one thread colour.
We have used contrasting threads for photographic purposes only.

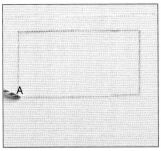

1 Mark the shape to be filled onto the fabric. Bring the thread to the front at A on the left side of the shape.

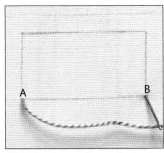

2 Take the needle to the back at B on the other side of the shape.

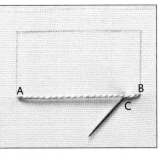

3 Pull the thread through. Completed laid stitch. Bring needle to the front at C directly under the laid stitch.

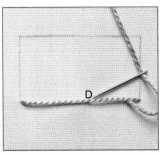

4 Take the needle over the laid stitch and to the back at D forming a diagonal stitch.

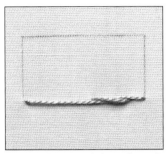

5 Pull the thread through until it sits loosely over the laid stitch. First completed couching stitch.

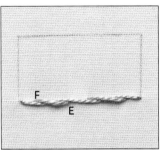

6 Work a second diagonal couching stitch from E to F in the same manner.

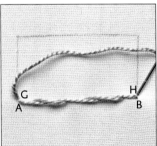

7 Bring the thread to the front at G, just above A on the marked line. Take the needle to the back at H just above B.

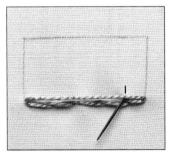

8 Pull through to form a second laid stitch. Bring the needle to the front at I, angling the needle to emerge between the two laid stitches.

9 Take the needle over the second laid stitch and to the back at J, forming a diagonal stitch. Make a second diagonal stitch from K to L.

10 Pull the thread through. Keep an even tension and the stitches loose so they do not distort the fabric. Continue to work in the same manner.

11 **Completed Roumanian couching.**

The petals of this variegated flower are embroidered with Roumanian couching.

Cretan Stitch

Also known as long-armed feather stitch, cretan stitch is a filling or border stitch with a plaited appearance along the centre. The stitches can be worked close together or spaced apart.

1 Rule four lines on the fabric to help with stitch placement. Bring the thread to the front at A, at the top of the first line.

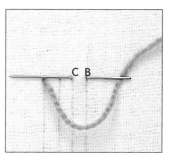

2 Take the needle from B to C. Ensure the thread is below the needle.

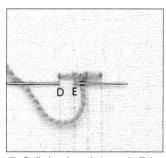

3 Pull the thread through. Take the needle from D to E. Ensure the thread is under the tip of the needle.

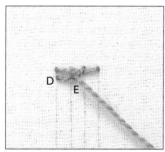

4 Pull the thread through until it lies snugly against the emerging thread.

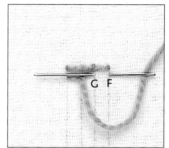

5 Take the needle from F to G. Ensure the thread is under the tip of the needle.

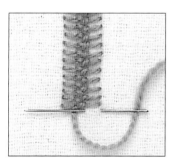

6 Pull the thread through. Continue working stitches in the same manner alternating from right to left.

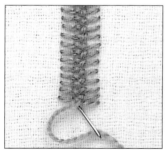

7 To finish, take the needle to the back just below the last stitch very close to where it emerged.

8 Pull the thread through and end off on the back of the fabric.

9 Cretan stitch worked within a shape.

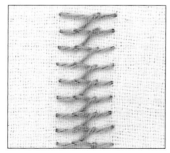

10 Cretan stitch with the stitches spaced apart.

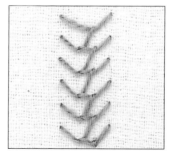

11 Cretan stitch worked with the needle angled.

CREWEL EMBROIDERY

The name 'crewel' refers to the type of thread that is used – a two ply worsted wool yarn that is available in a variety of thicknesses and a huge range of colours. Crewel embroidery is often called Jacobean embroidery, a reference to the flowing motifs that were employed in crewel work during this period in history. These motifs remained popular and are still common in traditional crewel designs.

Many of these beautiful designs, such as the 'Tree of Life', have their origins in India. After the East India company began to trade in the 16th century, there was a steady exchange of design ideas. The exotic flowers, fruits, animals and birds seen in Jacobean designs are evidence of this cultural melting pot.

Crewel work was most commonly used for dressing beds. Houses were cold and draughty, so a four poster (tester) bed would be hung with heavily embroidered curtains. A matching valance and bedspread would complete the set. Other common uses for crewel work were wall-hangings, pockets and petticoats.

Cross Stitch

Cross stitch is probably the oldest and best known of all embroidery stitches. It is usually worked on evenweave fabric, using a tapestry needle. Once the work has begun, ensure the upper stitch of each cross lies in the same direction. Using guidelines or counting fabric threads ensures even-sized stitches.

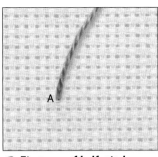

1 **First row of half stitches.** Secure the thread on the back or begin with a waste knot. Bring the thread to the front at A. Pull the thread through.

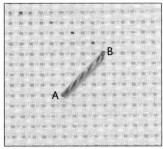

2 Take the thread to the back at B, above and to the right of A. Pull the thread through to form a diagonal stitch.

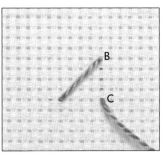

3 Re-emerge at C, directly below B. Pull the thread through.

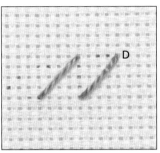

4 Take the needle to the back at D, forming a second stitch parallel to the first stitch. Pull the thread through.

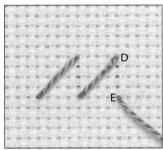

5 Re-emerge at E, directly below D. Pull the thread through.

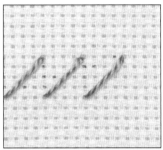

6 Continue in the same manner until the required number of half stitches is worked.

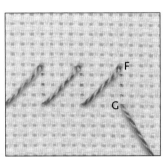

7 Re-emerge at G, directly below the end of the last stitch, F. Pull the thread through. **Completed first row of half stitches.**

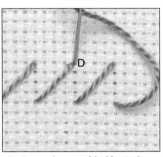

8 **Second row of half stitches.** Using the same hole in the fabric, take the needle to the back at D.

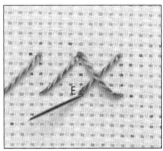

9 Pull the thread through to form the first cross stitch. Re-emerge at E through the same hole in the fabric.

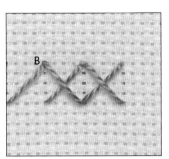

10 Pull the thread through. Take the needle to the back at B using the same hole in the fabric. Pull the thread through.

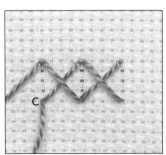

11 Re-emerge at C through the same hole in the fabric. Pull the thread through.

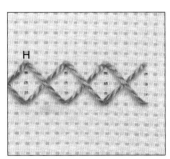

12 Take the needle to the back at H and pull the thread through. Complete the row in the same manner. **Completed cross stitches.**

Cross Stitch – Double

Also known as Leviathan stitch or Smyrna cross stitch, it is most commonly used in canvas embroidery or can form flower centres in surface embroidery.

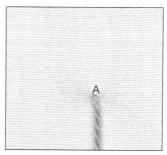

1 Bring the thread to the front at A, in the lower right hand corner of the stitch.

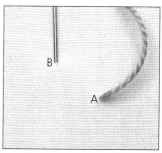

2 Take the needle to the back at B, in the upper left hand corner of the stitch.

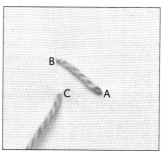

3 Pull the thread through to form the first diagonal stitch. Re-emerge at C, in the lower left hand corner of the stitch.

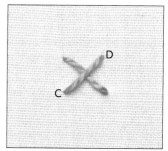

4 Take the needle to the back at D, diagonally opposite. Pull the thread through.

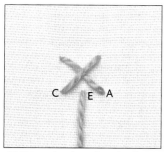

5 Bring the thread to the front of the fabric at E, halfway between A and C.

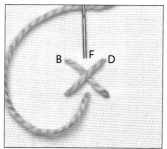

6 Take the needle to the back of the fabric at F, halfway between B and D.

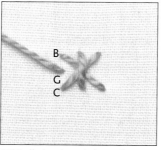

7 Pull the thread through. Re-emerge at G, halfway between B and C.

8 Take the needle to the back of the fabric at H, halfway between A and D.

9 Pull the thread through. **Completed double cross stitch.**

Cross Stitch – Long-armed

This stitch is known by several different names - long-legged cross stitch, plaited Slav stitch, Portuguese stitch and twist stitch. It is worked from left to right, usually on canvas but also on evenweave fabrics. Like cross stitch, once the work has begun, all the top half stitches should lie in the same direction.

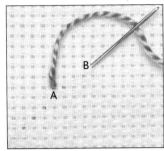

1 Bring the thread to the front at A. Take the needle to the back at B, above and to the right of A.

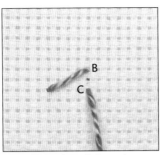

2 Pull the thread through to form a long diagonal straight stitch. Re-emerge at C, directly below B. Pull the thread through.

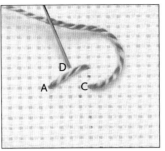

3 Take the needle to the back at D, approximately half the distance between A and C.

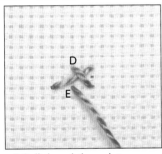

4 Pull thread through to complete the first stitch. Bring the needle to the front at E, directly below D. Pull thread through.

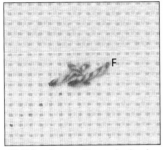

5 Take the needle to the back at F. Pull the thread through forming a second long diagonal straight stitch.

6 Continue working stitches in the same manner. **Completed long-armed cross stitch.**

HINTS

STITCHING CANVAS WORK

Do not pull the stitches too tight. When working on canvas, correct tension is very important. Always maintain the correct stitch order, angle and direction.

HINTS

FINISHING OFF CANVAS WORK

Take the thread to the back of the worked canvas and weave backwards and forwards through several stitches. Alternatively, run the thread under the stitches on the back for approximately 2cm (3/4"). Take care not to alter the tension of the stitches on the front. Trim the thread.

Cross Stitch – Straight Stitch Combination

Here we show cross and straight stitch combination worked with each stitch being completed individually. This stitch can also be worked in separate steps across a row. Ensure the top stitches all lie in the same direction.

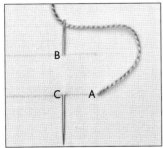

1 Bring the thread to the front at A. Take the needle to the back at B, diagonally opposite A. Re-emerge at C, below B and to the left of A.

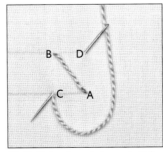

2 Pull the thread through. Take the needle to the back at D, directly above A. Re-emerge at C to begin the straight stitch.

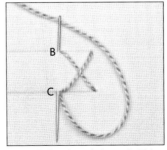

3 Pull the thread through. Take the needle from B to C using the same holes in the fabric.

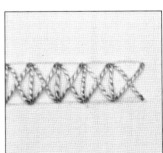

4 Pull thread through. Continue working stitches following steps 1–3. **Completed cross stitches with straight stitches in between.**

Crow's Foot

A crow's foot is a tailoring technique, similar to an arrowhead, which is used to strengthen the stress points on a garment.

Here it is worked as a surface stitch to produce a small decorative triangular motif on plain weave fabric.

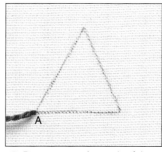

1 Draw a triangle on the fabric. Bring the thread to the front at A on the lower left hand corner.

2 Insert the needle at B and re-emerge at C, picking up one fabric thread.

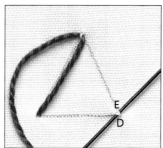

3 Pull the thread through.

4 Take the needle to the back at D on the lower right hand corner and re-emerge at E picking up one fabric thread.

5 Pull the thread through. Take the needle from F to G through the fabric.

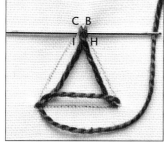

6 Pull the thread through. Take the needle from H to I, just below B and C, picking up a slightly larger piece of fabric.

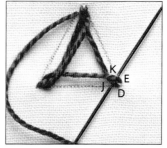

7 Pull the thread through. Take the needle from J to K, just next to D and E, picking up slightly more of the fabric as before.

8 Pull the thread through. Take the needle from L to M, picking up slightly more of the fabric.

9 Continue working stitches in a clockwise direction, picking up slightly larger pieces of fabric in each round.

10 **Completed crow's foot.**

Cutwork

Cutwork is a form of openwork embroidery which includes detached blanket stitch bars and eyelet holes. The embroidery is completed before cutting away any fabric.

CUTWORK EMBROIDERY

Cutwork generally refers to a form of embroidery in which blanket stitch is used to outline a motif or design. Some of the background fabric is then cut away.

After the fabric is cut away, the resulting space is often decorated with cross bars. These are blanket stitched or buttonholed over and then joined to each other.

It appears to have originated from Flanders and Italy and its influence can be seen in the white-work samplers of the 17th century.

A large quantity of cutwork was produced in Venice, initially in ecclesiastical vestments and altar cloths stitched by nuns in convents.

Gradually the nuns taught the art to pupils who spread the technique outside the Church for adornment of houses and clothing.

Cutwork became so popular in England that Mary Tudor passed an edict in 1555 restricting its importation. She also designated who could wear it. A man had to hold the title of Baron or higher to enjoy the privilege of wearing imported cutwork. Ladies married to men lower than a knight were forbidden to wear imported cutwork.

1 Work a running stitch outline around all areas to be blanket stitched. When reaching the first bar, take the needle to the inside of the shape and take a small stitch.

2 Pull the thread through. Take a long stitch back to the beginning of the bar, then across to the inside of the shape again in the same manner.

3 Blanket stitch over these three strands until they are completely covered and the thread is back at the start. The stitches do not pierce the fabric. Do not stretch the bar.

4 Continue working running stitch and the blanket stitch bars until the outer section is complete. Work running stitch around the inner section.

5 Starting on the outside of the design, work close blanket stitch around the areas to be cut. The purl of the blanket stitch lies against the area to be cut away.

6 Work blanket stitch along the inner line of the design covering the opposite ends of the bars. You may wish to turn your work as you stitch.

7 **Completed blanket stitching.**

8 **Cutting the fabric.** Using the point of a pair of very sharp, fine embroidery scissors, pierce the fabric in the centre of one area to be cut away. With the right side up, clip towards the blanket stitch edge.

9 Cut away the fabric as close to the blanket stitching as possible. Angle the scissors under the purl edge and take great care not to cut any of the edging stitches or bars. **Completed cutwork heart.**

Danish Knot

This easy knot can be worked singly as an accent stitch or close together to create textured clusters.

It is a delightful pebbly knot adding quite heavy texture when worked en masse in thick, shiny thread such as perlé cotton.

The substantial nature of this knot gives subtle contrasts between light and shade when different weights and colours of thread are used.

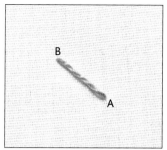

1 Bring the thread to the front at A and take a short diagonal straight stitch to B. This is the foundation stitch.

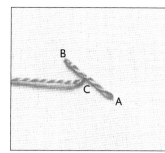

2 Bring the needle to the front at C to the left of the foundation stitch, halfway between A and B. Pull the thread through.

3 With the thread below the needle, slide the needle under the foundation stitch above C. Take care not to catch the thread or the fabric.

4 Pull the thread gently.

5 Continue pulling the thread through until the knot lies gently around the foundation stitch.

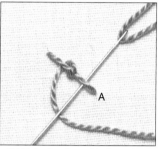

6 With the thread below the needle, slide the needle under the foundation stitch, just above A. The needle is at a right angle to the foundation stitch.

7 Begin to pull the thread through gently.

8 Continue pulling the thread through until the second knot rests on the foundation stitch.

9 Take the needle to the back close to the knot and finish off.

10 **Completed Danish knot.**

Detached Back Stitch

Also known as spider's web stitch, this filling stitch gives the appearance of rows of bullion knots. Work with a loose tension and keep the rows of back stitches packed close together.

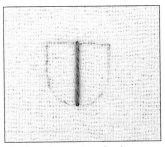

1 Foundation. Work a long straight stitch through the centre of the shape.

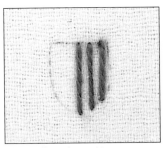

2 Working from this centre stitch, fill one side of the shape with parallel straight stitches no more than 2.5mm (⅛") apart.

3 Fill the remaining half of the shape in the same manner.

4 Detached back stitches. Using a tapestry needle, bring a new length of thread to the front at the lower edge on the right hand side.

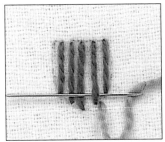

5 Take the needle from right to left under the foundation stitch. Do not go through the fabric.

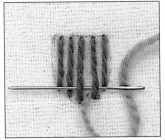

6 Pull the thread through. Take the needle from right to left under the first two foundation stitches.

7 Pull the thread through but do not distort the straight stitches.

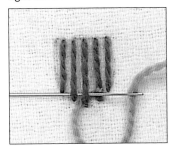

8 Take the needle from right to left behind the second and third straight stitches.

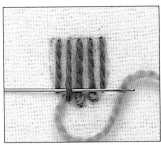

9 Pull the thread through. Continue in the same manner to the end of the row, always going behind one new and one used straight stitch.

10 At the end of the row, take the needle from right to left behind the last straight stitch.

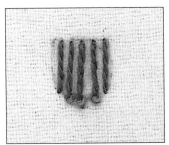

11 Pull the thread through. Take the needle to the back of the fabric on the marked outline.

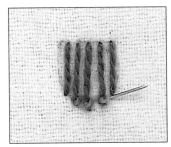

12 Pull the thread through. Bring the needle to the front on the right hand side of the shape, just above the previous row of back stitches.

13 Pull the thread through. Work across the row in the same manner as before.

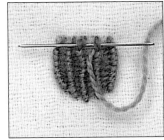

14 Always working in the same direction, continue stitching rows close together.

Detached Chain

This stitch is also commonly known as lazy daisy stitch. Other names are daisy stitch, knotted knot stitch, loop stitch, picot stitch, tied loop stitch, tail stitch and link powdering stitch.

Detached chain stitch is a looped stitch, which can be worked alone or in groups. It can also be used as a filling stitch with individual stitches placed at regular intervals over the space to be filled.

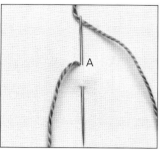

1 Bring the needle to the front at the base of the stitch at A. Take the needle to the back as close as possible to A. Re-emerge at the tip of the stitch.

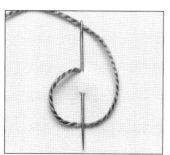

2 Loop the thread in an anti-clockwise direction under the tip of the needle.

3 Keeping your left thumb over the loop, pull the thread through (thumb not shown). The tighter you pull, the thinner the stitch will become.

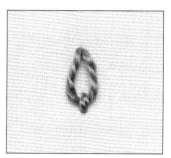

4 To anchor the stitch, take the thread to the back just over the loop. **Completed detached chain.**

Detached Chain – Flowers

Detached chain stitch can be used to create a variety of flowers and leaves.

Here we show two methods to stitch different daisies, with each petal being a single detached chain.

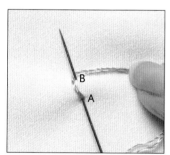

1 **Five petal daisy.** Bring the needle to the front at A (centre). Take it to the back at A and re-emerge at B. Loop the thread under needle tip.

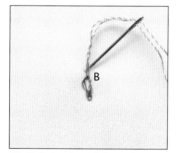

2 Pull the thread through gently. Anchor the stitch by taking the needle to the back over the loop, just above B. **Completed first detached chain petal.**

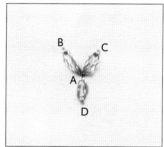

3 Pull the thread through and bring the needle up at A. Work two more stitches from A–C and A–D. The three petals form a 'Y' shape.

4 Work the fourth and fifth stitches midway between C and D and B and D. **Completed five petal daisy.**

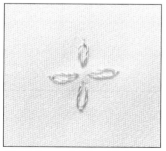

1 **Eight petal daisy.** Mark a tiny circle for the flower centre. Work four petals from the centre circle in the form of a cross.

2 Work four more petals in the spaces between the previous four. You may wish to fill the centre with French knots. **Completed eight petal daisy.**

THREADING NEEDLES

Ensure that the end of the thread has been cut cleanly– on an angle may help. Any stray fibres can push the thread away from the needle when you try to thread it.

Moisten the end of the thread and flatten it between your fingers. The eye of the needle is an elongated shape, not round, so you need to make the thread fit the eye. After threading, cut the moist piece off.

If you are having real difficulty, try a size larger needle.

Are you using the right end of the thread? Make sure you are threading with the grain running down the thread. The wrong end will 'frizz up' as you try to push it through the eye.

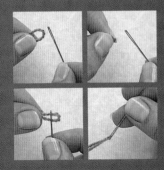

Try folding the end of the thread around the needle. Pinch it tightly and slide it off the needle. Push the folded piece through the eye. This method is particularly useful for wool threads.

Detached Chain–French Knot Combination Flower

This combination of stitches is used to complete detached chain flowers. The French knots form the tips of the petals.

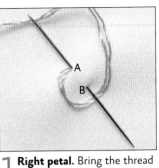

1 **Right petal.** Bring the thread to front at A. Take the needle to the back at A and re-emerge at B. The needle is angled to the right. Loop the thread under needle tip.

2 Wrap the thread twice in a counter-clockwise direction around the needle tip.

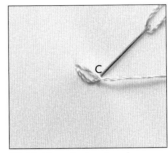

3 Holding the knot under your thumb (thumb not shown), pull thread gently towards you. Pull the knot to the right. Take the thread to the back at C. This forms a small 'foot'.

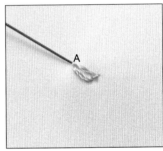

4 **Completed right petal.** The detached chain is now anchored with a French knot. To begin the left petal, bring the needle and thread to the front at A.

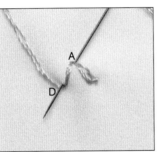

5 **Left petal.** Take the needle from A to D. The needle is angled to the left. Loop the thread clockwise under the needle tip.

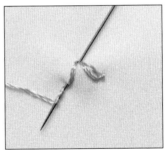

6 Wrap the thread around the needle twice in a clockwise direction.

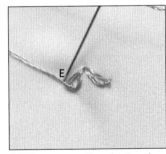

7 Repeat step 3 anchoring the chain to the left at E forming a small 'foot'.

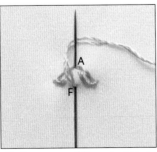

8 **Centre petal** (detached chain only). Bring the thread to the front at F. Take the needle to the back at F again and re-emerge at A. Loop the thread under the needle tip.

9 To anchor the petal take the needle to the back just over the loop at A and end off.

10 **Completed flower.**

Detached Chain – Twisted

Twisted detached chain is a variation of detached chain and can be worked with either ribbon or thread.

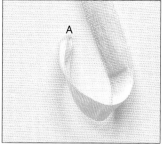

1 Bring the ribbon to the front at A. Make a counter-clockwise loop. Hold the loop on the fabric with your thumb (thumb not shown).

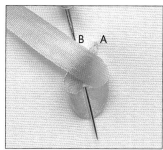

2 Take the needle to the back at B, just to the left of A. Re-emerge through the loop at C.

3 Ensure the ribbon is smooth and untwisted. Carefully pull the needle through until the loop gently tightens around the ribbon.

4 Take the needle to the back of the fabric just over the loop. Pull the ribbon through. Completed twisted detached chain.

Drizzle Stitch – Flower

Drizzle stitch is best worked with a milliner's (straw) needle. It is created from cast-ons like those used in cast-on stitch. The stitches are very effective when clustered together as shown below.

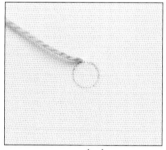

1 Draw a 6mm (¼") circle on the fabric. Knot the thread and bring it to the front on the edge of the circle.

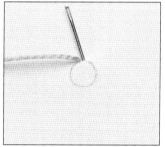

2 Insert the needle halfway into the fabric just next to the thread. Unthread the needle.

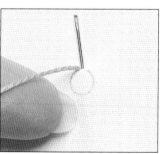

3 With your finger facing you, place the thread over your left index finger.

4 Rotate your finger towards you. Keep the thread taut and looped around your index finger.

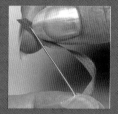

Drizzle Stitch—Flower CONTINUED

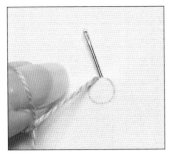

5 Continue to rotate your finger until the thread is wrapped around the finger.

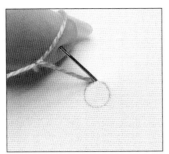

6 Keeping tension on the thread, place the tip of your finger on the end of the needle.

7 Slip the loop off your finger and onto the needle.

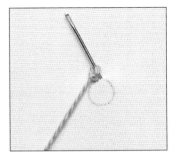

8 Pull the thread tight, slipping the loop down the needle onto the fabric. This is the first cast-on.

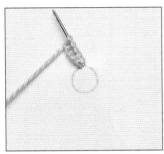

9 Work four more cast-ons in the same manner. Pull each one firmly and pack them down onto the needle.

10 Re-thread the needle. Pull the needle and thread through the cast-ons. First completed drizzle stitch.

11 Continue working stitches around the circle in the same manner.

12 Fill the centre of the circle with drizzle stitches. **Completed drizzle stitch flower.**

HINTS

EMBROIDERY ON CLOTHING

Embroidered embellishment can be as simple as a single, bold line of stitching over a seam, or a complex design that covers large areas of the garment. Embroidery adds a wonderful personal touch to your clothing and you can create something truly unique from an ordinary mass produced item.

Many embroidery designs can be adapted for use on garments. Trace the design and move it around on the garment to find the position that suits it best. You may find that you only need to use part of the design to achieve the desired effect.

Some ideas you can try are -

> *Pants*—around the leg edge, down the side seams, along the pocket edges
> *Shirts and blouses*—on collars, cuffs and pocket edges, down the front button bands
> *Skirts*—around the lower edge
> *Jackets*—down the lapels and front openings, on pocket edges, around lower sleeves
> *Cardigans and jumpers*—around the neckline and cuffs, along the lower edge
> Sprays of bullion roses and other small embroidered motifs add a lovely touch to underwear and sleepwear

Ermine Filling Stitch

Ermine filling stitch is an easy stitch to work. If worked in black thread on white fabric, it looks very much like ermine tails, hence the name. Mark two parallel lines on the fabric to help keep the stitches even.

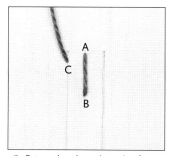 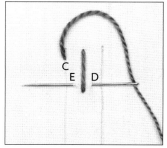 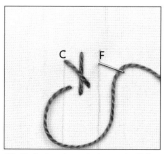 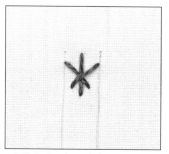

1 Bring the thread to the front at A. Take it to the back at B and re-emerge at C, slightly lower than A. Pull through to form the centre straight stitch.

2 Take the thread through the fabric from right to left, D to E, just above the end of the central straight stitch.

3 Pull the thread through. Take the needle to the back at F, directly opposite C.

4 Pull the thread through. **Completed ermine filling stitch.**

Eyelet

These embroidered holes are the basis of traditional white-on-white broderie anglaise or Swiss embroideries. They are also used in Madeira and Venetian embroidery.

Eyelets have a small central hole, which is surrounded by running stitches and then covered by short, regular, over-casting stitches. The beauty of this technique is in the regularity of the stitches.

Mark a tiny circle on the fabric.

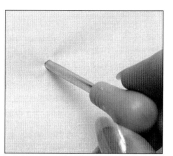 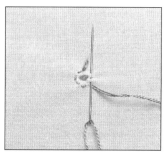 

1 With right side up, and using a dressmaker's awl, pierce the fabric on the marked circle. Do this carefully. The awl should gently separate the fabric fibres.

2 With the right side of the work facing, work small running stitches around the circle, leaving a tail of approx 3mm (1/8").

3 On the last stitch, take the needle through the first stitch, splitting the stitch. Pull the thread through.

 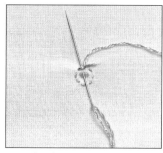 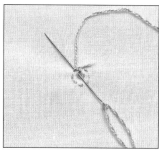

4 Re-pierce the hole with the awl. Bring the needle and thread to the front of the work just outside a running stitch.

5 Take the needle through the pierced hole and bring it to the right side directly alongside the emerging thread. Pull the thread through.

6 Holding the emerging thread under the thumb, take the needle through the pierced hole and bring to the right side alongside the previous stitch (thumb not shown).

Eyelet CONTINUED

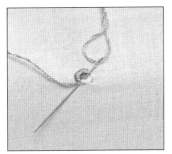  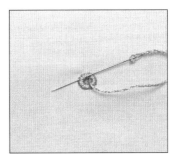 

7 Closely overcast the edge of the eyelet as shown. Keep turning the work to maintain consistent fanning of the stitches. Keep an even tension on the closely worked stitches.

8 Finish overcasting and take the thread to the back through the hole.

9 To end off, take the thread under the overcast stitches on the back.

10 If necessary, use the awl to carefully re-punch the hole from the back. This helps to 'settle' the thread and fabric.

Eyelet Flowers

These flowers consist of an eyelet centre and granitos petals.
The overcast stitches of the eyelet need to be worked very firmly, while the petals require a looser tension.

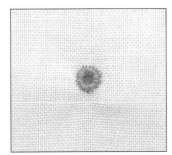 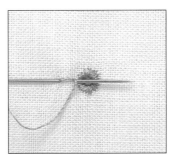 

1 Work an eyelet centre following the instructions above.

2 **Petals.** Each petal is a granitos. Work 3 stitches into the same two holes, positioning the stitches each side of the first stitch.

3 Work 13 more stitches in the same manner. The granitos should have a full, rounded look. **Completed petal.**

4 Work the remaining five petals in a similar manner. Re-pierce the eyelet from the back to settle the stitches. **Completed flower.**

HINTS

SIGNING YOUR WORK

When a piece is complete many embroiderers, like artists, often sign their name or initials. This is important because it identifies the embroiderer.

Initials are often added to the right hand corner of a finished piece. The placing of a signature or initials is just a matter of choice.

A signature should never detract from the finished piece nor take the viewer's eye from the work.

Eyelet–Shaped

Large eyelets can be worked in a variety of shapes. Leaves, petals, ovals, triangles or large circles are some of the shapes appearing in broderie anglaise or cutwork designs. These are stitched in a similar manner to the eyelets, however the fabric is cut rather than pierced. Lengthen the overcasting stitches on the points and corners of the tear-drop and triangular eyelets. Always work on a fabric with a fine, firm texture and use twisted threads such as stranded cotton and silk.

1 Draw the shape onto the fabric. Work running stitch just outside the outline. For a tear-drop or petal, cut fabric into segments within the outline as shown.

2 Cut larger circles and triangles into segments as shown.

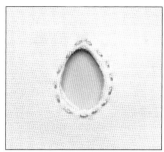

3 Turn the fabric flaps to the back in the centre of the shape and finger press.

4 Overcast the eyelet, catching the flaps with the stitches. Clip away any excess fabric on the wrong side. **Completed eyelet.**

Faggoting

Faggoting, or twisted insertion stitch, can be used to join together two pieces of fabric, producing an attractive join with an open, lacy look. Strong cotton or linen thread should be used. The measurements given are intended as a guide only.

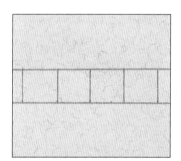

1 On a piece of stiff paper, rule two parallel lines 3mm (⅛") apart. Rule vertical lines (crossbars) between the parallel lines at 3mm (⅛") intervals.

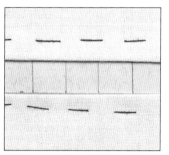

2 Press under and finish the seam allowance on each piece of the fabric. Align the folded edges with the parallel lines and tack the fabric to the paper.

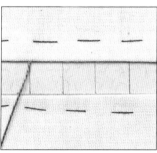

3 Knot the thread. Take the thread through the fold of the seam allowance in the upper piece of fabric, emerging at the top of a crossbar.

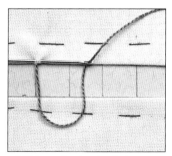

4 Take a tiny back stitch near the fold to secure the thread.

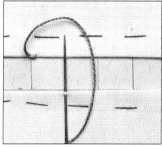

5 Pull the thread through. Loop to the right above the needle tip. Keeping needle vertical, pick up a few threads on the fold of the lower fabric at the next crossbar.

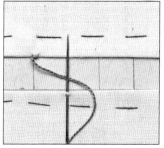

6 Ensure the thread loop is behind the tip of the needle.

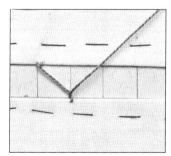

7 Pull the thread through.

Faggoting CONTINUED

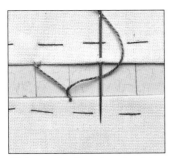

8 Loop the thread to the right. Pick up a few threads on the fold of the upper fabric at the top of the next crossbar.

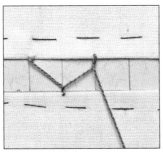

9 Ensure the loop is behind the needle. Pull the thread through.

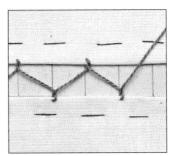

10 Continue in the same manner to the end.

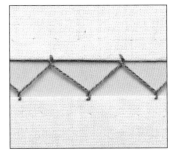

11 To end off, work two tiny back stitches near a folded edge on wrong side. Remove the tacking stitches and paper. Press and spray starch the stitches to set them. **Completed faggoting.**

Faggoting – Single

This stitch is also known as diagonal line stitch and diagonal square stitch.

The arrow indicates the top of the fabric.

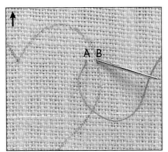

1 Bring the thread to the front in the top right hand corner at A. Take the needle to the back over four threads at B.

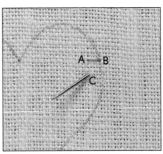

2 Pull the thread through. Re-emerge at C, four threads down from A.

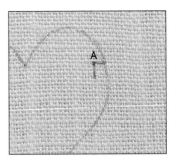

3 Pull the thread through. Take the needle to the back at A and pull through.

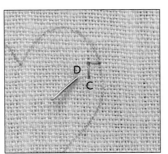

4 Re-emerge at D, four threads to the left of C.

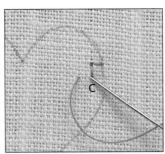

5 Pull the thread through. Take needle to the back at C. Continue in this manner pulling each stitch tightly.

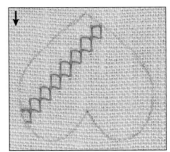

6 To work the second row, turn the fabric upside down, repeat the process, using some of the holes of the first row.

7 Continue stitching until the heart is filled. **Completed single faggoting.**

Fine single faggoting worked on a handkerchief

Feather Stitch

Feather stitch is a delicate stitch, often used to decorate baby and children's clothing.

The stitch can vary greatly in appearance, depending on the angle of the needle and the length of the stitches.

The tension, needle angle and stitch length must be kept consistent throughout to ensure even stitches.

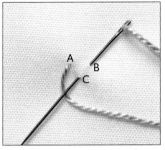

1 Bring the needle to the front at A. Loop the thread to the right and take the needle from B to C. The loop is under the needle.

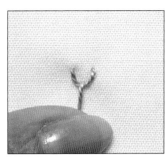

2 Pull the thread through in a downward movement, holding the thread firmly with the thumb. **Completed first stitch.**

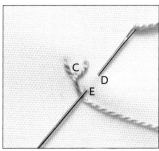

3 Take the needle from D to E. Loop the thread under the needle tip.

4 Pull the thread through. **Completed second stitch.**

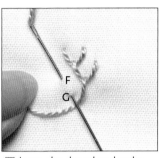

5 Loop the thread under the needle and hold in place. Take the needle from F to G.

6 Continue, following steps 3–5. Finish with a tiny stitch over the last loop. **Completed feather stitch.**

Feather Stitch–Closed
This stitch is worked downwards between two parallel lines.

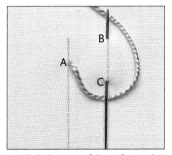

1 Rule lines on fabric. Bring the thread to the front at A. Pull the thread through. Take the needle from B to C. Loop thread under the needle tip.

2 Pull the thread through in a downward motion until the loop rests snugly on the emerging thread.

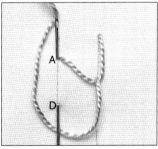

3 Take the needle from A to D, using the same hole in the fabric at A. Ensure the thread is looped under the tip of the needle.

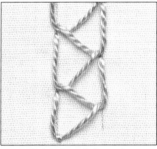

4 Pull the thread through as before. Continue working stitches from side to side in the same manner. **Completed closed feather stitch.**

Feather Stitch– Double and Triple

The double and triple styles of feather stitch are attractive variations of basic feather stitch. Usually worked in a regular pattern these variations produce a delightful lacy effect. To keep the stitches even, rule three parallel lines on the fabric for double feather stitch and four lines for triple feather stitch.

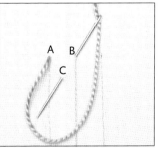

1 Double feather stitch. Emerge at A. Insert the needle at B, directly opposite A. Re-emerge at C, halfway between and slightly lower than A and B.

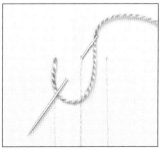

2 Loop the thread to the right and under the needle.

3 Pull the thread through in a downward movement. Hold the thread firmly with your thumb.

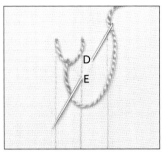

4 Keeping the thread taut, loop it to the right. Take the needle from D to E. Ensure the loop is under the tip of the needle.

5 Pull the thread through in a downward movement and hold it firmly with your thumb (thumb not shown).

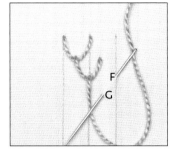

6 Keeping the thread taut, loop it to the right. Take the needle from F to G. Ensure the loop is under the tip of the needle.

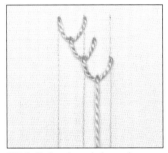

7 Pull the thread through as before.

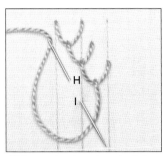

8 Loop the thread to the left and hold in place firmly with your thumb. Take the needle from H to I, ensuring the loop is under the tip of the needle.

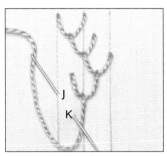

9 Pull the thread through as before. Again, loop the thread to the left and hold in place firmly with your thumb. Take the needle from J to K.

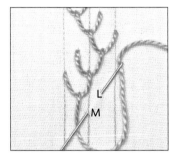

10 Pull the thread through as before. Loop the thread to the right and hold in place firmly with your thumb, taking the needle from L to M.

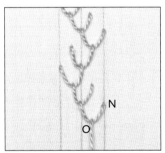

11 Pull the thread through as before. Again, loop the thread to the right. Holding the thread firmly, take a stitch from N to O and pull through.

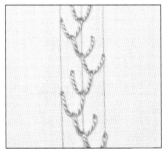

12 Continue in this manner, working the sequence of two stitches to the left and two stitches to the right each time.

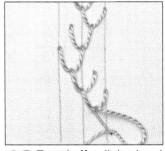

13 To end off, pull the thread through for the last stitch. Take the needle to the back over the looped thread, just below where it emerged.

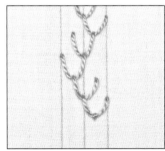

14 Pull the thread through and secure on the back. Completed double feather stitch.

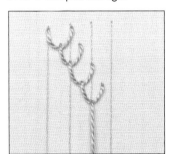

1 **Triple feather stitch variation.** Work steps 1–7 and then work one more stitch.

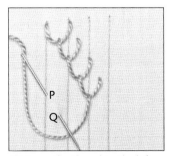

2 Loop the thread to the left and hold firmly. Take the needle to the back at P, on the left hand side directly opposite the last stitch. Re-emerge at Q.

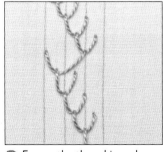

3 Ensure the thread is under the tip of the needle and pull through as before. Work three stitches with the thread looped to the right.

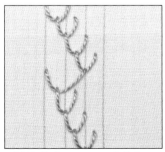

4 Work the next stitch following step 16. Continue in this sequence to the end of the row. **Completed triple feather stitch variation.**

Fishbone Stitch

Fishbone stitch is a close filling stitch with a plaited centre suitable for working shapes such as borders, leaves, feathers or wings. When used for leaves the stitches cross at the centre and the plaited effect forms the central vein.

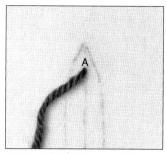

1 **Straight fishbone stitch.** Mark the outline of the shape and central line on the fabric. Bring the thread to the front at A on the centre line.

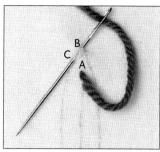

2 Take the needle from B, at the end of the line, to C. The thread is to the right of the needle.

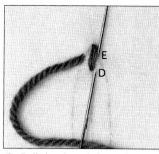

3 Pull the thread through. With the thread to the left, take the needle from D to E.

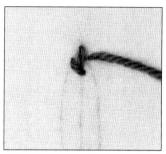

4 Pull the thread through. This forms the first half of the first fishbone stitch.

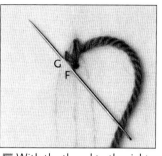

5 With the thread to the right, take the needle from F to G.

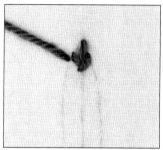

6 Pull the thread through. Completed first fishbone stitch.

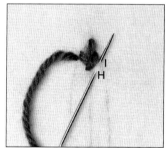

7 With the thread to the left, take the needle from H to I.

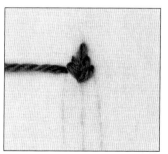

8 Pull the thread through, and repeat steps 5 and 6. **Completed second fishbone stitch.**

9 Continue stitching alternating from left to right, forming a straight line of fishbone stitch. Completed straight fishbone stitch.

10 **Curved fishbone stitch.** Follow steps 1 to 8, until the shape begins to curve. On the curve, begin to increase the distance between the stitches on the outside edge.

11 Work down the shape, decreasing the distance between the stitches on the inside curve as well as increasing the distance on the outside curve.

12 Continue stitching. The sharper the curve, the greater the distance between the stitches on the outside line. **Completed curved fishbone stitch.**

Fishbone Stitch– Raised

Also known as overlapping herringbone stitch, this stitch is a simple variation of basic fishbone stitch.

Here the stitches are taken right across the shape, rather than to a central line, to make a raised effect.

Draw a shape on the fabric and mark the centre.

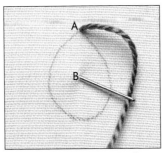

1 Bring the thread to the front at A at the top of the shape. Take the needle to the back at B.

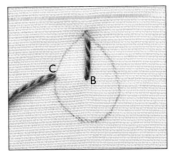

2 Pull the thread through. Bring the thread to the front at C, on the outline directly across from B. Pull the thread through.

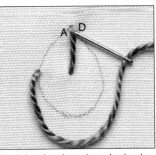

3 Take the thread to the back at D on the marked line, very close and to the right of A.

4 Pull the thread through. Emerge at E, on the marked line, very close and to the left of A. Pull the thread through.

5 Take the needle to the back at F, on the outline directly opposite C.

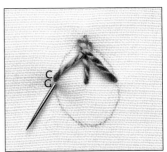

6 Pull the thread through and emerge at G, on the marked line just below C.

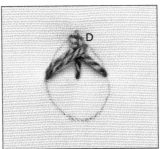

7 Pull the thread through. Take the thread to the back on the opposite side just below D.

8 Pull the thread through. Bring the needle to the front on the opposite side just below E.

9 Pull the thread through. Take the thread to the back on the opposite side just below F.

10 Pull the thread through and re-emerge on the opposite side just below G.

11 Continue working stitches in the same manner, ensuring they cross near the centre.

12 **Completed raised fishbone stitch.**

Fly Stitch

Fly stitch is an open detached chain stitch with many possible variations.
It is worked in the shape of a 'V' or 'Y' depending on the length of the anchoring stitch.

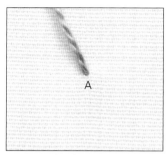

1 Bring the thread to the front at A. This will be the left hand side of the stitch.

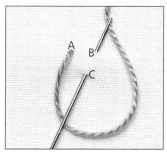

2 Take the needle to the back at B and re-emerge at C. Loop the thread under the tip of the needle and to the right.

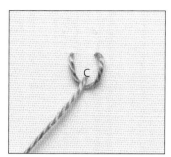

3 Hold the loop in place under the left thumb (thumb not shown). Pull the needle through until the looped thread lies snugly against C.

4 Take the thread to the back at the required distance below C to anchor the fly stitch. **Completed fly stitch.**

Fly Stitch– Twisted

A variation of fly stitch, this stitch can be used to form the calyxes for buds. The stalks can be varied in length to suit the design.

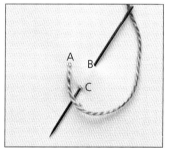

1 Bring the needle to the front at A. Take the needle to the back at B and re-emerge at C. The needle is under the thread.

2 Gently begin to pull the needle through. The loop is over the thread.

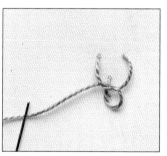

3 Take the needle over and through the loop. Begin to pull the thread through.

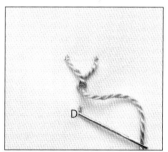

4 Pull thread through until the stitch lies flat on the fabric. To anchor the twisted fly stitch, take the needle to the back at D for the required length.

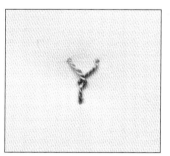

5 Pull the thread through. **Completed twisted fly stitch with long anchoring stitch.**

Fly stitch is often used to work the calyx of flowers

Fly Stitch Leaf

These effective leaves are created with several fly stitches worked closely together. They can be made to curl to either the right or left.

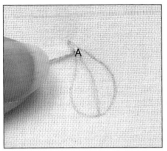

1 **Leaf curling to the left.** Bring the thread to the front at A, a short distance from the tip of the leaf. Hold it to the left.

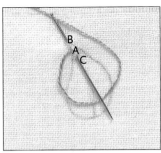

2 Take the needle from B to C. A, B and C are aligned and B is at the tip of the leaf.

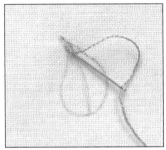

3 Pull the thread through, ensuring it goes under the tip of the needle. Take the needle to the back of the fabric just over the loop of thread.

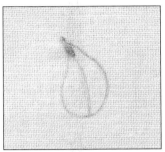

4 Pull the thread through to anchor the loop.

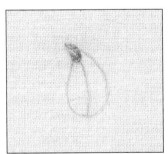

5 Work a second fly stitch around the first.

6 Work several more fly stitches in the same manner until the leaf is the desired width.

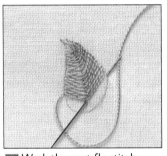

7 Work the next fly stitch directly below the previous stitch. This stitch is the same width as the previous one.

8 Continue working stitches following step 7 until the leaf is the desired length.

9 End off the last stitch. **Completed fly stitch leaf.**

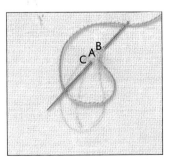

10 **Leaf curling to the right.** Bring the thread to the front at A. Hold it to the right and take the needle from B to C.

11 Work the stitches in the same manner but as a mirror image of those for a leaf curling to the left.

Folded Ribbon Rose

These decorative roses can be made from different widths and types of ribbon. The size of the rose is determined by the width of the ribbon and the number of folds. Each rose is formed individually and attached to the fabric.

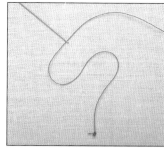

1 Prepare a needle threaded with matching machine sewing thread. Put a small knot in the end.

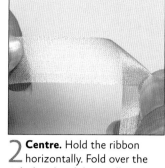

2 **Centre.** Hold the ribbon horizontally. Fold over the right hand end diagonally so you have a tail of ribbon approx 1.5cm (⅝") long.

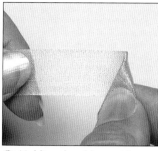

3 Holding the ribbon with your left hand and the folded tail with your right, roll the fold firmly in a clockwise direction for one turn.

4 Roll twice more to form the centre of the rose.

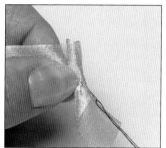

5 Still holding firmly and using the thread, take the needle through all layers of ribbon at the lower edge.

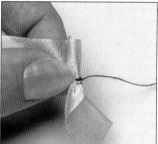

6 Pull the thread through. Take two more stitches through all layers. Leave the thread hanging free.

7 **Petals.** Hold the centre in your right hand. Fold the top edge of the ribbon back and down with your other hand.

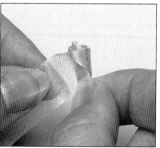

8 Wrap the folded ribbon once around the centre.

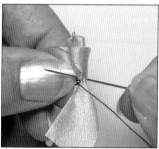

9 Using the thread, take the needle through all layers at the base of the rose.

10 Pull the thread through. Work a second stitch through all layers.

11 Fold the top edge of the ribbon back and down once again.

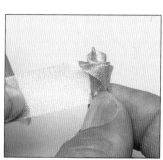

12 Wrap the folded ribbon once around the centre.

Folded Ribbon Rose CONTINUED

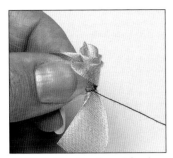

13 Pulling the thread firmly, work two stitches through all layers at the base of the rose to secure the petal.

14 Continue folding, wrapping and stitching until the rose is the desired size.

15 Cut off the excess ribbon leaving a tail that is the width of the ribbon plus 1.5cm (⅝") long. Fold the ribbon back and down as before.

16 Wrap the ribbon to form a partial petal.

17 **Securing the rose.** Turn the rose upside down. Pulling firmly, take several stitches through the base to secure.

18 End off the thread.

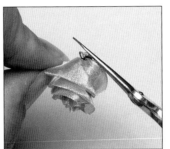

19 Trim away the tail as close as possible to the base without cutting the stitching.

20 **Completed rose.**

Folded Ribbon Rosebud

Folded rosebuds are worked in a similar manner to the roses. The centre of the bud is identical to the centre of the rose but only one petal is formed to complete the bud.

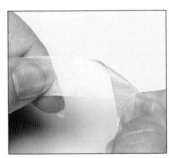

1 **Centre.** Fold the right hand end of the ribbon over at a 90° angle (refer to step 1 on the previous page).

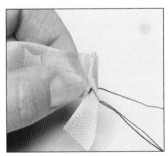

2 Holding the ribbon in your left hand and the folded tail in your right hand, roll ribbon firmly for 3 turns. Secure as for folded rose.

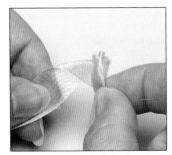

3 **Petal.** With the left thumb and forefinger, fold the top edge of the ribbon back and down.

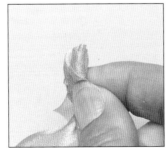

4 Wrap the ribbon in a counter-clockwise direction, allowing the folded edge to angle towards the base of the bud.

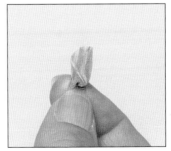

5 Stitch through all layers to secure. End off the thread. Trim the excess ribbon close to the stitching.

6 **Completed folded ribbon roses and rosebuds.**

Four-Legged Knot Stitch

Four-legged knot stitch has the appearance of a cross with a knot in the centre. The knots can be worked close together or sprinkled randomly. The foundation stitches were worked longer for photographic purposes only.

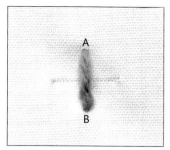

1 Bring the needle to the front at A at the top of a cross. Take the thread to the back at B to form the first stitch.

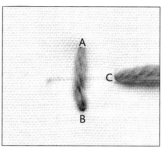

2 Bring the needle to the front at C and pull the thread through.

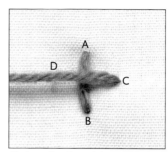

3 Lay the thread from C to D, and hold in position with the thumb (thumb not shown).

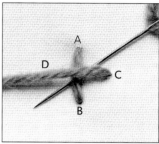

4 With the thread looped below, slide the needle from the upper right to the lower left under both threads at the centre.

5 Pull the thread through gently, ensuring the loop is under the tip of the needle.

6 Continue to pull through to tighten the knot.

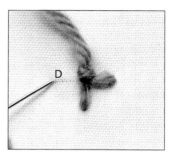

7 Take needle to the back at D.

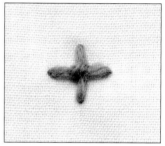

8 Pull the thread through and secure on the back.
Completed four-legged knot stitch.

Four Sided Stitch

Also known as square open work stitch and four sided open work stitch, four sided stitch forms an attractive border. This stitch is worked from right to left.

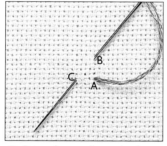

1 Bring the needle to the front at A. Take to the back at B, four threads above A. Emerge at C, four threads below and four to the left.

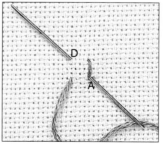

2 Pull the needle through and insert at A, through the same hole in the fabric. Bring to the front at D, four threads above and four to the left.

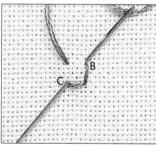

3 Insert the needle at B and re-emerge at C.

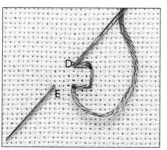

4 Insert the needle at D and emerge at E, four threads below and four to left.

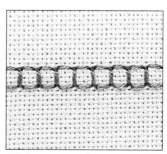

5 Continue in this manner to the end of the row.
Completed four sided stitch.

French Knot

The traditional French knot was worked with only one wrap, however today it is often worked with more.
A larger knot will look neater worked with more strands of thread rather than too many wraps.

1 Bring the thread to the front.

2 Hold the thread firmly with your left thumb and index finger 3cm (1¼") away from the fabric.

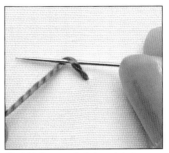

3 With your left hand, bring the thread over the needle. Ensure the needle points away from the fabric.

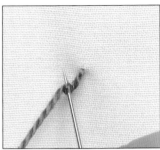

4 Wrap thread around the needle. Keeping the thread taut, begin to turn the point of the needle towards the fabric.

5 Take the needle to the back approx 1–2 fabric threads away from the emerging thread.

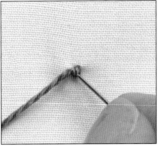

6 Slide the knot down the needle onto the fabric. Pull the thread until the knot is firmly around the needle.

7 Slowly push the needle to the back of the fabric while holding the knot in place under your thumb. Begin to pull the thread through.

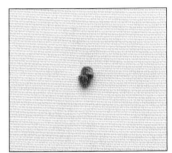

8 Continue to pull until the thread disappears under your thumb and is completely pulled through. **Completed French knot.**

French Knot – Colonial Knot Berry

Berries created from a dense mass of French and colonial knots are perfect for raised embroidery.
Using different sized knots gives texture and character to the berries. We used 4 shades of crewel wool
and tiny glass beads for added highlights.

1 Draw a circle slightly smaller in diameter than the desired size of the finished berry. Using the darkest shade, work 4 French knots in one third of the circle.

2 Using the same colour thread, scatter 2–4 colonial knots in the same area. Leave the thread hanging free.

3 Using a paler shade of thread, stitch 6–8 French or colonial knots among those already worked. Leave the thread hanging free.

4 Using the next palest shade, work knots along the upper edge of this section, merging the three shades. The lower section is completely filled.

French Knot – Colonial Knot Berry CONTINUED

5 Using the same shade, densely fill the middle third of the circle with French and colonial knots. Leave the thread hanging free.

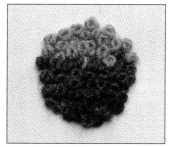

6 With the lightest shade, work French and colonial knots in the remaining section of the circle. Leave the thread hanging free.

7 Re-thread the darkest shade and work 5–6 knots on top of those already worked in the first third of the circle. Leave the thread hanging free.

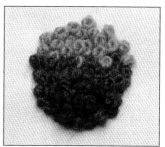

8 Re-thread the second shade and work knots in the first third of the circle and merge into the middle of the circle. Leave the thread hanging free.

9 Re-thread the third shade and continue working knots over those already stitched, merging from the middle third to the last third. Leave the thread hanging free.

10 Finally, re-thread the lightest shade in the berry and work French and colonial knots in the last section of the circle.

11 To smooth the edges, work knots in any gaps around the edge. Use the shade that matches the adjacent knots. End off the threads on the back.

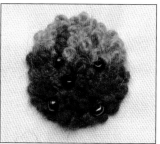

12 Securely attach 5 beads using doubled sewing thread. Pull the thread firmly so the beads nestle among the knots. **Completed berry.**

French Knot – Ribbon Flower

Ribbon French knot flowers are created by working a loose French knot with ribbon and then anchoring this with a firm French knot using thread.

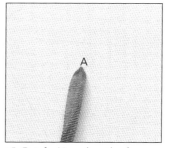

1 **Petals.** Use a length of ribbon approx 30cm (12") long. Bring the ribbon to the front at A, leaving a short tail, approx 1cm (³⁄₈") on the back.

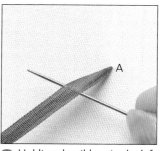

2 Holding the ribbon in the left hand, place the needle under the ribbon approx 1.5cm (⁵⁄₈") away from A.

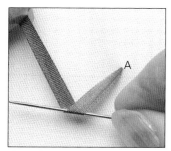

3 Holding the ribbon in the left hand, take the ribbon behind the needle towards A.

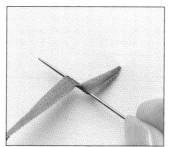

4 With the left hand, take the ribbon over the needle, forming one wrap.

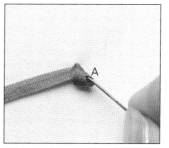

5 Place the needle in the fabric very close to A, allowing the wrap to slide gently down the needle onto the fabric. Do not pull the knot tight.

6 Begin to pull the ribbon through gently.

French Knot – Ribbon Flower CONTINUED

7 Continue pulling the ribbon through gently, leaving a very loose French knot on the fabric. Leave the ribbon hanging free.

8 **Centre.** Thread a needle with a thread and secure on the back. Bring to the front in the centre of the ribbon French knot.

9 Pull thread through. Work a French knot in the centre. Take the thread to the back. Trim the ribbon and secure the tail with thread. **Completed flower.**

Ribbon French knot flowers, with and without thread French knot centres.

Gathered Ribbon Blossom

These beautiful flowers can be made with any number of petals. When dividing the ribbon into evenly spaced sections each section will form one petal - the more sections the more petals.

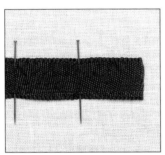 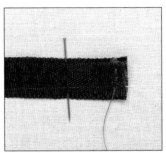 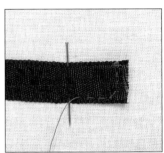

1 Cut a piece of ribbon the required length. Mark the ribbon at evenly spaced intervals.

2 Knot a length of sewing thread. Starting approx 3mm (1/8") from one end, work tiny running stitches until almost at the opposite edge.

3 Turn the corner and work running stitch along the edge until reaching the first mark.

  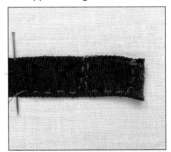 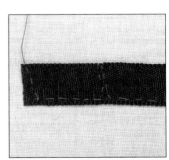

4 Turn the corner again and continue stitching to the opposite edge, ending with the needle on the back.

5 Bring the needle to the front over the fold and continue working running stitch back to the opposite edge.

6 Turn the corner and work running stitch to the second mark.

7 Continue working running stitch in the same manner to the end of the ribbon.

8 Pull up the gathers to form the petals.

9 Place the ends right sides together and stitch. End off the thread.

10 Position the petals on the fabric and attach them with tiny stab stitches around the centre.

11 Fill the centre with a cluster of beads or knots. **Completed blossom.**

Gathered Ribbon Rose

To make this superb rose, two widths of ribbon are stitched together, gathered and couched in a spiral to the fabric.

We used two 46cm (18") lengths of silk ribbon.

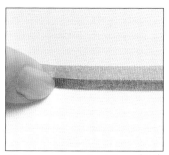

1 Cut one length of 7mm (5/16") ribbon. Cut a piece of 4mm (3/16") ribbon the same length. Place the ribbons together so they match along one edge.

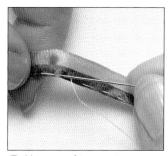

2 Using machine sewing thread, work a tiny running stitch through both ribbons close to the edge.

3 Pull up the running stitch to gather the ribbons until they measure 23cm (9"). Leave the needle and thread hanging free.

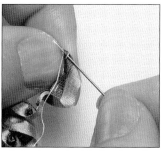

4 At the end with the thread, fold the corner down diagonally to meet the gathered edge. Using the thread, secure with two tiny stitches.

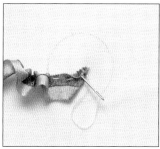

5 Using the same thread, position this end in the centre of the shape to be filled. Couch in place with a tiny stitch just through the edge of the ribbons.

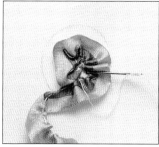

6 Begin folding the ribbons around the centre. Couch in place at 3–4mm (1/8"–3/16") intervals using tiny stitches.

7 Continue spiralling the ribbon ensuring the gathers are even. Couch in place as you go until all the ribbon is attached. Place the last stitch very close to the end.

8 At the end, fold the top edge of the wider ribbon down diagonally. Attach it to the fabric with two tiny stitches.

9 Take the thread to the back and end off. **Completed gathered rose.**

Gathered roses are used along with other techniques to create this eye-catching floral display.

Ghiordes Knot

Ghiordes knots are also known as Turkey work and single knot tufting.

The velvety pile is formed by leaving every second stitch as a loop that is later cut and combed. Rows of knots are worked from left to right either away from you or towards you.

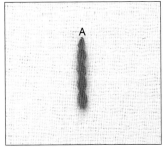

1 **First row.** Take the needle to the back at A on the left hand side. Pull the thread through, leaving a tail on the front of the fabric.

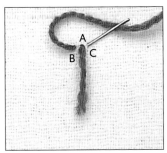

2 Re-emerge at B, just to the left of A. Take the needle to the back at C, just to the right of A.

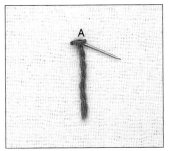

3 Hold the tail taut and pull the thread through. Re-emerge at A just below the previous stitch.

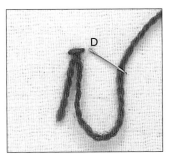

4 Pull the thread through. With the thread below the needle, take the needle to the back at D.

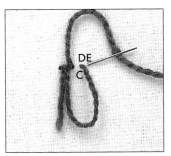

5 Pull the thread through leaving a loop the same length as the tail. Bring the needle to the front at C and pull through. Take the needle to the back at E.

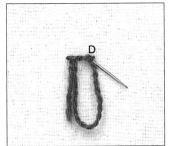

6 Pull the thread through. Bring the needle to the front at D, just below the previous stitch.

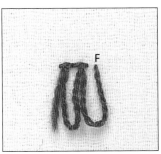

7 Pull the thread through. With the thread below the needle, take it to the back at F, leaving a loop on the front.

8 Continue to the end of the row. Ensure the last stitch is not a loop. Finish with the thread on the front. Trim, leaving a tail the same length as the loops.

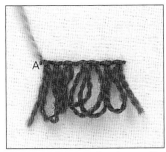

9 **Second row.** Take the needle to the back of the fabric, directly above A. Pull the thread through, leaving a tail on the front.

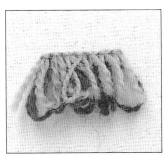

10 Work the second row in the same manner as the first row.

11 Continue working the required number of rows in the same manner. Stand the loops up and trim them evenly. Do not trim them too short.

12 Alternate between combing and trimming until the stitches are the desired height and appearance. **Completed Ghiordes knots.**

Glove Stitch

Traditionally used in the making of fine kid gloves, this stitch is similar in appearance to the first row of zigzag stitch. It is often used to stitch the edges of chatelaines and boxes together as it makes a very pretty edge. Marking two parallel lines on the fabric will help to keep the stitches even.

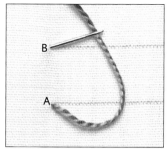

1 Bring the thread to the front at A and take it to the back at B.

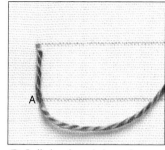

2 Pull the thread through to form a vertical straight stitch. Re-emerge at A through the same hole in the fabric.

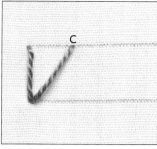

3 Take the needle to the back at C. Pull the thread through to form a diagonal straight stitch.

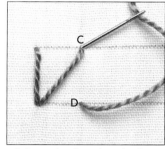

4 Bring the thread to the front at D, directly below C. Take the needle to the back at C through the same hole in the fabric.

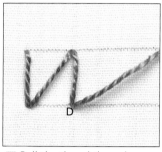

5 Pull the thread through. Re-emerge at D through the same hole in the fabric.

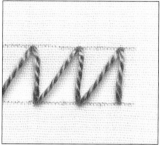

6 Continue in the same manner for the required distance ending on a vertical stitch. **Completed glove stitch.**

Grab Stitch with Ribbon Bud

Grab stitch can be used to form the stem and calyx on buds. It needs to be worked in association with a stitch such as ribbon stitch. Here it is worked using six strands of thread.

1 Bring the thread to the front. Take the needle back through the ribbon selvedge, next to where it came up, without going through the fabric.

2 Take the needle under the ribbon and up through the selvedge on the left side. Pull the thread through leaving the loop that is formed.

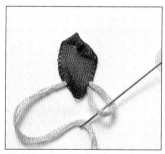

3 Take the needle through the loop. Holding the ribbon bud with left thumb, pull the grab stitch tight towards the left (thumb not shown).

4 **Stem.** Anchor the stitch by taking the needle to the back of the fabric approx 1cm (³/₈") away from the base of the bud. **Completed bud with grab stitch calyx and stem.**

Gobelin Stitch

Gobelin stitch is also known as diagonal gobelin stitch, oblique gobelin stitch and gros point.
This stitch forms horizontal and vertical rows.
It is often used when a wider line is required in a particular design.

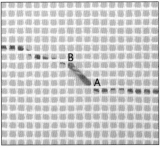

1 **Working horizontally.** Bring the thread to the front at A. Take the needle to back at B diagonally over two threads. Pull the thread through.

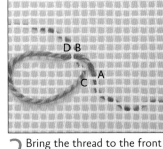

2 Bring the thread to the front at C, one hole to the left of A. Take it to the back at D, one hole to left of B.

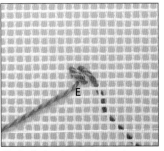

3 Pull the thread through. Bring the thread to the front at E.

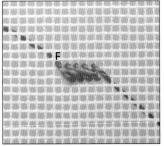

4 Continue working stitches in the same manner until reaching the first corner at F.

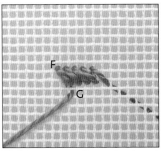

5 **First corner.** Bring the thread to the front at G, one hole below the beginning of the previous stitch.

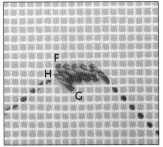

6 Take the needle to the back at H, one hole below F. Pull the thread through.

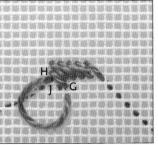

7 **Working vertically.** Bring the needle to the front at I, one hole below G. Take it to the back at J, one hole below H.

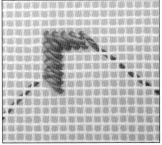

8 Pull the thread through. Continue in the same manner until reaching the next corner.

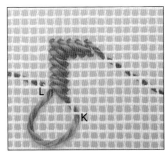

9 **Second corner.** Bring the thread to the front at K, one hole to the right and two holes down from the start of the previous stitch. Take it to the back at L.

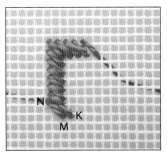

10 Pull the thread through. Bring the needle to the front at M, one hole to the left of K and to the back at N. Pull the thread through.

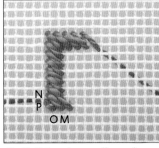

11 Bring the needle to the front at O, one hole to the left of M. Take the needle to the back at P, one hole below N. Pull the thread through.

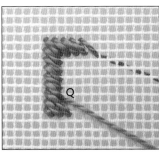

12 Bring the needle to the front at Q. This is a shared hole at the beginning of the last stitch worked before working the long stitch at the corner.

Gobelin Stitch CONTINUED

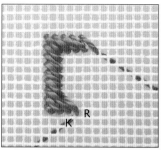

13 Take the needle to the back at R, one hole to the right of K. Pull the thread through.

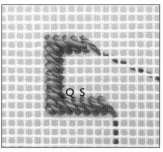

14 Bring the needle to the front at S, just to the right of Q. Continue working in the same manner until reaching the next corner.

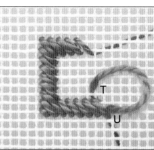

15 **Third corner.** Bring the needle to the front at T, directly above the beginning of the last stitch. Take the needle to the back at U.

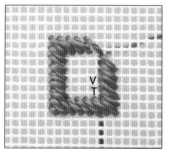

16 Pull the thread through. Bring the needle to the front at V, one hole above T. Continue working until reaching the next corner.

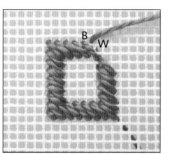

17 **Fourth corner.** Bring the needle to the front at W, one hole to right of B.

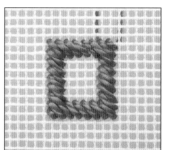

18 Work the last three stitches as a mirror image of the second corner. **Completed square of gobelin stitch.**

Gobelin Stitch – Straight

Straight Gobelin stitch is worked on canvas from right to left and is made up of a series of vertical straight stitches worked over two or more canvas threads.

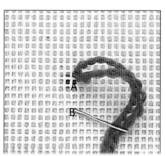

1 Bring the thread to the front at A on the right hand side. Take the needle to the back at B.

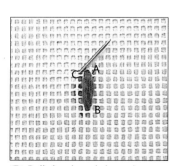

2 Pull the thread through. Re-emerge at C, in the next hole to the left of A.

3 Pull the thread through. Take the needle to the back at D, one hole to the left of B.

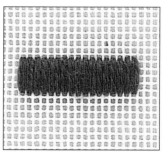

4 Pull the thread through. Continue working the desired number of stitches in the same manner.

Often mistakenly called 'tapestry', needlepoint is a type of counted thread embroidery worked on canvas. The canvas can be made from cotton, linen, silk or plastic and varies in size from silk gauze – 46 threads to the inch (2.5cm), to rug canvas – 4 threads to the inch (2.5cm).

Needlepoint designs can be worked onto unmarked canvas using a chart, or onto printed or trammed canvas. Tramming is a method of putting the design onto the canvas by working long straight stitches in the required colours, parallel to the weft.

Needlepoint can be worked in a variety of threads and the most commonly used stitches are those referred to as tent stitch.

Granitos

These quick and easy stitches are created by working several straight stitches using the same holes in the fabric.

It is important to ensure the stitches lie alongside each other.

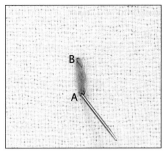

1 Bring the thread to the front at A. Take the needle to the back at B and pull through. Re-emerge at A, taking care to use exactly the same hole in the fabric.

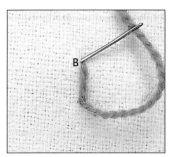

2 Pull the thread through. Loop the thread to the left and take the needle to the back at B.

3 Gently pull the thread through ensuring the stitch is positioned to the left of the first stitch.

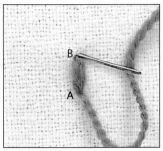

4 Bring the thread to the front at A and loop it to the right. Take the needle to the back at B.

5 Gently pull the thread through, placing the stitch to the right of the previous stitches.

6 Work the required number of stitches alternating them from the left side to the right side. After the last stitch, end off on the back of the fabric.

A small bouquet of granitos rosebuds

Granitos – Blossom

A combination of stitches is used to create this beautiful blossom. Each petal is a granitos. Fly and straight stitches add detail to the petals and French knots fill the centre.

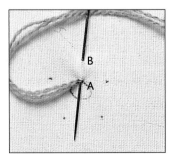

1 **Petals.** Draw a circle for the blossom centre. Mark five dots for the tips of the petals. Bring the thread to the front at A. Take the needle from B to A.

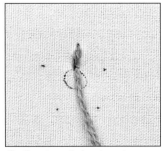

2 Gently pull the thread through to form a straight stitch.

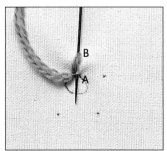

3 With the thread to the left of the needle, take a second stitch from B to A.

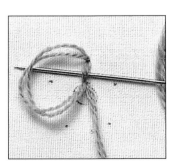

4 Pull through. Leaving the thread loose, place the needle under the stitch. This helps to create even, plump petals.

Granitos – Blossom

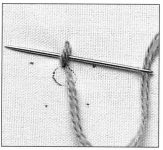

5 Keeping the needle under the stitch, pull the thread until the second stitch lies to the left and snug against the first stitch.

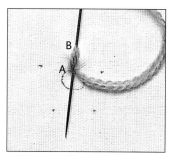

6 Remove the needle from under the stitches. With the thread to the right, take a third stitch from B to A.

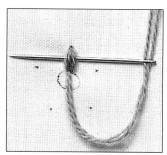

7 Pull the thread through, placing the needle under the stitches as before. Pull until the stitch lies to the right of and snug against the first stitch.

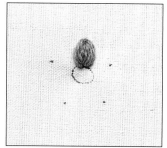

8 Work 3–5 more stitches in the same manner. Lay the last three stitches over the top of the petal.

9 Work four more petals following steps 1–8. The petals just touch each other on the centre circle.

10 **Straight stitches between petals.** Change thread. Work a straight stitch between each petal, stitching from the centre to where the petals separate.

11 **Petal tips.** Change thread. Work a straight stitch from the centre of the petal to the tip and then a fly stitch around the tip of each petal.

12 Work three straight stitches over the petals for highlights. Fill the centre with closely packed French knots. **Completed Granitos blossom.**

Granitos – Bud

A combination of granitos, couching, whipping, straight stitch and fly stitch is used to create this lovely bud.

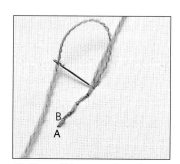

1 **Stem.** Bring two threads to the front at A and place along the marked line. Bring a second thread to the front at B and couch the laid threads in place. Leave the threads hanging free.

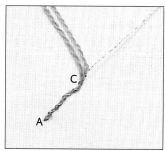

2 Bring the whipping thread to the front near A. Whip the couched threads to C. Leave the threads hanging free.

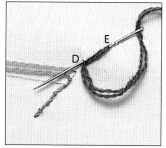

3 **Inner petal.** Using the darkest thread, bring it to the front at D. Work a straight stitch from E to D. Take the needle from E to D again.

4 Work 4–5 more straight stitches in the same manner as the blossom petals to form a granitos.

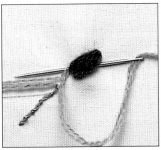

5 **Outer petals.** Change thread. Bring it to the front, just left of the base of the first petal. Take the needle to the back on the right hand side approx two thirds up the side.

6 Pull the thread through. Work 2–3 more stitches using the same holes in the fabric.

7 Change thread. Bring it to the front just to the right of D. Work this petal in the same manner as the previous petal but to the left.

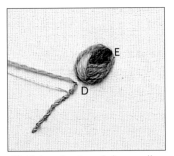

8 **Calyx.** Re-thread the needle with the laid thread. Take it to the back at D and re-emerge at E. Work two straight stitches on each side of the bud.

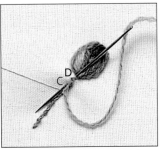

9 Work three straight stitches over the top of the bud. Re-thread the couching thread. Take the needle to the back at D and re-emerge at C.

10 Work a granitos of 4–5 stitches between D and C. End off the yarn.

11 **Highlights.** Using the whipping thread, work three straight stitches over the granitos for the calyx and 8–10 straight stitches over the petals.

12 **Stamens.** Bring the same thread to the front near E. Turn the fabric upside down. Work two fly stitches, one long and one short, at the tip of the bud.

Granitos flowers and buds used in a heart shaped floral design

WHY WOOL SHRINKS

Wool is an amazing fibre but one disadvantage it does have is that it can shrink and once shrunk it cannot be returned to its original state. Woollen fibres have thousands of tiny overlapping scales which all face the same way. Air is trapped between these scales. The outside of a wool fibre repels water but at a certain point of getting wet the inside of the fibre, which is hollow, attracts water. When this happens and heat and the twisting, churning motion of a washing machine are added, the scales move and lock together. And so shrinking occurs!

Hem Stitch–Antique

Antique hem stitch is worked from right to left on the wrong side of the fabric. Hemstitching is worked in a similar way, but on the right side of the fabric. This drawn thread stitch is both pretty and functional as it secures the hem while providing decoration.

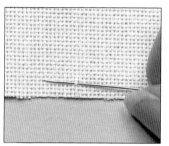

1 **Drawing the threads.** Using a pin, carefully ease one vertical thread from the fabric near the raw edge.

2 Very gently pull the thread, drawing it from the fabric. The fabric will gather as you pull.

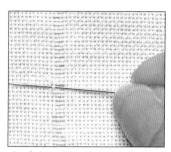

3 If thread breaks, remove the broken piece. Ease remaining end out of the weave and continue drawing out the thread.

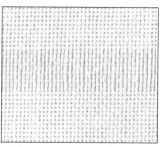

4 Draw out several adjacent threads until the band is the required depth.

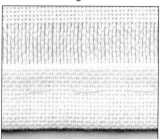

5 **Preparing the hem.** Fold and press a double hem. Align the folded hem edge with the edge of the band of drawn threads. Tack in place.

6 **Hemstitching.** Take the needle between the two layers of the hem, a short distance away from the lower fold. Emerge on the upper fold.

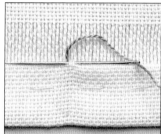

7 Pull the end of the thread between the layers of fabric. Work a tiny back stitch to secure the thread.

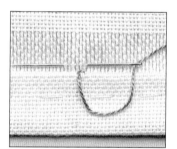

8 Take the needle from right to left behind the fabric threads. Collect required number of threads onto the needle. Bring the needle to the front.

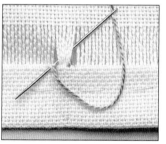

9 Pull the thread through. Take the needle from right to left behind the bundle of threads. Re-emerge below the last thread in the bundle, just catching the hem.

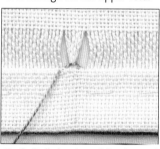

10 Pull the thread firmly until the bundle of threads is tightly grouped together. **Completed first stitch.**

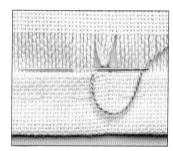

11 Take the needle through the hole that has been formed, to right side of fabric. Collect the same number of threads onto the needle as for the first stitch.

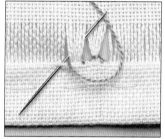

12 Pull the thread through. Take needle from right to left behind the bundle of threads. Re-emerge below the last thread in the bundle, just catching the hem.

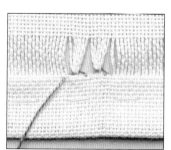

13 Pull the thread firmly until the bundle of threads is tightly grouped together. **Completed second stitch.**

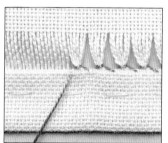

14 Continue working stitches following steps 11–13.

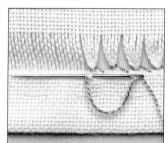

15 To finish off, work a tiny back stitch close to the fold just below the last bundle.

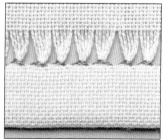

16 **Completed antique hem stitch on the right side of the fabric.**

Hem Stitch– Serpentine

Also known as trellis hem stitch, it can be worked on either the right or wrong side of the fabric.

Always bundle an even number of threads in the first row in order to have the same number when you divide the threads in the second row. For drawing out the threads, see page 91.

The arrow indicates the top of the fabric.

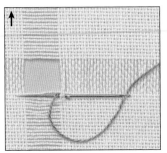

1 Starting on the left hand edge, secure the thread with a tiny back stitch on the wrong side.

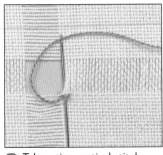

2 Take a tiny vertical stitch emerging below the edge of the drawn thread area. Count an even number of threads to the right of this stitch (usually 4, 6, 8 or 10).

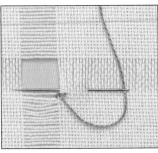

3 Take the needle from right to left behind the counted fabric threads. Bring the needle tip to the front.

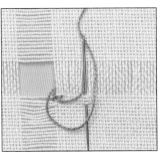

4 Pull the thread through. Take the needle to the back just to the right of the last thread. Re-emerge directly below in the fabric.

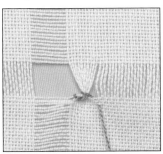

5 Pull the thread firmly until the bundle of threads is tightly grouped together. **Completed first stitch.**

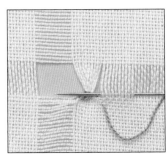

6 Take the needle from right to left behind the same number of threads as for the first stitch. Bring the needle tip to the front.

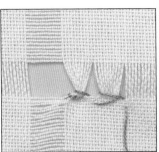

7 Pull the thread through. Take the needle to the back just to the right of the last thread. Re-emerge directly below in the fabric.

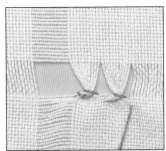

8 Pull the thread firmly until the bundle of threads is tightly grouped together. **Completed second stitch.**

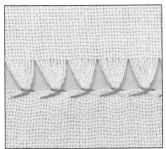

9 Following steps 6–8, continue to the end of the row.

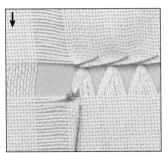

10 Turn fabric upside down. Secure the thread to the fabric as in step 1. Work a hem stitch, picking up half the number of threads only from first bundle.

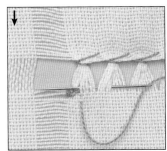

11 Take the needle behind the fabric threads, picking up half the number of threads from the second bundle and the remaining threads from the first bundle.

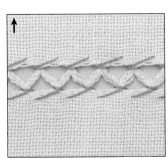

12 Complete the stitch as for steps 4–5. Continue working, regrouping threads in the bundles. **Completed serpentine hem stitch.**

Herringbone Stitch

Also known as plaited stitch and catch stitch, it is often used to work decorative borders. Mark two parallel lines to help keep your stitches even. Space the stitches closer or wider apart according to the desired effect.

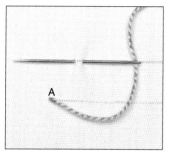 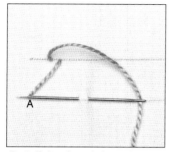 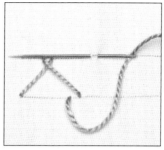 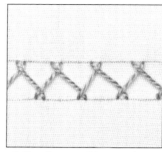

1 Bring the thread to front at A. With the thread below needle, take the needle from right to left on the upper line, approx 6mm (¼") to the right of A. Pick up approx 2mm (1/16") of fabric.

2 Pull the thread through. With the thread above the needle take the needle from right to left for 2mm (1/16") on the lower line, approximately 1cm (3/8") to the right of A.

3 Pull the thread through. With the thread below the needle, pick up 2mm (1/16") of fabric on the upper line, the same distance away as before.

4 Continue working evenly spaced stitches, alternating between the lower and upper lines. **Completed herringbone stitch.**

Herringbone Stitch – Double

Also known as Indian herringbone stitch, this stitch is formed from two rows of herringbone. A second row using the same spacing is worked over the first, interlacing the stitches together.

Using contrasting coloured threads highlights the decorative effect of the interlacing.

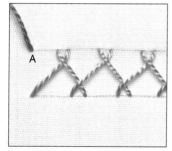 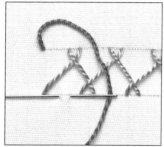 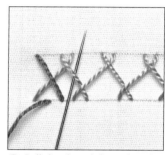

1 Work a foundation row of herringbone stitch. Bring a second thread to the front at A, directly above the beginning of the previous row.

2 Take the needle from right to left on the lower line, between the stitches of the previous row. Pick up approximately 2mm (1/16") of fabric.

3 Pull the thread through. Take the needle under the second diagonal stitch of the previous row. The needle does not go through the fabric.

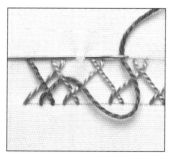 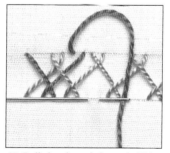 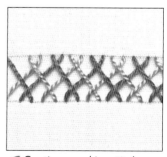

4 Pull the thread through. Picking up 2mm (1/16") of fabric as before, take the needle from right to left between the stitches on the upper line.

5 Pull the thread through. Take the needle from right to left on the lower line. The thread will cross over the diagonal stitch on the foundation row.

6 Continue working stitches, weaving the thread under or over the diagonal stitches in the foundation row. **Completed double herringbone stitch.**

Herringbone Stitch – Detached

First work a foundation of back stitch along the design lines. The length of the back stitches will determine the denseness of the herringbone stitch. Use a tapestry needle when working the interlacing to avoid splitting the stitches.

We used contrasting colours for photographic purposes only.

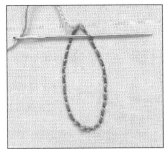

1 Bring the thread to the front just under the first back stitch on the left hand side. Slide the needle from left to right under the second back stitch on right.

2 Pull the thread through. Slide the needle under the first back stitch on the right hand side from right to left.

3 Taking the needle over the lacing, slide it under the second back stitch on the left hand side. Pull the thread through.

4 Slide the needle under the first stitch on the left. Take it over the lacing and under the third stitch on the right hand side.

5 Pull the thread through. Continue until all back stitches have been laced.

6 To finish, take the thread to the back just under the last back stitch and end off. **Completed detached herringbone stitch.**

Herringbone Stitch – Shadow Work

Detached herringbone stitch can be used as a variation of shadow work. The outlines are worked in back stitch before the detached herringbone stitch is worked in a darker shade on the wrong side of the fabric.

1 **Outline.** Work the outline around the shape with small, regular back stitches on the right side of the fabric.

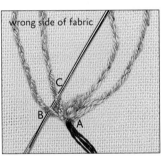

2 **Detached herringbone.** Secure a new thread on the wrong side at A. Slide the needle under both rows of back stitch at B and C.

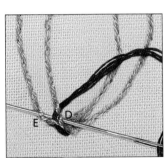

3 Pull the thread through. Slide the needle under the stitches at D and E.

4 Continue working the detached herringbone stitches to fill the shape.

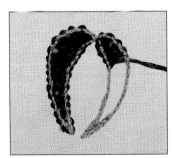

5 Stitch into the new shape, ensuring that the thread does not trail over the background fabric at the crossover.

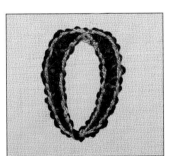

6 Complete the second part of the shape. To secure, weave the thread through the previous stitches.

Holbein Stitch

Also known as double running stitch, this stitch is created in two stages following a chart. Work one row of evenly spaced running stitches and then a second row to fill the remaining spaces in the first row. Worked carefully, this stitch is identical on the front and back.

We used two thread colours for photographic purposes. The arrow indicates the top of the fabric.

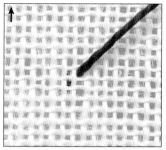

1 Bring the thread to the front at the right hand end of the line to be covered.

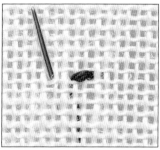

2 Count two fabric threads to the left. Take the needle to the back through the next hole. Pull through and re-emerge two fabric threads further to the left.

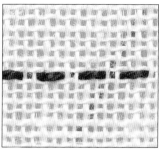

3 Continue in this manner to the end of the line, leaving two fabric threads between each stitch.

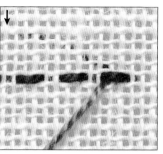

4 Turn the fabric upside down. Working from right to left again, bring the thread to the front through the same hole in the fabric as the previous running stitch.

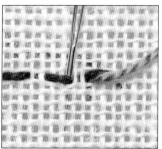

5 Take the needle to the back at end of the next running stitch. Use the same hole in fabric and take the needle through just above the thread.

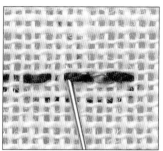

6 Re-emerge at the left hand end of the stitch. Use the same hole in the fabric and bring the needle through just below the thread.

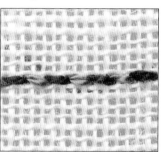

7 Continue in this manner, ensuring the second stitch is slightly angled. This is important for achieving a smooth line. **Completed Holbein stitch.**

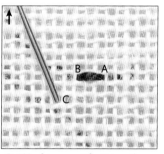

8 **Working motifs.** Bring the thread to the front at the top right corner at A. Take to back two threads to the left at B. Count two threads across and two down. Re-emerge at C.

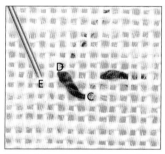

9 Pull the thread through. Take the needle to the back two threads across and two threads up at D. Re-emerge two fabric threads to the left at E.

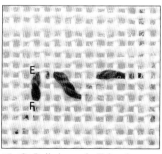

10 Pull through. Take the needle to the back two threads directly below at F.

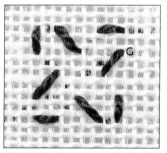

11 Continue to work stitches following the design carefully, until you are one stitch from the starting point at G.

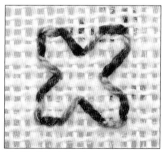

12 Stitch in the reverse direction, following steps 5–7, to complete the motif outline.

Kloster Blocks

Kloster blocks form the basis of Hardanger embroidery. They are worked in satin stitch and consist of five parallel stitches over a grid of four by four fabric threads.

Each block is worked at a right angle to the previous one. The corners of the two blocks share the same hole in the fabric.

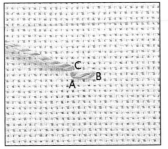

1 Bring the thread to the front at A. Take to the back at B and bring to the front at C.

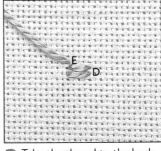

2 Take the thread to the back at D and bring it to the front at E.

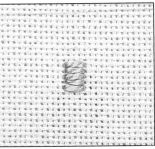

3 Continue in this manner until five stitches have been worked. **Completed kloster block.**

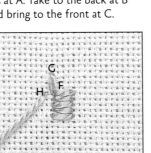

4 Bring the thread to the front at F and take it to the back at G. Emerge at H.

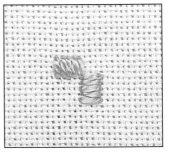

5 Continue in this manner until five stitches have been worked. **Completed pair of kloster blocks.**

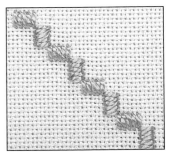

6 Continue working blocks following the chart.

Kloster Blocks – Cutting away the fabric threads

In preparation for needleweaving (see page 104), the fabric threads are cut and removed after the relevant kloster blocks have been completed. Do not remove all the threads at once as this may destabilise the fabric. Work approximately 5cm (2") at a time. Use a pair of very sharp fine embroidery scissors when cutting the threads.

1 Carefully cut the vertical threads below the top left kloster block.

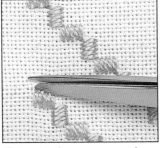

2 In a similar manner, cut the fabric threads of the kloster block directly opposite.

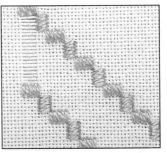

3 Remove the fabric threads cut in steps 1 and 2.

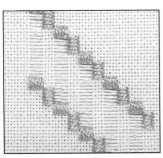

4 Repeat in a similar manner for all the vertical fabric threads to be removed.

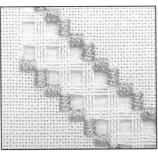

5 Remove all relevant horizontal threads in a similar manner.

HARDANGER EMBROIDERY

Hardanger, an historic Norwegian embroidery, is typically seen on table linen and as a decorative border on traditional costumes. The basis of the design is satin stitch, worked in squares known as kloster blocks, which alternate with squares of cut threads, connected by needlewoven bars. Satin stitch is also used for the other traditional shapes, while the outer border is worked in blanket stitch, to form a decorative edging, before being cut from the fabric.

Lacing Embroidery

Before being placed into its frame, the embroidery needs to be laced over cardboard to hold the surface flat and free from wrinkles.

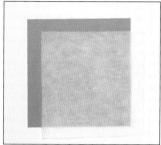

1 Cut a square of acid-free cardboard at least 1cm (⅜") larger on all sides than the opening required in the mount. Cut a square of thin wadding the same size as the cardboard.

2 Place the square of thin wadding over the cardboard.

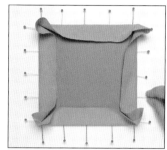

3 Centre the embroidered fabric over the wadding. Fold the excess fabric to the wrong side. Pin in place by pushing pins into the ends of the cardboard around all four sides.

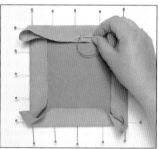

4 Thread a long length of doubled quilting thread into a sharp pointed needle. Secure it to the middle of one overlapping piece of fabric.

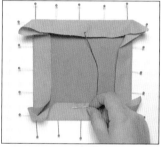

5 Take a 6mm (¼") horizontal stitch through the overlapping fabric on the opposite edge. This type of stitch reduces the stress to any one spot in the fabric.

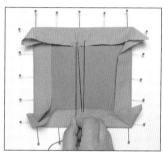

6 Pull the thread firmly. Take a 6mm (¼") stitch on the opposite side. Again, pull firmly. Check that the front is smooth and free from wrinkles as you work.

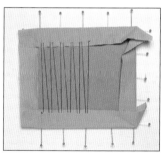

7 Continue working stitches in the same manner until reaching the end of the cardboard. Tighten the lacing and tie off the thread securely.

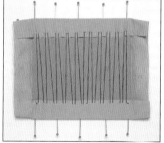

8 Return to the middle and repeat the procedure to the opposite end. Check the two laced edges are free from wrinkles and adjust if necessary.

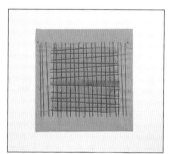

9 Join the thread to the middle of one unworked side. Repeat steps 4–8, ensuring the front is smooth and free from wrinkles. Remove the pins. **Completed lacing.**

Laid Work

Laid work is a useful method to cover large areas. It is a technique often used in goldwork where the maximum amount of expensive gold thread remains on the front. Always work on a strong, firm fabric and use a hoop.

In laid work a combination of stitches are worked, one over the other, to add texture to the shape. This example is worked with a foundation of split stitch and satin stitch padding. A layer of couched lattice completes the design.

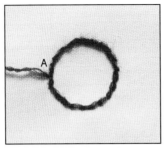

1 **Foundation.** Work the outline using split stitch. Bring the thread to right side at A.

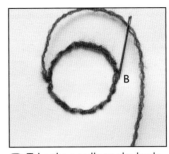

2 Take the needle to the back at B on the opposite side of the shape to work the first long stitch.

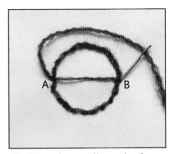

3 Bring the needle to the front of the work just above A and take to the back just above B.

4 Continue filling the upper half. Keep the stitches very close. Take the thread to the back and weave under the stitches on the back to begin the lower half.

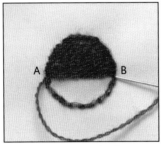

5 Bring needle to the front just below A. Take the needle to the back just below B. Work the lower half of the shape to complete the foundation.

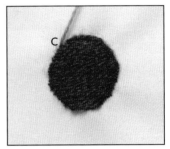

6 **Lattice.** Change to a new colour. Bring the thread to the front at C to begin working the long diagonal stitches for the lattice work.

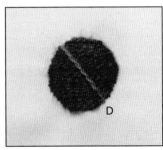

7 Take the needle to the back of the work at D.

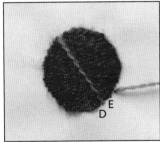

8 Bring the needle to the front at E approx 4mm (³/₁₆") above D. The trellis stitches will be spaced approx 4mm (³/₁₆") apart.

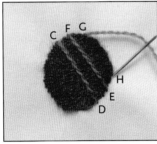

9 Pull the thread through. Take the needle to the back at F. Pull the thread through. Continue working the lattice, G to H.

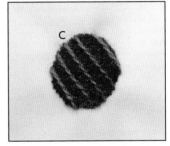

10 Weave the thread on the back and emerge 4mm (³/₁₆") below C to begin second half. **Completed first layer.**

11 The top layer of lattice is worked in the same manner, placing the stitches at right angles to the first layer. **Completed trellis.**

12 **Couching.** Work through all layers. Change thread, bring to the front close to a lattice intersection. Take the needle to the back over the intersection.

13 Pull the thread through. **First completed couching stitch.**

14 Continue couching the intersections working one row at a time.

15 **Completed laid work.**

Lattice Couching

Lattice couching is one of the many variations of couched fillings. The design area is covered with a foundation of evenly spaced laid threads. The spacing of the diagonal stitches is determined by the thickness of the thread used.

Where two laid threads cross, they are secured to the background with a small straight stitch.

Lattice couching can be worked directly onto the fabric or over a satin-stitched shape.

Lattice couching worked over the base of the thistles

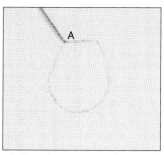

1 **Foundation.** Bring the thread to the front near the left side of the shape at the upper edge, A.

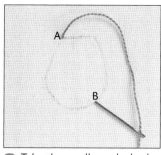

2 Take the needle to the back at B, on the lower right side of the shape.

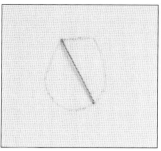

3 Pull the thread through to form a diagonal stitch.

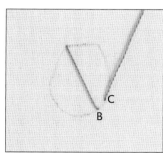

4 Bring the thread to the front at C, above B.

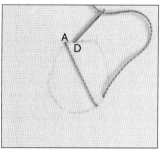

5 Take the needle to the back at D, to the right of A.

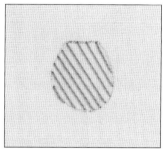

6 Pull the thread through. Continue working evenly spaced parallel stitches in the same manner until the entire area is covered.

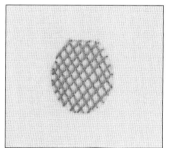

7 Work a second set of diagonal stitches over the design area in the opposite direction to form a pattern of diamonds.

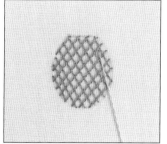

8 **Couching.** Using a new thread, bring it to the front directly below the first inter-section on the upper right of the shape.

9 Take the needle to the back directly above the intersection. Pull through to complete the first couching stitch.

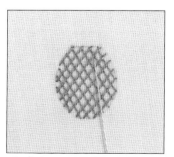

10 Re-emerge directly below the next intersection to the left.

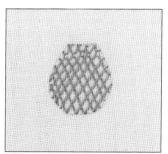

11 Take the needle to the back directly above the intersection and continue across the row in the same manner.

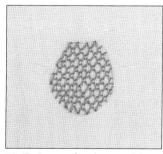

12 Repeat for the remaining intersections. Take the thread to the back and end off. **Completed lattice couching.**

Long and Short Stitch

Long and short stitch and its variations are known by many names such as embroidery stitch, plumage stitch, shading stitch, tapestry shading stitch, brick stitch, leaf stitch, Irish stitch, featherwork and Opus Plumarium.

Long and short stitch is used in thread painting to achieve gradual colour changes.

See also soft shading, page 134 and thread painting, page 147.

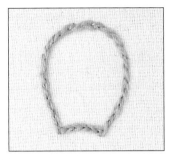

1 Outline the shape to be filled with split stitch. This helps to create a neat edge.

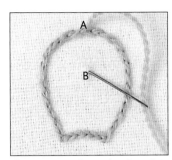

2 **First row.** Bring the thread to the front on the left hand side just beyond the centre top of the outline at A. Take the needle to the back of the fabric at B.

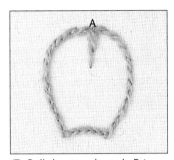

3 Pull the yarn through. Bring the yarn to the front just to the right of A. Work a shorter straight stitch alongside the previous stitch.

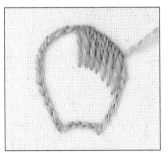

4 Continue working parallel straight stitches across the row in the same manner, alternating a long stitch with a short stitch.

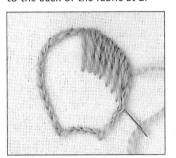

5 Ensure the last stitch goes to the back of the fabric just beyond the outline. Pull the thread through and end off.

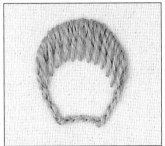

6 Beginning at the centre, work the remaining half of the row in the same manner.

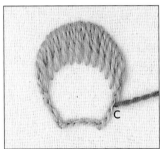

7 **Second row.** Bring a new length of thread to the front at C. Leave enough distance for this stitch to be the same length as the long stitches in the first row.

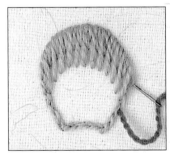

8 Take the needle to the back of the fabric at the base of the first stitch from the right in the first row. This is just beyond the outline.

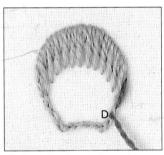

9 Pull the thread through. Re-emerge at D to begin the second stitch. This stitch will be the same length as, and parallel to, the previous stitch.

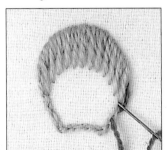

10 Take the needle to the back at the base of the second stitch from the right in the first row.

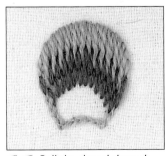

11 Pull the thread through. Continue across the row in the same manner and end off. All the stitches are the same length but are staggered.

12 **Subsequent rows.** Work remaining rows, except for the last row, in the same manner. In the last row, the lower end of each stitch just covers the outline.

Lazy Stitch

This bead embroidery filling stitch is like a beaded satin stitch and allows larger areas to be covered relatively quickly.

1 Bring the needle to the front at A. Thread the required number of beads and settle them in place.

2 Take the needle to the back at B, allowing beads to lie comfortably, and secure with a back stitch at the back of the fabric.

Loop Stitch

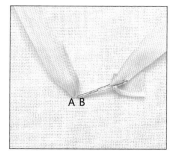

1 Bring the ribbon to the front at A. Spread the ribbon out flat with the needle and take the needle to the back at B, very close to A.

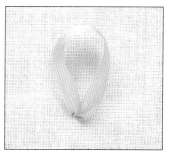

2 Begin to pull the ribbon through, making sure it does not twist.

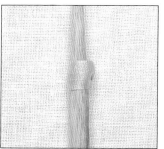

3 Place a skewer or similar into the loop. Continue pulling the ribbon, tensioning it slightly with the skewer, until the loop is the desired size.

4 Remove the skewer. Secure the ends of the ribbon on the back of the fabric. **Completed loop stitch.**

Loop Stitch–Bow

A neat little ribbon bow can easily be created from a simple loop stitch.

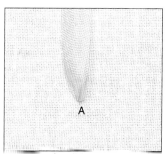

1 Bring the ribbon to the front at A.

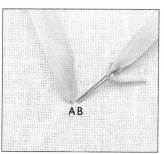

2 Spread the ribbon out flat with the needle and take the needle to the back at B, next to A.

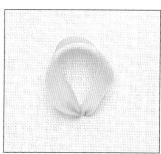

3 Pull the ribbon through until the loop is the desired length.

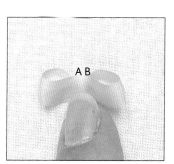

4 Flatten the loop onto the fabric so the centre of the loop lies over A and B.

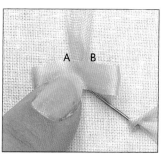

5 Bring the ribbon to the front just above A and B. Take the needle to the back just below A and B.

6 Pull the ribbon through to form a small straight stitch. **Completed bow.**

HINTS

LOOP STITCH

The ribbon must be very smooth before taking the needle to the back of the fabric to complete the stitch. Drawing it over the shaft of a large needle (eg a no. 18 tapestry needle) will help to achieve this.

Secure the stitches on the back with thread so they cannot be inadvertently pulled out of shape.

Loop Stitch Flower 1

A small loop stitch secured with a French knot creates a simple flower.

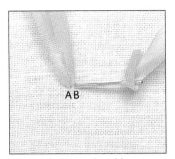

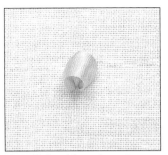

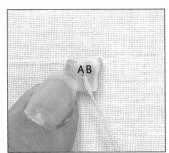

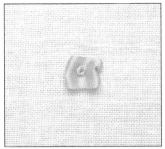

1 **Petals.** Bring the ribbon to the front at A. Spread the ribbon out flat with the needle and take the needle to the back at B, next to A.

2 Pull the ribbon through, making sure it does not twist. Pull until a tiny loop is left on the right side of the fabric.

3 **Centre.** Flatten the loop so the centre is over A and B. Holding the loop in place, bring the desired thread to the front through the centre of the loop.

4 Work a French knot in the centre. **Completed loop stitch flower.**

Loop Stitch Flower 2

This flower is created with several loop stitch petals arranged around a centre filled with knots or beads.

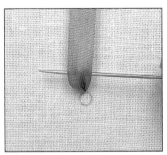

1 **Petals.** Mark a tiny circle for the centre of the flower. Bring the ribbon to the front at A.

2 Spread the ribbon out flat with the needle.

3 Keeping your thumb or finger on the ribbon, fold it over towards the centre to form a loop.

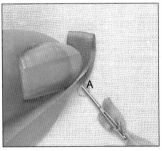

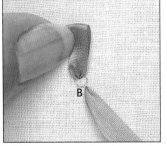

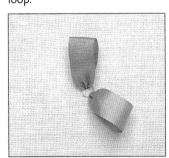

4 Reposition your thumb or finger to hold both layers of ribbon. Take the needle to the back next to A.

5 Gently pull the ribbon through until a small loop is formed.

6 Keeping your thumb over the loop to prevent it pulling through, bring the ribbon to the front at B.

7 Form a second loop by following steps 2–5.

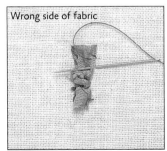

8 Keeping your thumb on the second loop, bring the ribbon to the front at C. Form a loop in the same manner.

9 Repeat the procedure for the desired number of petals.

10 End off the ribbon and secure each petal on the back of the fabric.

11 Fill the centre with a colonial knot, French knot or beads. **Completed loop stitch flower.**

Moss Stitch

These isolated stitches create an interesting texture when scattered within a shape.

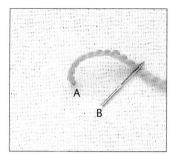

1 Bring the thread to the front at A. Take the needle to the back at B.

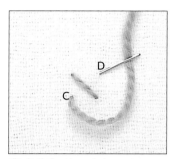

2 Pull the thread through to form a diagonal straight stitch. Bring the needle to the front at C. Pull the thread through and take the needle to the back at D.

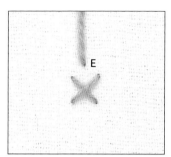

3 Pull the thread through to form a cross stitch. Bring the thread to the front at E, above the centre of the cross.

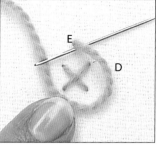

4 Loop the thread to the left. Hold the loop in place and slide the needle from left to right under the thread between D and E. Do not pierce the fabric.

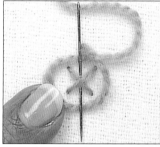

5 Still holding the loop in place, slide the needle from top to bottom behind the centre of the cross. Do not pierce the fabric.

6 Ensure the loop is under the tip of the needle. Pull the thread through until a small loop lies at the centre of the cross.

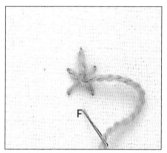

7 Take the needle to the back at F.

8 Pull the thread through and end off on the back of the fabric. **Completed moss stitch.**

HINTS

CLEANING AND PRESSING

Cleaning

Once the embroidery is complete it will need to be 'finished'. This may involve washing if the work has become marked from continual handling. If the fabric or threads are not suitable for washing, you may need to visit the dry cleaner.

Be careful with silk fabric or thread as they have a nasty habit of not looking dirty when you finish working but marks may develop over time.

If your work needs to be washed, do this by hand using pure soap (or a detergent specially developed for this purpose) and lukewarm water. Be careful not to rub the surface of your stitching as this will cause unsightly pilling.

Rinse the work in clean water, preferably demineralised, then roll it up in a clean towel and gently squeeze the excess water out. Dry quickly away from direct sunlight to keep the colours from running or fading, then press.

Pressing

Pressing your embroidery makes an enormous difference to the overall finish of the work.

Avoid pressing the right side as this will flatten the threads too much.

Make a pressing pad from a soft smooth fabric. A piece of flannelette, folded into several thicknesses, is excellent.

Place the embroidery face down onto the pad and iron the back using a setting suitable for the fabric. The stitches will sink into the pad and you will be able to press the fabric flat. Steam is beneficial for silk as it increases the lustre of the thread.

Needlelace – Woven Bar

Needlewoven bars link the kloster blocks in Hardanger embroidery.
See page 96 for working the kloster blocks and removing the fabric threads.

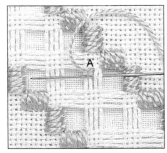 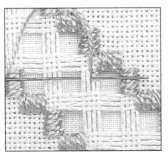 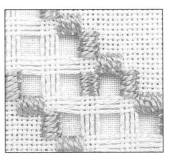 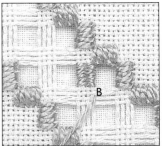

1 Bring the thread to the front at A. Take the needle around two threads on the right. Come up through the centre again.

2 Tighten the stitch. Take the needle around the two threads on the left and come up through the centre

3 Tighten the stitch. Continue in this manner until the bar is filled with six stitches on each side.

4 Carry the thread behind the fabric and bring to the front at B to begin the next bar.

Needleweaving – Bar

Needlewoven bars are most often used in needlelace and raised embroidery. In flower or fruit embroidery, they make lovely sepals or tiny leaves. Each needlewoven bar is detached from the fabric. The length of the bar can be varied and the bar gently manipulated and anchored to the fabric to give the desired effect.

 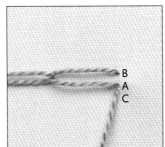  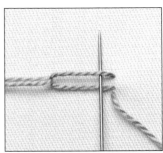

1 Bring the thread to the front at A and take to the back at B, leaving a loop of the desired length.

2 Re-emerge at C, just below A taking care not to pull the loop through. Pass a piece of waste thread through the loop.

3 With your left hand, hold the waste thread taut, slightly above the surface of the work. Continue to hold this taut while you work.

4 Weave the needle over the lower thread of the loop and under the upper thread. Do not pierce the fabric.

 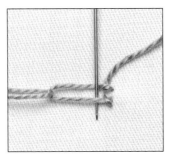  

5 Pull the thread through firmly and push the wrap down onto the fabric with the tip of the needle.

6 Weave the needle over the upper thread and under the lower thread. Do not pierce the fabric.

7 Pull through firmly and push the wrap down the loop with the tip of the needle so it sits snugly against the first wrap.

8 Continue working steps 4–7, weaving the stitches over and under the threads of the loop. Push each wrap firmly against the previous one.

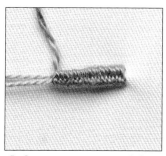

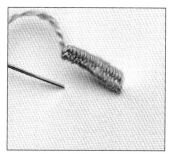

9 Continue weaving until the loop is completely filled and the wraps are firmly packed.

10 Remove the waste thread. Take the needle to the back at the desired position.

11 Pull the thread through. The bar slightly curves and does not lie flat against the fabric. **Completed needlewoven bar.**

The green sepals below the raspberries are formed with needlewoven bars.

Needleweaving— Closed Base Picot

This picot features a narrow, closed base with the tip of the picot detached from the fabric.

The length of the picot is determined by the distance between A and B.

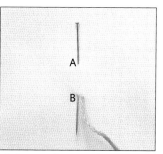

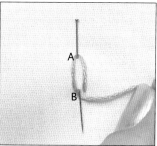

1 Insert a long pin from A to B, for approx 1cm (³⁄₈"). This is the picot length. Bring the thread to the front at the right of the pin.

2 Wrap the thread in an anti-clockwise direction around the pinhead at A and under the tip at B. Keep the loop plump and do not pull too tightly.

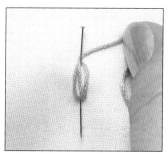

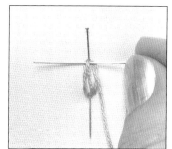

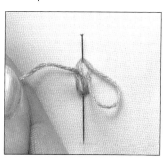

3 Take the thread diagonally across the pin and wrap it clock-wise around the pinhead. There are now three foundation threads around the pin.

4 Begin weaving. Slide the needle from the right to the left under the centre thread (over, under, over).

5 Begin to pull the thread through.

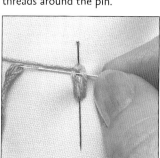

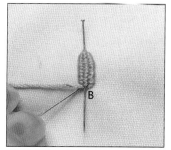

6 Pull the thread through firmly against the pin. Weave the needle from the left to right (under, over, under).

7 Pull the thread through. Continue weaving, packing each row firmly as you work towards the base. To end off, take the needle to the back close to B.

8 Remove the pin. **Completed closed base needlewoven picot.**

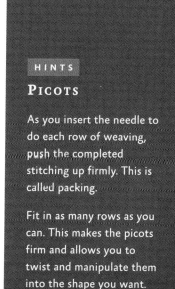

HINTS

PICOTS

As you insert the needle to do each row of weaving, push the completed stitching up firmly. This is called packing.

Fit in as many rows as you can. This makes the picots firm and allows you to twist and manipulate them into the shape you want.

Be careful not to pull the vertical working threads too firmly as this will pull the picot into a thin 'mean' shape.

Needleweaving – Open Base Picot

This picot is a lace-making technique used to create raised embroidery. The picot is worked around a pin inserted in the fabric and is only attached to the fabric at one end. Beautiful picots depend on even tension and tightly packed stitches.

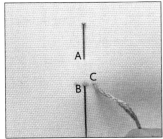

1 **Foundation threads.** Insert a long pin from A to B. This is the picot length. Bring the thread to the front at C and pull through.

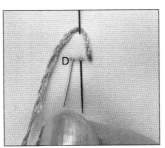

2 Wrap the thread counter-clockwise under the head of the pin. Take the needle to the back at D.

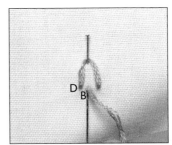

3 Pull the thread through. Re-emerge just to the right of B. Pull the thread through.

4 Wrap the thread clockwise around the head of the pin. The centre thread crosses the pin and becomes the third foundation thread.

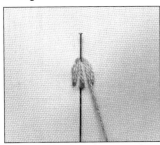

5 Hold the thread taut to the right. Give a firm tug.

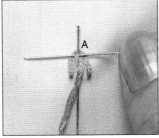

6 Towards the top of the pin (A) weave the needle from right to left under the foundation threads (over, under, over).

7 Pull the thread through.

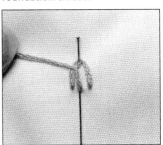

8 Pull the thread firmly up against the pin.

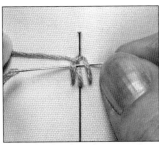

9 Hold the thread taut to the left, weave the needle from left to right (under, over, under). You may find it easier to turn the work slightly to do this.

10 Pull the thread through until the loop is snug against the first foundation thread.

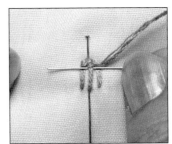

11 Weave the needle from right to left under the centre thread. Push the needle up towards the top of the picot. Pack threads as tightly as possible.

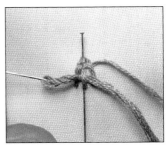

12 Begin to pull the thread through.

13 Before the thread is completely through, place the point of the needle in the loop being formed. (This helps to maintain the shape, keeping outer line of foundation threads even).

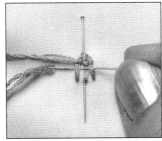

14 Weave from left to right, sliding the needle under, over, under. Continue weaving towards the base of the picot, packing each left-to-right row firmly.

15 Continue weaving until the foundation threads are firmly packed. Take the needle to the back at the base of the picot, close to C.

16 Pull through and end off on the wrong side. Remove the pin. **Completed picot.** The picot can now be twisted and manipulated into shape.

Needleweaving – Heartsease

The petals of this heartsease flower have been created using a five thread picot for each petal. Ensure that the base of the petal is not as wide as the main section.

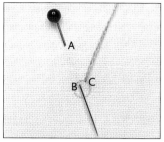

1 **Back petals.** Insert a long pin from A to B for approx 1cm (⅜"). This is the picot length. Bring thread to the front at C and pull through.

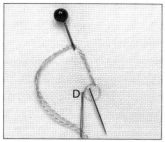

2 Wrap the thread counter-clockwise under the head of the pin. Insert the needle at D.

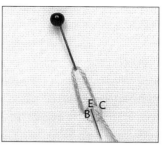

3 Pull the thread through. Bring the thread to the front between C and B at E.

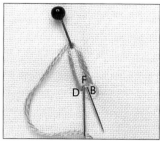

4 Wrap the thread counter clockwise under the head of the pin. Insert the needle at F, half way between D and B.

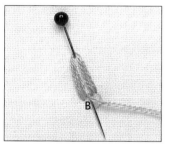

5 Pull the thread through. Re-emerge at B. Pull the thread through.

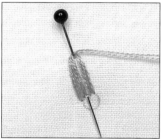

6 Wrap the thread clockwise around the head of the pin. The centre thread crosses the pin and becomes the fifth foundation thread.

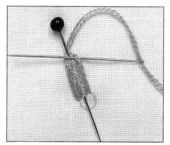

7 Take the needle and thread under the first thread and begin weaving as for the open base picot.

8 Continue weaving, packing the threads firmly, until all the foundation threads are filled.

9 Take the thread to the back at the base of the picot , close to C and secure. Remove the pin.

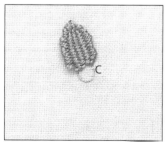

10 Catch the tip with a tiny stitch each side of the tip to give a more rounded look. **Completed petal.**

11 Work the second back petal in the same manner, slightly overlapping at the base of the petal.

12 **Front petals.** Work two side front petals in the same manner.

13 Work the centre front petal in the same manner, overlapping the side petals.

14 Work the highlights in straight stitch, then the French knot centre. **Completed heartsease.**

A needlewoven heartsease is featured on this Elizabethan Sweetbag

Net Stitch

Net stitch is completely detached from the fabric except at the beginning and end of a row. It requires a stitch such as blanket stitch for the first row of stitching. Each row uses a continuous length of thread and is worked from the same side of the shape. Couch a cord at the top of the shape for the foundation.

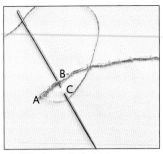

1 **Blanket stitch.** Using a new thread, start at the left side of the cord. Bring the needle to the front at A. Take a small stitch from B to C. The thread is under the needle.

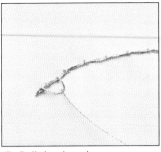

2 Pull the thread through.

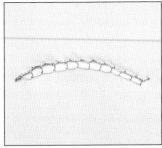

3 Work loose blanket stitches to the end of the row, taking one stitch between each couching stitch. Take the needle to the back and end off.

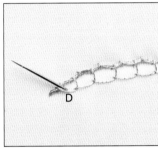

4 **First row of net stitch.** Using a new thread, bring the needle to the front at D on the left side of the work.

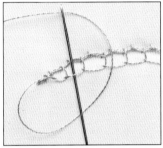

5 With the thread under the needle, take the needle through the loop of the second blanket stitch. Do not go through fabric.

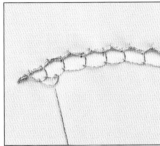

6 Pull thread through until the stitch wraps loosely around the centre of the blanket stitch loop.

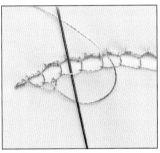

7 Again, with the thread under the needle, take the needle through the loop of the third blanket stitch.

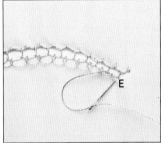

8 Pull the thread through. Continue to the end of the row. Take the needle to the back at E and end off.

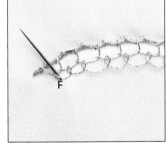

9 **Second row.** Using a new thread and starting on the left side of the work, bring the needle to the front at F.

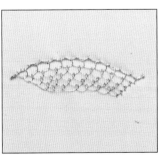

10 Continue to the end of the row. Continue working rows from left to right for the required shape using a new thread for each row.

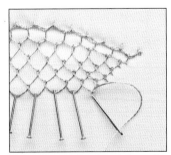

11 **Secure final row.** Stretch the net and hold in place with pins. Using a new thread, work a tiny stitch through the fabric at the first pin, catching a loop of the net stitch.

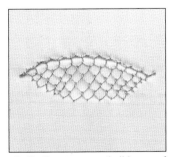

12 Continue until all loops of the final row are anchored to the fabric. **Completed net stitch shape.** For straight sides, add a net stitch at start and end of each row.

Outline Stitch

This stitch is very similar to stem stitch and is worked in a similar way. The difference is in the position of the thread. In outline stitch the thread is always kept above the needle.

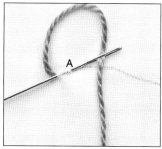

1 Bring the needle to the front at the left end of the line. With the thread above the needle, take the needle to the back at A and re-emerge at the end.

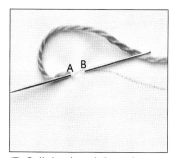

2 Pull the thread through. Again with the thread above the needle, take the needle from B to A. Ensure the tension is the same for each stitch.

3 Pull the thread through. Continue working stitches in the same manner, always keeping the thread above the needle and the stitches the same length.

4 To end off, take the thread to the back for the last stitch but do not re-emerge. Secure the thread on the back with tiny back stitches. **Completed outline stitch.**

Overlapping Sequins

Overlapping sequins create a solid flashing surface of colour. When attached in closely worked rows, large areas can be covered quickly.

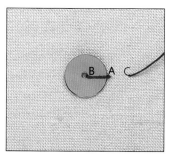

1 Attach the first sequin with a back stitch beginning at A, going down through the centre at B and emerging at C, half a sequin away.

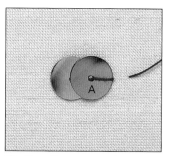

2 Place the next sequin to overlap the first. Work a back stitch down through the centre of the second sequin at A. Re-emerge half a sequin away.

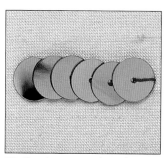

3 Continue to work in this manner. **Completed overlapping sequins.**

Oyster Stitch

Oyster stitch is a combination of twisted chain and chain stitch and can be used singly or in rows. It is an excellent stitch to add texture and is also suitable for outlines and borders.

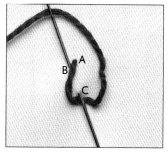

1 **First stitch.** Bring the thread to the front at A. Take to the back at B, and re-emerge at C. Take the thread under the needle tip in a counter-clockwise direction.

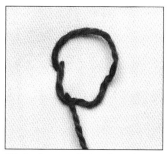

2 Begin to pull the thread through.

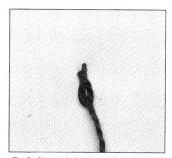

3 Pull until the loop lies firmly on the fabric.

4 Slide the needle under the right hand thread just below A. The needle does not go through the fabric.

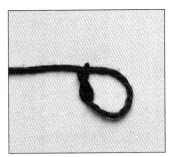

5 Pull the thread through. Allow the thread to lie alongside the twisted chain on the fabric.

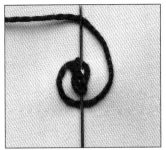

6 Take the needle to the back inside the loop and next to the twist of the twisted chain. Re-emerge at the base. Ensure the thread is under the tip of the needle.

7 Pull the thread through. The second loop encircles the first loop.

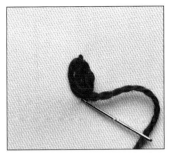

8 Take the needle to the back of the fabric just beyond the last loop to anchor the stitch.

9 **Completed first oyster stitch.**

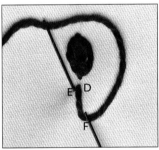

10 **Poppy.** Turn the fabric upside down. Bring the needle to the front at D. Take the needle from E to F and place the thread under the tip of the needle as before.

11 Work the stitch following steps 2–8. Work three more stitches in the same manner to form the five petals of a poppy.

12 Fill the centre with five French knots. **Completed oyster stitch poppy.**

Palestrina Stitch

Also known as old English knot, double knot stitch and tied coral stitch, Palestrina stitch produces a line of raised knots useful for outlines or borders.

It is important that the knots are evenly spaced and close together.

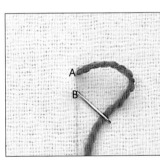

1 Bring the needle to the front at the top of the line at A. Take the needle to the back at B.

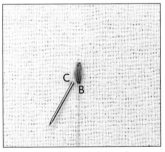

2 Pull the thread through. Bring the needle to the front at C, just to the left of B.

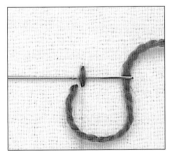

3 Pull the thread through. Slide the needle from right to left under the first stitch without going through the fabric.

4 Begin to pull the thread through.

5 Continue pulling the thread through gently until the loop hugs the straight stitch.

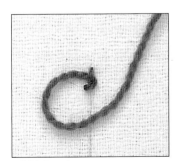

6 Make a loop to the left.

Palestrina Stitch

CONTINUED

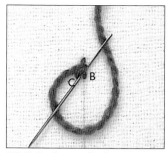

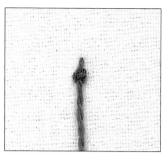

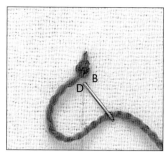

7 Slide the needle from right to left under the thread as shown. Emerge between B and C. Do not go through the fabric. Ensure the loop is under the tip of the needle.

8 Gently pull the thread through forming a soft knot. **Completed first knot.**

9 To begin the second stitch take the needle to the back at D a short distance below B, just to the right of the line.

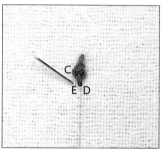

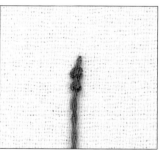

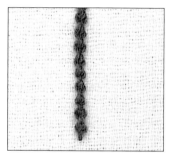

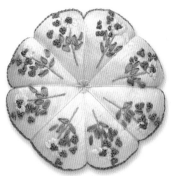

10 Bring the needle to the front at E, just to the left of the line opposite D, below C.

11 Complete the stitch following steps 3–8.

12 Continue working stitches in the same manner. End off by taking the needle to the back close to the base of the last stitch. **Completed Palestrina stitch.**

Palestrina stitch used as edging on a pumpkin pincushion

Pekinese Stitch

This is also known as Chinese stitch, blind stitch and forbidden stitch. It can be worked as a single line or as a filling stitch.

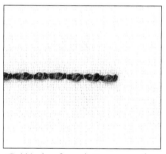

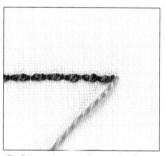

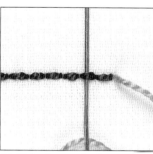

1 Work a foundation row of evenly spaced back stitches.

2 Bring the needle to the front at the end of the row.

3 Slide the needle, from bottom to top, under the second stitch.

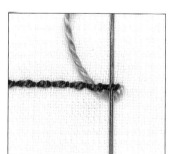

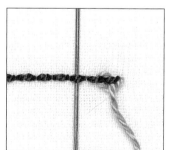

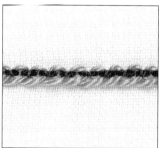

4 Pull the thread through. Slide the needle from top to bottom, under the first stitch and over the working thread.

5 Slide the needle from bottom to top, under the third stitch.

6 Slide the needle from top to bottom, under the second stitch and over the working thread.

7 Continue working in this manner to the end of the row.

Pin Stitching

Pin stitching is also referred to as point de Paris. It may be used to create a neat and decorative hem, as in fine handkerchiefs, when it is worked on the wrong side, or to appliqué one piece of fabric to another, as in Madeira embroidery, when it is worked on the right side.

The arrow indicates the top of the fabric.

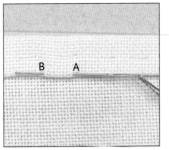

1 Take the needle through the fold of the hem from A to B. Slowly pull the thread through to conceal the tail inside the hem.

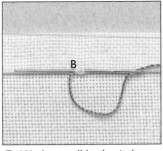

2 Work a small back stitch to secure.

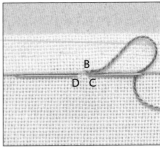

3 Take the needle from C to D below the fold.

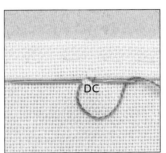

4 Pull the thread through firmly. Take the needle from C to D again, using the same holes in the fabric.

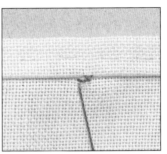

5 Pull firmly to draw the fabric threads together. A small hole will form.

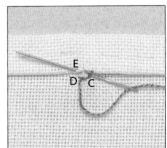

6 Take the needle to the back at C and emerge at E through the fold of the hem.

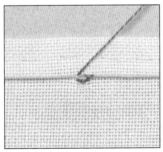

7 Pull the thread through.

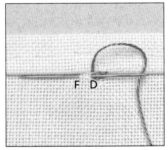

8 To begin the second stitch, take the needle to the back at D and emerge at F.

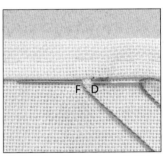

9 Pull the thread through. Take the needle to the back at D and re-emerge at F.

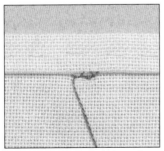

10 Pull the thread through firmly until a small hole forms.

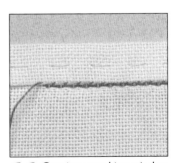

11 Continue working stitches in the same manner.

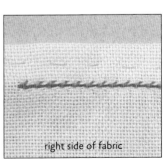

12 To secure, take a back stitch in the fold of the hem.

Pistil Stitch

Pistil stitch is a French knot on a stem. Varying the length of the stem and the number of wraps in the knot will give different effects.

Pistil stitches are often used for flower stamens and petals. For a curved effect, loosen the tension as you place the stitch for the stem.

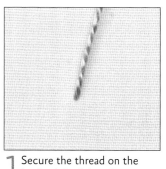

1 Secure the thread on the back of the fabric. Bring it to the front at the base of the stitch.

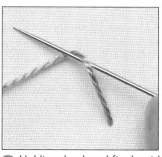

2 Holding the thread firmly with the left thumb and forefinger, wrap the thread over the needle (thumb and finger not shown).

3 Keeping the thread taut, wind it around the needle in a counter-clockwise direction for the required number of wraps.

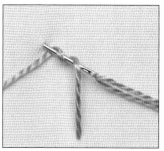

4 Still holding the thread taut, turn the needle towards the fabric. Place the tip of the needle onto the fabric at the position for the end of the stitch.

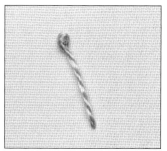

5 Slide the wraps down the needle onto the fabric. Push the needle through the fabric, maintaining a firm tension on the thread.

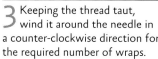

6 Pull the thread through keeping the thumb over the knot. **Completed pistil stitch.**

Plaiting   The number of threads must be divisible by three.

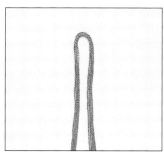

1 Separate the strands of thread and put them back together. Fold the threads in half to find the centre.

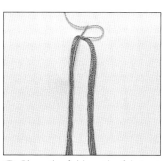

2 Place the fold on the fabric at the position for the base of the plait. Using one strand of thread, secure the strands of thread with three stitches over the fold.

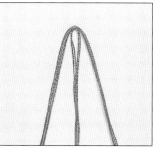

3 Finish with the thread on the back and secure. Separate the strands into three equal groups.

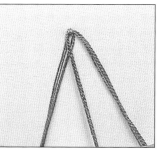

4 Take the left hand group of threads over the middle group. The left hand group now becomes the middle group.

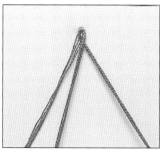

5 Take the right hand group of threads over the middle group. The right hand group now becomes the middle group.

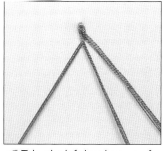

6 Take the left hand group of threads over the middle group.

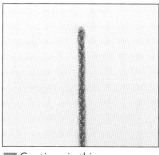

7 Continue in this manner, alternating from side to side until reaching the end of the threads.

8 Knot the threads. Trim the ends to 8mm (5/16") below the knot. **Completed plait.**

Pompom

Pompoms created in a variety of shades and sizes add a three dimensional touch and are a useful trimming.

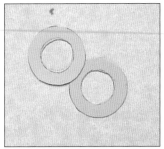

1 Cut two circles of cardboard to the required size of the pompom. Within each circle, cut a second circle so you have two doughnut shapes.

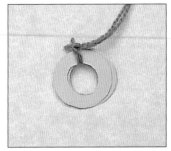

2 Thread a long length of thread into a chenille needle. Place the pieces of card together. Take the thread through the hole and knot it at the outer edge.

3 Take the thread through the hole again and around the outer edge.

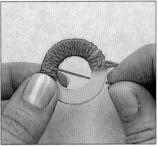

4 Always working in the same direction, continue taking the thread through the hole so it wraps around the cardboard.

5 To join in a new piece of thread, knot the new length to the end of the old piece, positioning the knot at the outer edge.

6 Continue wrapping the thread around the cardboard in the same manner until the hole is firmly packed.

7 Place small sharp scissors between the two pieces of card at the outer edge and cut through the thread.

8 Cut a length of thread. Take it between the two pieces of card so it encircles the cut pieces of thread at the centre. Tie in a firm secure knot.

9 Cut through each piece of cardboard and carefully remove them.

10 Fluff out the cut strands with your fingers to make a ball shape.

11 Carefully trim away any knots or uneven pieces of thread except for the length used to tie the pompom.

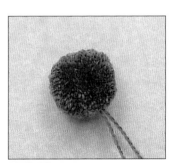

12 The pompom is now ready to use.

Raised Cup Stitch

Raised cup stitch is a buttonhole stitch worked on a thread base. It is used in stumpwork to create raised sections of a design. It gives a rich, textured effect.

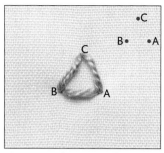

1 Base. Take a stitch from A to B. Re-emerge at C. Take to the back at A and re-emerge at B. Take to the back at C to complete the base.

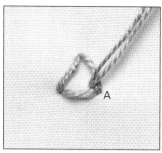

2 Buttonhole stitch. Bring the needle to the front inside the triangle near A.

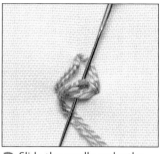

3 Slide the needle under the base thread (the thread is to the right of the needle). Wrap the thread around the needle in a counter-clockwise direction.

4 Gently pull the thread through in an upward direction. A knot will form around the base stitch. **First completed buttonhole stitch.**

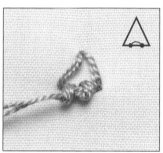

5 On the same base stitch, work a second buttonhole stitch in the same manner as before.

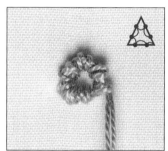

6 Continue around the triangle, working two buttonhole stitches on each base stitch. The completed round of stitches now appears circular.

7 Begin a second round of stitches at A. Slide the needle under the linking thread between the first and second stitch of the first round. Wrap thread counter-clockwise around the needle.

8 Gently pull the thread through.

9 Work four more stitches. To work the last stitch slide the needle under the linking thread between the first and second stitch of the second round. Wrap the thread around the needle as before.

10 Gently pull the thread through.

11 To end off, take the needle to the back through the centre. Pull through to the wrong side and secure.

12 Completed raised cup stitch.

Rhodes Stitch

Rhodes stitch was invented by British needlework designer, Mary Rhodes. The size of the stitch can vary, covering anything from three to twenty-four horizontal and vertical canvas threads. Here the stitch is worked over four horizontal and four vertical canvas threads (five holes). Begin each Rhodes stitch with a stitch at the same angle so every square looks the same.

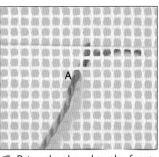

1 Bring the thread to the front at A. This is one hole below the top left hand corner of the square to be covered.

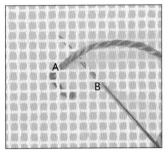

2 Take the needle to the back at B (on the opposite side of the square and one hole up from the lower right hand corner).

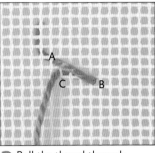

3 Pull the thread through. Re-emerge at C, directly below A.

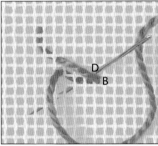

4 Take the needle to the back at D, directly above B.

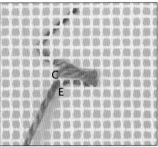

5 Pull the thread through. Re-emerge at E, directly below C.

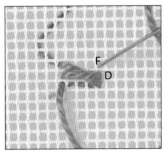

6 Take the needle to the back at F, directly above D.

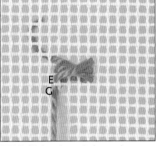

7 Pull the thread through. Re-emerge at G, directly below E.

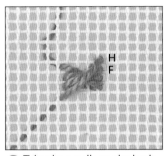

8 Take the needle to the back at H, directly above F. Pull the thread through.

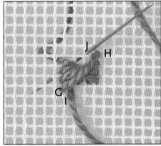

9 Re-emerge at I, one hole to the right of G. Take the needle to the back at J, one hole to the left of H.

10 Pull the thread through. Re-emerge at K, one hole to the right of I. Take the needle to the back at L, one hole to the left of J.

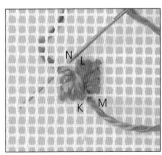

11 Pull the thread through. Re-emerge at M, one hole to the right of K. Take the needle to the back at N, one hole to the left of L.

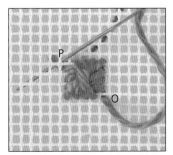

12 Pull the thread through. Re-emerge at O in the lower right hand corner. Take the needle to the back at P, in the upper left hand corner.

13 Pull the thread through. **Completed Rhodes stitch.**

Rhodes Stitch – Circular

This variation of Rhodes stitch is worked on plain fabric and forms a circle. You may find it easier to gradually turn the fabric as you progress around the circle.

1 Draw a circle onto the right side of the fabric. Outline the circle with tiny split stitches.

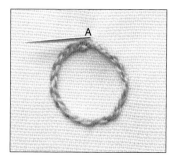

2 Bring the needle to the front at the top of the circle, just out-side the split stitch outline at A.

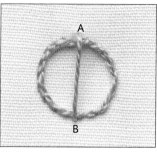

3 Pull the thread through. Take the needle to the back on the opposite side of the circle, just over the split stitch outline at B. Pull the thread through.

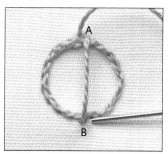

4 Re-emerge just to the left of A. Pull the thread through. Take the needle to the back just to the right of B.

5 Pull through. Continue in a counter-clockwise direction keeping the stitches close together. Ensure stitches start and finish on opposite sides.

6 Continue until the outline is covered. The last stitch lies next to the first stitch. **Completed circular Rhodes stitch.**

Ribbon Stitch

This stitch can be worked with any width of ribbon. The stitches should be longer than the width of the ribbon.

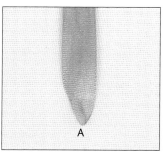

1 Leaving a 1cm (³⁄₈") tail of ribbon on the back of the fabric, bring the ribbon to the front at the position for the base of the stitch at A.

2 Hold the ribbon flat on the fabric with your thumb.

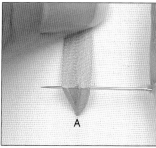

3 Place the needle under the ribbon near A. Using a slight upward pressure, move the needle towards your thumb to spread the ribbon.

4 Place the point of the needle in the centre of the ribbon at the position for the tip of the stitch at B.

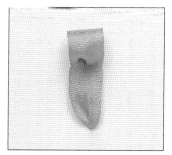

5 Take the needle to the back. Place your thumb over the stitch to keep it flat and untwisted. Begin to gently pull the ribbon through.

6 Pull until the ribbon folds back on itself at the tip and the edges curl. Pulling too far will result in a thin stitch. **Completed ribbon stitch.**

Ribbon Stitch – Folded This stitch is useful for creating leaves and petals.

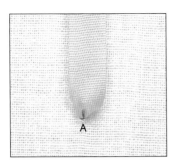

1 Bring the ribbon to the front at the position for the base of the stitch at A.

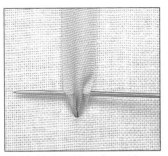

2 Hold the ribbon flat with your thumb (thumb not shown). Spread it by moving the needle behind while applying a slight upwards pressure.

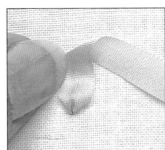

3 Fold the ribbon under a short distance from the base of the stitch.

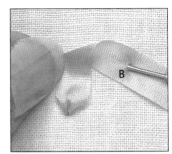

4 Hold the fold in place. Place the tip of the needle in the centre of the ribbon at the position for the tip of the stitch at B.

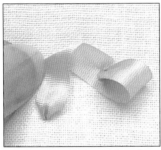

5 Still holding the fold in place, begin to gently pull the ribbon through.

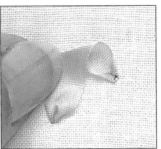

6 Pull until the ribbon folds back on itself at the tip and the edges curl.

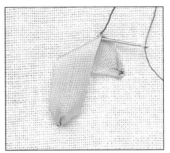

7 If desired, couch the ribbon to the fabric at the fold with matching thread.

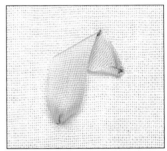

8 **Completed folded ribbon stitch.**

Ribbon Stitch – Looped

Looping the ribbon before completing a ribbon stitch adds further dimension to your finished embroidery.

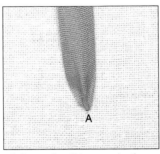

1 Bring the ribbon to the front at the position for the base of the stitch at A.

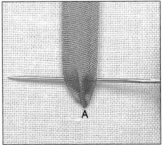

2 Place the needle under the ribbon near A. Using a slight upward pressure, move the needle towards your thumb to spread the ribbon (thumb not shown).

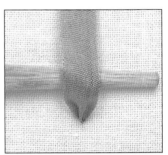

3 Place a chopstick or similar object under the ribbon, close to where it emerged from the fabric.

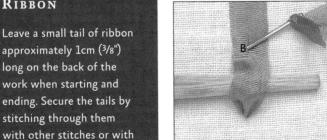

4 Holding the ribbon over the chopstick, place the tip of the needle at B, in the centre of the ribbon at the position for the tip of the stitch.

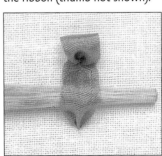

5 Still holding the ribbon in place, take the needle to the back of the fabric and begin to gently pull the ribbon through.

6 Pull until the ribbon folds back on itself at the tip and the edges curl. Remove the chopstick. **Completed looped ribbon stitch.**

Ribbon Stitch – Side

Side ribbon stitch is a variation of ribbon stitch. It creates a stitch that curls to one side depending on the placement of the needle at the tip.

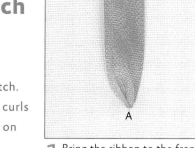

1 Bring the ribbon to the front at the position for the base of the stitch at A.

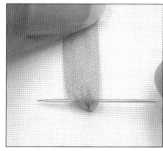

2 Hold the ribbon flat with your thumb. Spread it by moving the needle behind it while applying a slight upward pressure.

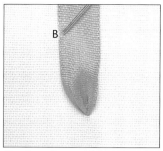

3 Place the tip of the needle just in from the edge of the ribbon at the position for the end of the stitch at B.

4 Take the needle to the back of the fabric. Place your thumb over the stitch to keep it untwisted (thumb not shown). Begin to gently pull the ribbon through.

5 Pull until the ribbon folds back on itself at the tip and the upper edge curls. **Completed side ribbon stitch.**

6 By placing the needle on the other side of the ribbon, the tip of the stitch will curl in the opposite direction.

Rolled Ribbon Rose
To begin, thread a needle with matching machine sewing thread.

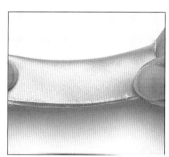

1 Cut a strip of fabric on the bias or use bias cut ribbon. Fold the ribbon in half along the length.

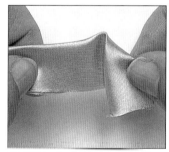

2 With the folded edge at the top, fold down one end diagonally so that a tail of approx 1.5cm (⅝") extends below the raw edge.

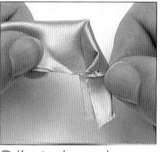

3 Keeping the raw edges even, fold over the end. Take 2 or 3 tiny stitches through the base to secure.

4 Leave the thread hanging free. Still keeping the raw edges even, begin to roll the folded end.

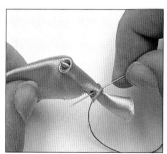

5 Secure the roll with 2 or 3 tiny stitches through all layers at the base.

6 Continue rolling and securing until the rose is the desired size. Cut off excess, leaving a tail the width of the folded ribbon plus 1.5cm (⅝") long.

7 Diagonally fold the ribbon back and down so a 1.5cm (⅝") tail extends below the lower edge.

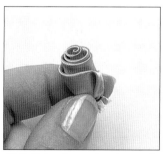

8 Roll the diagonal end onto the rose. Tightly wrap the thread around the base 3 or 4 times and secure. Trim the tails close to the base. **Completed rolled rose.**

Rope Stitch

Different looks can be achieved with rope stitch by varying the width. Place the needle diagonally when working a wide rope stitch and vertically when working a narrow rope stitch.

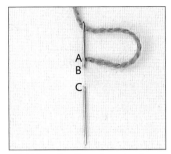

1 Bring the thread to the front at the top of the line at A. Take the needle from B to C.

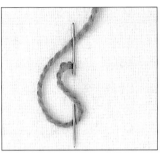

2 Take the thread from left to right over the needle and then pass it from right to left under the tip of the needle.

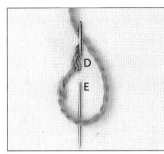

3 Pull the thread through. Take the needle from D to E. D is just below B and E is below C.

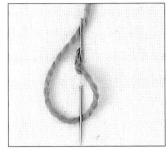

4 Take the thread from right to left under the tip of the needle.

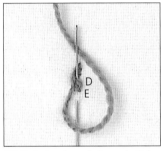

5 Pull the thread through. Take the needle to the back just below D and re-emerge just below E.

6 Continue working stitches in the same manner for the desired distance.

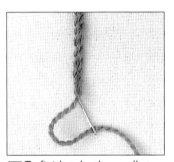

7 To finish, take the needle to the back of the fabric just below the loop of the last stitch.

8 Pull the thread through and end off on the back of the fabric. **Completed rope stitch.**

EMBROIDERY ON CLOTHING

Almost any piece of clothing can be decorated with embroidery but there are a few things to keep in mind.

Try not to position the embroidery where it will receive excessive wear. You want your embroidery to last as long as possible.

The embroidery threads that you use should have the same care requirements as the garment. Putting a dryclean only silk thread onto a washable cotton or linen shirt will result in the garment having to be drycleaned.

If you wish to stitch onto a lined garment, unpick the lining in the area that you have chosen to stitch then re-attach it once the embroidery is complete. This will conceal the back of the embroidery and maintain the correct shape of the garment.

Knitwear is a great surface to embroider but it requires special care because of the large amount of stretch in the knitted fabric. Avoid stitching on areas that are designed to stretch when worn, such as the elbow area. When stitching on knits you can use waste canvas or stabilising paper if you need extra help in preventing the fabric from stretching.

Rosette Stitch

The needle is inserted into the fabric to form the framework around which the thread is wound. After winding, the thread is couched in place.

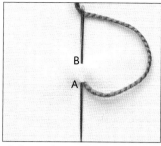

1 Bring the needle to the front at A. Insert the needle at B and emerge at A. Leave the needle in the fabric.

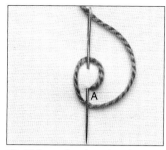

2 Pick up the thread at A. Wrap the thread under each end of the needle in a counter-clockwise direction.

3 Work 2–3 more wraps. Ensure the wraps lie side-by-side and not on top of each other.

4 Holding the wraps in place with your left thumb near the top, gently pull the needle through.

5 Still holding the wraps with your thumb, take the thread over the wraps and to the back of the fabric.

6 Pull the thread through. Bring the needle to the front at the top, just inside the last wrap.

7 Take the needle to the back just over the last wrap and pull the thread through. **Completed rosette stitch.**

Roumanian Stitch

Also known as Roman stitch, Roumanian stitch can be used as a filling to create a broad outline.

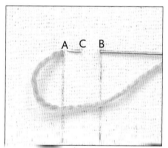

1 Draw two lines on the fabric. Bring the thread to the front at A. Take the needle from B to C. Ensure the thread is below the needle.

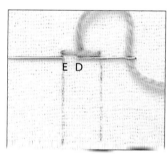

2 Pull the thread through. With the thread above the needle, take the needle from D to E.

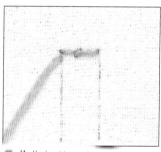

3 Pull the thread through.

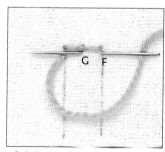

4 Take the needle from F to G. Ensure the thread is below the needle.

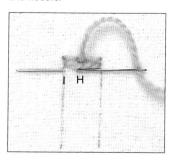

5 Pull the thread through. With the thread above the needle, take the needle from H to I.

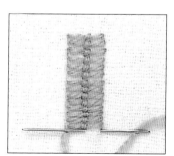

6 Pull the thread through. Continue working stitches in the same manner.

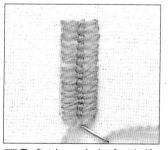

7 To finish, work the first half of the last stitch. Take the needle to the back below the straight stitch but do not re-emerge on the left hand side.

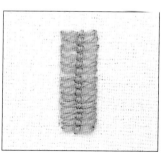

8 Pull the thread through and end off on the back of the fabric. **Completed Roumanian stitch.**

Running Stitch

Running stitch is quick and easy to work and is often used to form the foundation of other stitches such as whipped running stitch and Holbein stitch. When working on plain weave fabrics, make the stitch on the right side of the fabric slightly longer than the stitch on the wrong side.

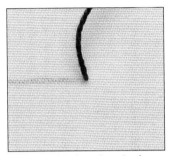

1 Bring the thread to the front on the right hand end of the line to be stitched.

2 Take a small stitch, skimming the needle beneath the fabric along the line.

3 Pull the thread through. Take another stitch as before, ensuring the stitch is the same length as the previous stitch.

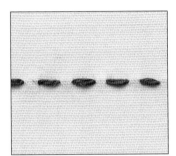

4 Continue in the same manner to the end of the line. **Completed running stitch.**

Running Stitch – Whipped

Also known as cordonnet stitch, whipped running stitch is worked in two stages and has a raised, corded appearance.

It is particularly effective when worked with two colours of thread.

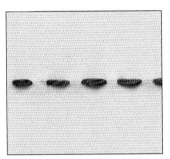

1 **Foundation.** Following the step-by-step instructions above, work a line of running stitch. Keep the spaces between the stitches small.

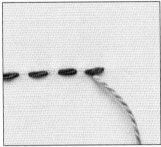

2 **Whipping.** Change thread. Bring the thread to the front just below the centre of the first running stitch on the right hand side.

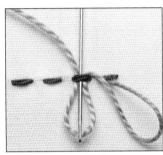

3 Take the needle from top to bottom under the second stitch. To ensure the needle does not go through the fabric or split the stitch, pass it under eye first.

4 Pull through using a loose tension. Take the needle from top to bottom under the third stitch.

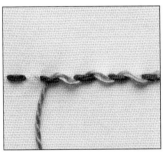

5 Pull through. Continue to the end of the row in the same manner.

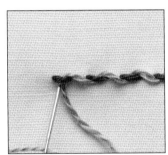

6 To end off, take the needle to the back of the fabric under the centre of the last stitch. **Completed whipped running stitch.**

Running Stitch – Double Whipped
Worked in ribbon, double whipped running stitch has a smooth raised appearance. The stitch can be workd in threads to achieve a raised cord.

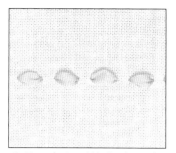

1 **Foundation.** Work a line of running stitch following the instructions on page 122.

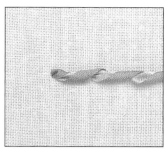

2 **First row of whipping.** Whip the running stitch following the instructions on page 122, keeping the ribbon smooth.

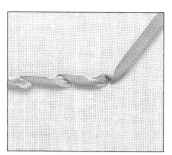

3 **Second row of whipping.** Change to a different ribbon. Bring it to the front at the right hand end of the line, close to where the first ribbon emerged.

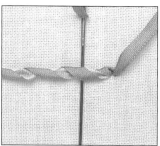

4 Take the needle from top to bottom behind the whipping ribbon between the first and second running stitches. Do not go through the fabric.

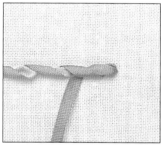

5 Keeping the ribbon smooth, pull it through loosely.

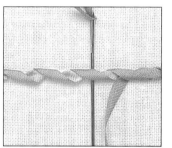

6 Take the needle from top to bottom behind the ribbon between the second and third running stitches. Do not go through the fabric.

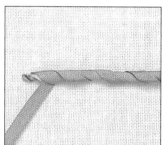

7 Pull the ribbon through loosely. Continue to the end of the line in the same manner.

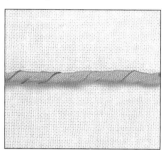

8 Take the needle to the back of the fabric near the end of the last running stitch and end off. **Completed double whipped running stitch.**

Running Stitch – Colonial Knot Combination Rose

A combination of running stitches and a colonial knot is used to create this ingenious rose. More running stitches can be used to form more petals but it is important to keep them all the same length.

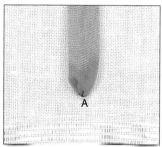

1 Bring the ribbon to the front of the fabric at A.

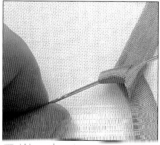

2 Wrap the ribbon around the needle as if making a colonial knot, but approximately 5–6cm (2–2⅜") from the fabric.

3 Take 6–8 running stitches, each approximately 6mm (¼") long, down the middle of the ribbon.

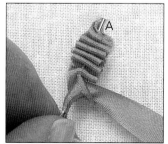

4 Insert the needle into the fabric close to A. Tighten the knot. Begin to pull the needle through to the back of the fabric.

5 Continue pulling until the ribbon folds up into petals with a colonial knot in the middle.

6 End off on the back of the fabric. Adjust the petals with the eye of the needle. **Completed rose.**

Satin Stitch

Satin stitch is also known as damask stitch. Work with the fabric in a hoop and angle the needle under the outline when coming to the front or going to the back. Split stitch is used to outline the shape and gives a smooth, stable edge. When working a curve, fan the stitches on the outer edge and keep them close together on the inner edge.

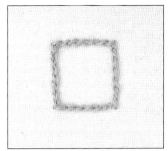

1 **Straight shape.** Outline the shape to be filled with split stitch. This helps to create a neat edge.

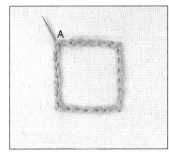

2 Bring the thread to the front at A, just outside the outline.

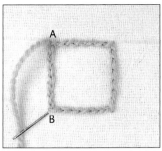

3 Take the needle to the back at B, just over the outline and directly opposite A.

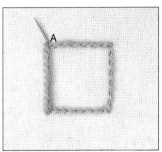

4 Pull the thread through. Re-emerge next to A, angling the needle from under the outline.

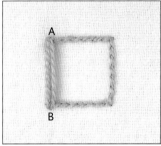

5 Pull the thread through. Take the needle to the back of the fabric next to B and pull the thread through.

6 Continue working stitches in the same manner until reaching the end of the shape. End off the thread on the back of the fabric.

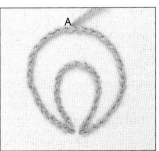

7 **Curved shape.** When working a curved or complex shape, begin near the centre. Bring the thread to the front at A.

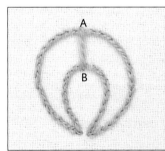

8 Take the needle to the back at B, directly below A. The stitch is at right angles to the shape at this point. Pull the thread through.

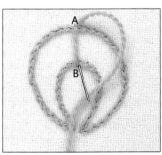

9 Re-emerge close to A and pull the thread through. Take the needle to the back near B, leaving a slightly narrower space between the stitches.

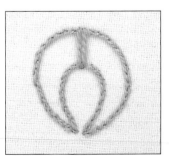

10 Pull the thread through to complete the second stitch.

11 Continue working stitches in the same manner, keeping each one at right angles to the outline. When one half is filled, end off the thread on the back.

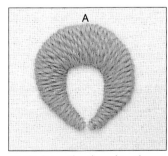

12 Bring the thread to the front close to A. Fill the remaining half of the shape in the same manner. **Completed satin stitch.**

Satin Stitch – Bow

Split stitch is used to outline the bow. It is important to angle the needle under the split stitch when coming to the front and going to the back.

The direction of the satin stitches follows the flow of the bow. The arrow indicates the top of the fabric.

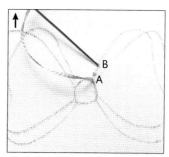

1 **Split stitch outline.** Bring the thread to the front at A. Take a small stitch from A to B.

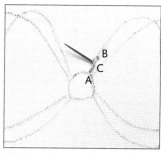

2 Bring the needle to the front at C, halfway between A and B, splitting the thread of the previous stitch.

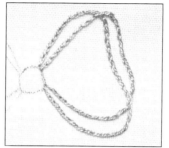

3 Work split stitch along one traced line and then work along the second traced line to complete the right loop outline.

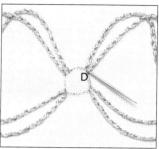

4 Work the outline of the left bow loop in the same manner. **Satin stitch.** Bring the needle to the front at D, just outside the split stitch outline.

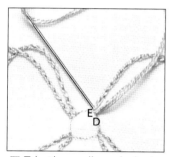

5 Take the needle to the back at E over the split stitch outline, opposite D. Angle the needle under the split stitch before taking it to the back.

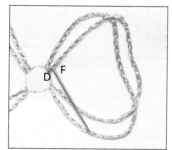

6 Pull the thread through, keeping an even tension. Bring the needle to the front at F, as close as possible to D.

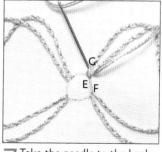

7 Take the needle to the back at G, as close as possible to E.

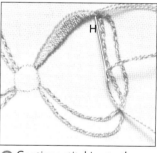

8 Continue stitching to the first ribbon twist keeping the stitches parallel. Complete the last stitch before the twist by taking the needle to the back at H.

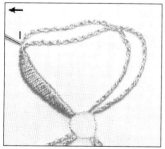

9 Rotate the fabric. Bring the needle to the front at I.

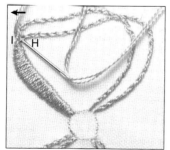

10 Pull the thread through. Take the needle to the back at H.

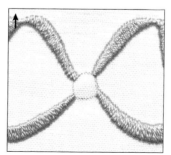

11 Continue stitching as before, rotating the fabric at each twist to complete the right loop. Complete the left bow loop in the same manner.

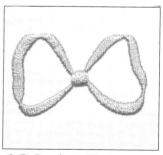

12 **Bow knot.** Work horizontal satin stitches across the bow knot. Work a layer of vertical satin stitches on top. **Completed bow.**

Satin Stitch Leaf

To create lustrous leaves the satin stitches are carefully angled towards the tip.

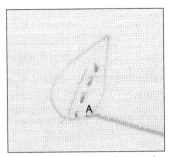

1 Work running stitches inside the leaf shape to secure the thread without a knot. Bring the thread to the front at A.

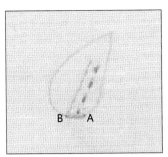

2 Take the thread to the back at B, on the centre vein.

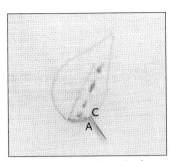

3 Bring the needle to the front at C, beside the first stitch and just above A.

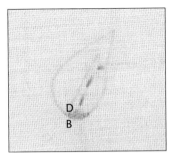

4 Take the thread to the back at D, just above B.

5 Following the leaf shape, continue working satin stitch up one side of the leaf vein.

6 Slightly fan the satin stitches until the first half of the leaf is filled.

7 Continuing on from the tip, work the second half as a mirror image of the first half.

8 End off the thread on the back of the fabric.
Completed satin stitch leaf.

Satin Stitch – Padded

A raised effect is achieved by filling a shape with stitches such as chain, stem, seed, straight or running stitch before working the satin stitches.

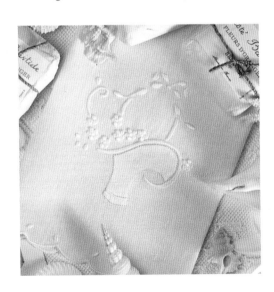

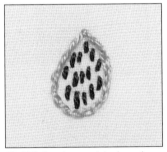

1 Stitch around the outline of the shape with split or back stitch.

2 Fill the shape with the selected filling stitches, ensuring they run opposite to the direction the satin stitches will go.

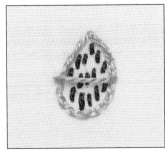

3 Beginning at the widest section of the shape, cover one half with satin stitches using the stabbing technique.

4 Cover the remainder of the shape in the same manner.
Completed padded satin stitch shape.

Satin Stitch – Padded Spot

Several layers of satin stitch can be worked to create a dome shape. Horizontal and vertical satin stitches build the surface over which the final layer of stitches is worked.

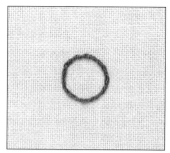

1 Work split stitch around the spot outline.

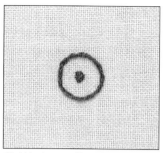

2 Work a small circle of horizontal satin stitches in the centre of the circle.

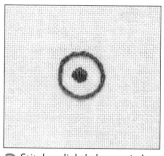

3 Stitch a slightly larger circle of vertical satin stitches over the previous circle.

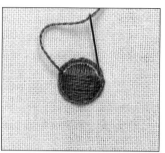

4 Continue working the circles, alternating between vertical and horizontal stitches.

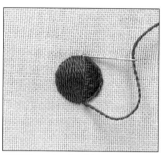

5 Work the final layer, covering the split stitch outline.

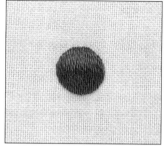

6 **Completed padded satin stitch spot.**

Scottish Stitch

Scottish stitch is a canvas stitch used for filling large spaces worked in blocks or squares.

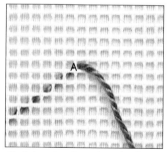

1 Bring the thread to the front at A leaving a tail of approx 5cm (2") on the back.

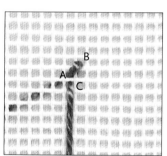

2 Take the thread to the back at B and re-emerge at C, one hole below A

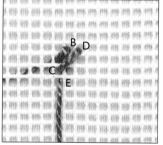

3 Take the thread to the back at D, one hole to the right of B and re-emerge at E, one hole below C.

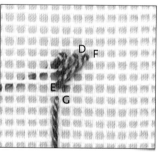

4 Take the thread to the back at F, one hole to the right of D and re-emerge at G, one hole below E.

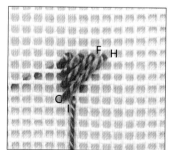

5 Take the thread to the back at H, one hole to the right of F and re-emerge at I, one hole to the right of G.

6 Take the thread to the back at J, one hole below H and re-emerge at K, one hole to the right of I.

7 Take the thread to the back at L, one hole below J and re-emerge at M, one hole to the right of K.

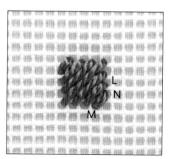

8 Take the thread to the back at N, one hole below L. End off both ends of thread on back by weaving under the stitches.

Scroll Stitch

Also known as single knotted line stitch, scroll stitch makes an attractive border.

Marking a line on the fabric will help keep the stitches straight.

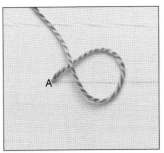

1 Bring the thread to the front at A. Make a loop to the right of A in a clockwise direction.

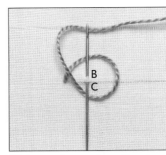

2 Insert the needle at B and re-emerge at C, taking a tiny stitch to the marked line. Ensure the circle of thread lies under both ends of the needle.

3 Pull the thread firmly so the loop tightens around the needle.

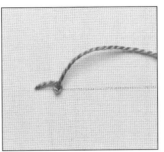

4 Pull the thread through. **Completed first stitch.**

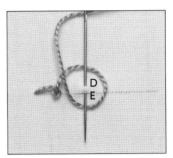

5 Loop the thread to the right. Insert the needle from D to E. Ensure the loop is under both ends of the needle.

6 Tighten the loop and pull the thread through. Continue working stitches in the same manner. **Completed scroll stitch.**

Seed Stitch

Also known as speckling stitch and isolated back stitch, seed stitch is a filling stitch. When used as a background or to fill a shape, the stitches should be scattered irregularly.

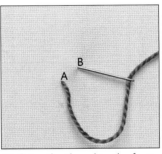

1 Bring the thread to the front at A. Take the needle to the back at B, a short distance away.

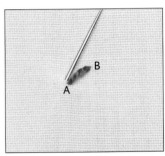

2 Pull the thread through and re-emerge next to A.

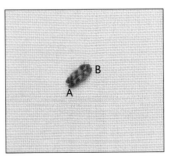

3 Pull the thread through. Take the thread to the back next to B. Pull the thread through.

4 Continue working random seed stitches in the area to be filled, varying the angle of the stitches. **Completed seed stitch.**

Shadow Work – Double Back Stitch

Shadow work creates a delicate effect of shading on fine fabrics. It can be worked from either the wrong or the right side of the fabric.

Here it is worked from the right side with the fabric in a hoop to help maintain an even tension.

Ribbons of shadow work and delicate sprays of flowers

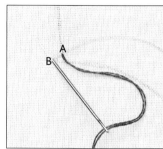

1 Begin with a waste knot. Bring the needle to the front at A, 1.5mm (1/16") away from the point of the shape. Pull through. Take the needle to the back at B, exactly on the point.

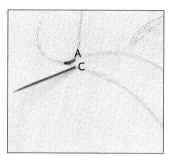

2 Pull the thread through. Re-emerge at C, on the lower line directly below A.

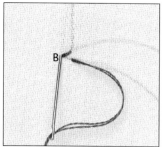

3 Pull the thread through. Take the needle to the back at B using the same hole in the fabric as before.

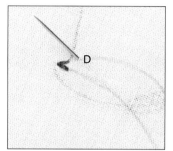

4 Pull the thread through. Re-emerge at D, on the upper line, 1.5mm (1/16") away from A.

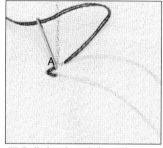

5 Pull the thread through. Take the needle to the back at A, using exactly the same hole in the fabric as before.

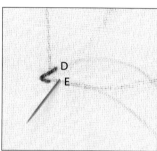

6 Pull the thread through and re-emerge at E on the lower line, opposite D.

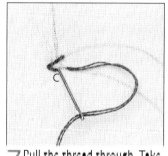

7 Pull the thread through. Take needle to the back at C, using the same hole in the fabric.

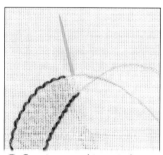

8 Continue working stitches in the same manner as steps 4–7. To work a curve, the stitches on the inside line are gradually reduced in length.

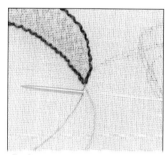

9 **Crossover.** To create the effect of twisting, the lower curve crosses over the upper curve. Work the first stitch of the crossover on the lower line.

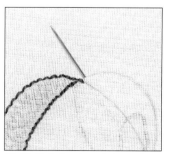

10 Pull the thread through. Bring the needle to the front on the upper line for the second stitch of the crossover.

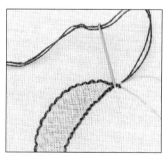

11 Take the needle to the back to the left of the intersection on the lower line.

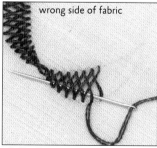

wrong side of fabric

12 Continue stitching as before. To end off or begin a new thread, weave through the threads on the wrong side, close to the edge.

Shadow Work – Closed Herringbone Stitch

When shadow work is stitched with the wrong side of the fabric facing, it is known as closed herringbone stitch. Work with the fabric in a hoop to help maintain an even tension. A tapestry needle parts the fabric threads rather than splitting them.

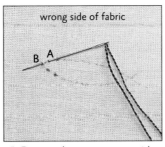

1 Draw a shape on wrong side of the fabric. On the upper line, take the needle from A to B.

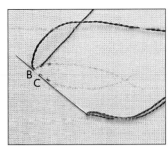

2 Pull thread through leaving a small tail approx 5cm (2") long. On the lower line, take the needle from C to B in the same hole.

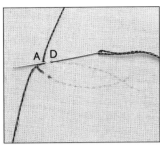

3 Pull the thread through. On the upper line take the needle to the back at D and re-emerge at A in the same hole.

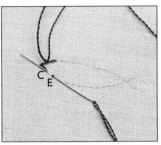

4 Pull the thread through. On the lower line take the needle from E to C in the same manner.

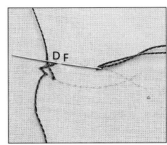

5 Pull the thread through. On the upper line take the needle from F to D in the same hole.

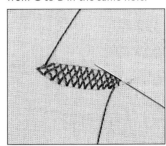

6 Continue closed herringbone stitch to the crossover point.

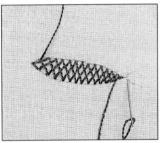

7 **Crossover.** When the crossover point is reached, make sure the upper line stitch at the intersection is worked first.

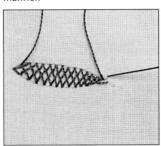

8 The lower line stitch will now cross over at the intersection. Check the right side of the fabric before proceeding.

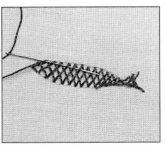

9 **Finishing off.** Weave the tails of thread under the stitches as close as possible to the edge.

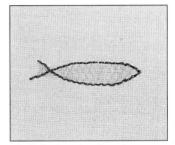

10 Right side of work. **Completed shadow work.**

Shadow Trapunto

Shadow trapunto is a form of Italian quilting. Two layers of fabric are stitched together with running stitch and the shapes filled with yarn. Work the running stitches using one strand of stranded cotton and the filling with a no. 20 tapestry needle and tapestry wool.

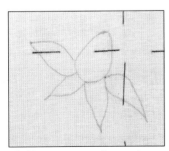

1 Using a contrasting sewing thread, tack both layers of fabric together, using long stitches in a grid formation.

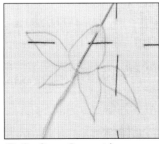

2 **Outlines.** Start with a waste knot approx 6mm (¹/₄") away inside the area to be filled. Slide needle between both layers, emerging on the traced line.

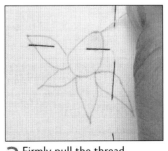

3 Firmly pull the thread through so the waste knot is buried between the two layers of fabric.

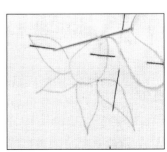

4 Take the needle through the fabric 2mm (¹/₁₆") away on traced line. Re-emerge 2mm (¹/₁₆") away, to form the first running stitch.

Shadow Trapunto CONTINUED

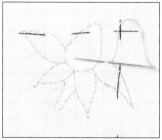

5 Pull the thread through. Continue working tiny running stitches approx 2mm (1/16") in length, along all traced lines of the design. End off on the back.

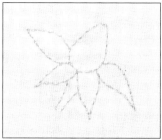

6 Remove all tacking threads. **Completed outlined design.**

7 **Filling.** Turn work to the wrong side. Insert the needle at the narrowest part of the shape between the two layers. Run the needle lengthwise, emerging at the end of the shape.

8 Pull through gently, leaving a very short tail of approx 1mm (less than 1/16") extending from the fabric.

9 Cut the yarn as close as possible to the fabric.

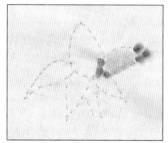

10 Continue filling the shape, keeping the lines of yarn parallel. Use shorter lengths as necessary until the shape is filled.

11 Trim all ends of yarn close to the fabric. Using the tip of the needle, hook the ends of yarn under the fabric.

12 Using the side of the needle, carefully stroke the fabric threads to conceal any holes.

13 **Two-tone rosebud.** On the wrong side and with the darker coloured yarn, work the first filling stitch. Begin at the tip of the upper part of shape. Take the yarn one third down the shape.

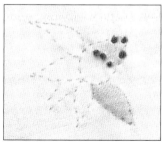

14 Continue filling the upper part of the shape with parallel lines of yarn.

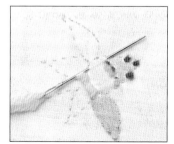

15 Using lighter coloured yarn, fill in the lower part of the shape. Begin from the opposite end, with the needle re-emerging approx 2mm (1/16") away from the darker yarn.

16 Trim and conceal ends. **Completed shadow trapunto.**

Sheaf Filling Stitch

Also known as faggot filling stitch, each sheaf filling stitch is worked separately and looks like a tiny sheaf of wheat.

Any type of thread can be used, depending on the effect desired. The stitch can be worked randomly or set in geometric patterns.

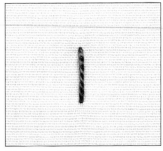

1 Secure the thread on the back. Work a vertical straight stitch.

2 Work a second vertical stitch on one side of the first stitch. Work another vertical stitch on the other side of the first stitch.

3 Bring the thread to the front at A, halfway along the left hand side of the left stitch.

4 Take the needle from right to left under all three stitches. Do not go through the fabric.

5 Pull the thread firmly. Take a second stitch from right to left under the vertical stitches.

6 Pull the thread through. Take the needle to the back very close to A. **Completed sheaf filling stitch.**

Shisha Stitch

Shisha stitch is a traditional Indian technique for attaching tiny round pieces of mirror or tin to fabric background. There are numerous forms of Shisha stitch. Here we show one form. We used two colours of thread for photographic purposes only.

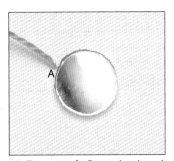

1 **Framework.** Bring the thread to the front at A approximately a third of the way down the left side.

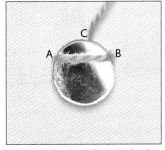

2 Take the thread to the back at B next to the edge of the glass. Re-emerge at C, slightly above. Pull the thread through.

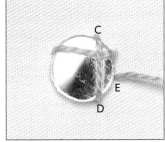

3 Take the thread to the back at D, below and directly opposite C. Re-emerge at E. Pull the thread through.

4 Take the thread to the back at F, on the opposite side. Re-emerge at G. Pull the thread through.

5 Take the thread to the back at H and re-emerge at I, just to the right of H. Pull the thread through.

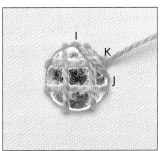

6 Take the thread to the back at J and re-emerge at K. Pull the thread through.

7 Take the thread to the back at L and re-emerge at M. Pull the thread through.

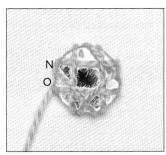

8 Take the thread to the back at N and re-emerge at O. Pull the thread through.

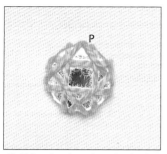

9 Take the thread to the back at P. Pull the thread through. **Completed foundation.**

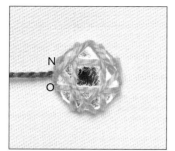

10 **Edging stitches.** Change to a new thread. Bring the thread to the front next to the glass on the left hand side between N and O.

11 Loop the thread to the right and hold in place with your left thumb (thumb not shown). Take the needle under two crossed foundation stitches.

12 Ensure the loop is under the tip of the needle. Begin to pull the thread through.

13 Continue pulling until firm. Loop the thread to the left.

14 Take a small stitch parallel to the glass, close to the edge. Ensure the loop is under the tip of the needle.

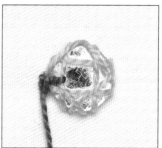

15 Pull the thread through. **First completed edging stitch.**

16 Loop thread to the right and hold in place. Take the needle under the next two crossed foundation stitches. Ensure the loop is under the tip of the needle.

17 Pull the thread through until the loop is firm.

18 Loop thread to left. Take a small straight stitch parallel to the edge of the glass, taking the needle under the first stitch. Ensure the loop is under the tip of the needle.

19 Pull the thread through until the loop is firm.

20 Loop the thread to the right. Take the needle under the next two crossed foundation stitches.

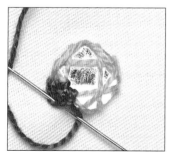

21 Pull the thread through. Loop the thread to the left. Take a small stitch through the previous stitch, picking up a small piece of fabric.

22 Continue working stitches in the same manner, turning the work as you proceed.

23 Take the last stitch into the back of the first stitch.

24 **Completed shisha stitch.**

Smocker's Knot

A smocker's knot is firmer than a French knot.

In smocking and other embroidery, it is often used as a secure technique for finishing off on the back of the work. It can also be used as a decorative stitch.

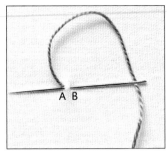

1 Bring the thread to the front at A. Take a back stitch from B to A, keeping the thread above the needle.

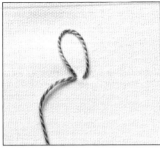

2 Pull the thread through leaving a small loop approx 1cm (³⁄₈") in diameter.

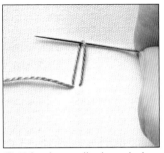

3 Take the needle through the loop.

4 Pull the thread through leaving a second small loop approx 1cm (³⁄₈") in diameter.

5 Holding the thread in the left hand and the second loop in the right hand, begin to pull the second loop.

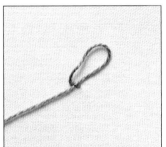

6 Pull until the first loop is tight and flat against the fabric. The second loop remains intact.

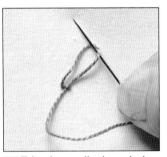

7 Take the needle through the remaining loop.

8 Begin to pull the thread through.

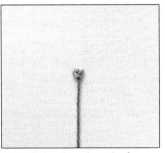

9 Pull the thread until a firm knot forms against the fabric.

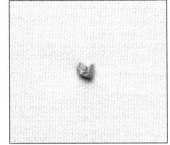

10 Take the needle to the back under the knot to end off.
Completed smocker's knot.

Soft Shading

Also known as thread painting, soft shading is a form of long and short stitch. Being a freer variation of this traditional stitch, the stitches are laid down with less uniformity and so it is possible to create a realistic blending of colour. See also long and short stitch, page 100 and thread painting, page 147.

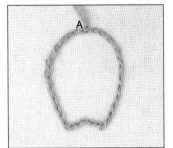

1 Outline the shape to be filled with split stitch. This helps to create a neat, well defined edge. Bring the thread to the front at A, just outside the outline.

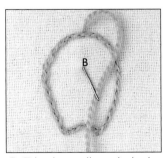

2 Take the needle to the back at B, within the shape.

3 Pull the thread through. Re-emerge just beyond the outline very close to A.

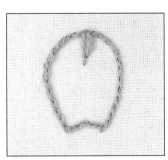

4 Pull the thread through. Work a second stitch which is slightly shorter than the first stitch.

Soft Shading

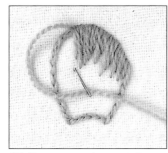

5 Continue working stitches very close together, fanning them to fit the shape. Alternate between long stitches and shorter stitches.

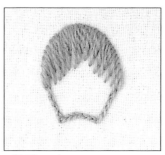

6 When the section is complete, take the thread to the back of the fabric and end off.

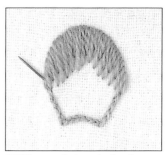

7 Using a darker shade of thread, bring the needle to the front, splitting a stitch of the previous row.

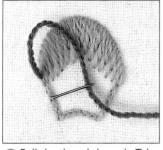

8 Pull the thread through. Take the needle to the back in the unembroidered area.

9 Work long and short stitches in the same direction as the first row, always emerging through a previous stitch. When complete, end off as before.

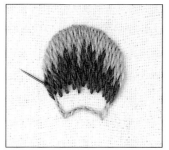

10 Using a darker shade of thread, bring the needle to the front, splitting a stitch of the previous row.

11 Repeat steps 8 and 9. When complete, end off as before. **Completed soft shading.**

HINTS

THREAD PAINTING

When choosing colours, use as many shades as you can, even if they are similar. The result is more realistic. Try blending shades in the needle to create new colours.

Work well into the previous row of stitches to achieve a smooth blend. Avoid finishing at the end of a previous row, as this will create a visible line.

Keep the stitch length as random as possible. This will help to blend the colours and create a smooth surface. Angle your needle into the fabric rather than pushing it straight through. This helps to blend the stitches. Observing your work from a distance will show up any problems not visible when viewed closely.

Spider Web Rose

This easy to stitch, textured rose is created by weaving ribbon or thread through a framework of straight stitch spokes. Always use an uneven number of spokes.

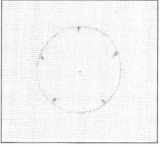

1 Draw a circle and mark the centre with a dot. Imagining the circle is a clock face, mark the outer edge with dots at 12, 2, 5, 7 and 10 o'clock.

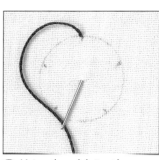

2 Using thread, bring the needle to the front at the 12 o'clock mark. Take it to the back at the centre.

3 Pull the thread through. Work straight stitches from the 5 o'clock and 7 o'clock marks to the centre.

4 Work straight stitches from the 10 o'clock and 2 o'clock marks in the same manner. Secure the thread on the back but leave it hanging free.

5 **Petals.** Bring the ribbon to the front between two spokes as close as possible to the centre.

6 Working in a counter-clockwise direction, weave the ribbon over and under the spokes of the framework until one round is complete.

7 Pull the ribbon firmly so the framework does not show at the centre.

8 Work 1 to 2 more rounds in the same manner, maintaining the over and under sequence. Take the ribbon to the back. Secure with the thread.

9 Bring a lighter shade of ribbon to the front, emerging next to where the previous ribbon went to the back.

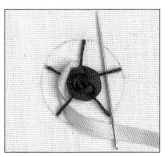

10 Using a looser tension and allowing the ribbon to twist, weave it over and under the spokes.

11 Continue weaving until the framework is entirely hidden. Take the needle over one more spoke, tuck it under the next spoke and take it to the back.

12 Pull the ribbon through and secure the uncaught tails with the dangling thread. **Completed spider web rose.**

Split Back Stitch

On the front of the fabric, split back stitch looks very much like split stitch. However, each stitch is split when the needle is taken to the back of the fabric rather than when it is emerging.

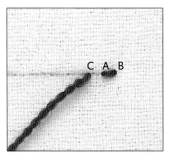

1 Bring the thread to the front at A, a short distance from the right hand end. Take the needle from B to C and pull through.

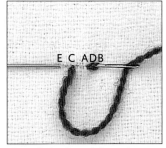

2 Pull the thread through. Take the needle from D to E, splitting the previous stitch. D is halfway between A and B.

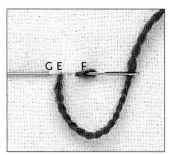

3 Pull the thread through. Take the needle from F to G, splitting the previous stitch.

4 Continue, keeping the stitches equal in length. For the last stitch, take the needle to the back through the previous stitch. End off. **Completed split back stitch.**

Split Stitch

Also known as Kensington outline stitch, split stitch can be used as an outline or as a filling stitch.

Used extensively in the Middle Ages for embroidering faces, it lends itself to subtle shading when it is worked in multiple rows to fill a shape.

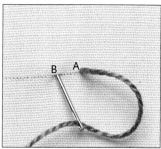

1 Bring the needle to the front at A. Take the needle to the back at B approximately 3mm (1/8") away.

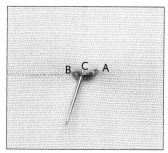

2 Pull the thread through. Emerge at C in the centre of the first stitch, splitting the thread with the needle.

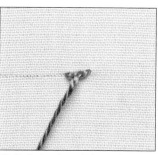

3 Pull the thread through to complete the first stitch and begin the second stitch.

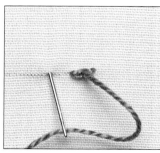

4 Take the needle to the back approximately 3mm (1/8") away.

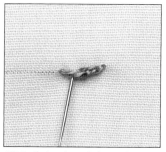

5 Pull the thread through. Re-emerge through the centre of the second stitch.

6 Pull the thread through. Continue working stitches in the same manner. **Completed split stitch.**

Star Stitch

Star stitch is an isolated stitch, often worked to add interest and texture to a background. Contrasting colours and different weights of thread can be used to create various effects.

It can be worked on canvas and evenweave fabrics as well as plain weave fabrics.

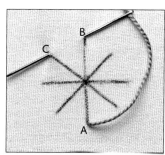

1 Mark the star onto the fabric. Bring the thread to the front at A. Take the needle from B to C.

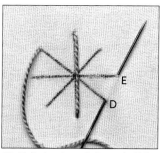

2 Pull the thread through. Take the needle from D to E. This stitch will cross over the first stitch.

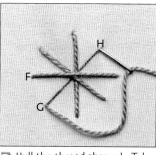

3 Pull the thread through. Take the needle from F to G and pull through. Take the needle to the back at H to form the final spoke of the star.

4 Bring the needle to the front very close to the centre, in between two spokes. Take the needle over the intersection of the spokes and to the back, close to the centre.

5 Pull the thread through to anchor the spokes at the centre. **Completed star stitch.**

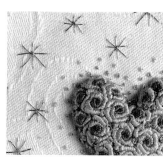

A background of star stitches, formed with spokes of various lengths.

Stem Stitch

Also known as crewel stitch, stem stitch is similar in appearance to outline stitch. The thread is always kept below the needle, whereas in outline stitch it is kept above.

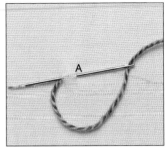

1 Bring the needle to the front at the left hand side of the line. With the thread below the needle, take it to the back at A. Re-emerge at the end of the line.

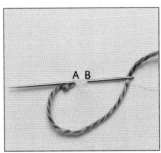

2 Pull the thread through. Again with the thread below the needle, take the needle from B to A.

3 Pull the thread through. Continue working the stitches in the same manner, always keeping the thread below the needle and the stitches the same size.

4 To end off, take the needle to the back for the last stitch but do not re-emerge. Secure the thread on the back with tiny back stitches. **Completed stem stitch.**

Stem Stitch – Encroaching

Encroaching stem stitch is a variation of stem stitch. When stitching, angle the needle across the design line rather than along it. This gives a wider stitch.

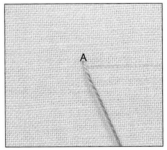

1 Following the design line on the fabric, bring the thread to the front at A. Lay the thread below the line.

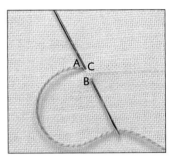

2 Take the needle from B, to C next to A. The needle is angled across the line.

Stem stitch is used extensively in redwork embroidery

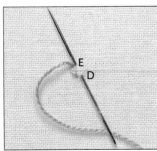

3 Pull the thread through. Take a second stitch from D to E.

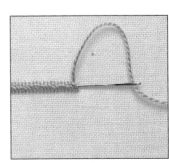

4 Continue in the same manner to the end of the line. To end off, take the needle to back on the line.

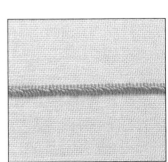

5 Pull the thread through and secure. **Completed encroaching stem stitch.**

Stem Stitch – Portuguese Knotted

This delightful scroll-like stitch forms a knotted line which is useful for outlining shapes. Two whipping stitches are worked around each stem stitch creating a line of knots.

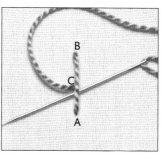

1 Work a stitch from A to D. Bring the needle to the front at C. With the thread above the needle, slide the needle from right to left under the stitch, below C.

2 Gently begin to pull the thread through.

3 Continue pulling the thread through. Pull upwards towards C, so a wrap is formed over the first stitch.

4 Keeping the thread above the needle, slide the needle under the first stitch again and below the first wrap.

5 Pull the thread through, so a second wrap is formed below the first.

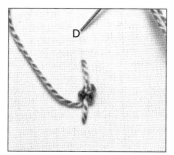

6 To begin the second stem stitch, take the needle through to the back at D.

7 Pull the thread through.

8 Bring the needle to the front at B on the left hand side of the second stem stitch.

9 Keeping the thread above the needle, slide the needle from the right to the left under the first and second stem stitches, below B.

10 Pull the thread through. Keeping the thread above the needle, slide the needle from right to left under the wrap just formed.

11 Pull the thread through so a second wrap is formed.

12 Continue working stitches. To end off, take the needle to the back under the last wrap and finish off on the wrong side.

Stem Stitch – Raised

Raised stem stitch is created from a base of straight stitches upon which rows of stem stitch are embroidered. It is best to work this stitch in a hoop, using a crewel needle for the base and a tapestry needle for the stem stitch.

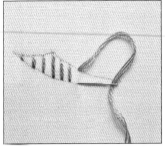

1 **Base.** Work evenly spaced parallel stitches at right angles to the shape outline and 2–3mm (⅛") apart. Start and finish the stitches exactly on the outline.

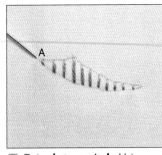

2 **Raised stem stitch.** Using a new thread, bring the needle to the front at A, on the left side of the shape.

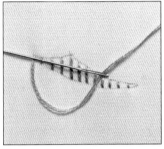

3 Pull through. Keeping thread below the needle, take the needle from right to left under the first straight stitch. The needle does not go through the fabric.

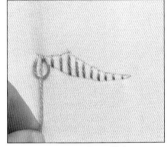

4 Begin to gently pull the thread downwards.

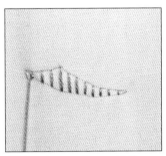

5 Continue pulling until the stem stitch wraps firmly around the straight stitch.

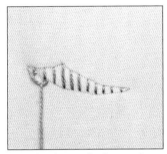

6 Take the needle from right to left under the next straight stitch. Holding it in place, pull the thread through in the same manner as the first stitch.

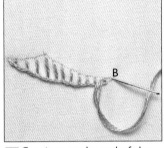

7 Continue to the end of the shape. Slide the needle behind the straight stitches and pack the stem stitches down. Take the needle to the back at B.

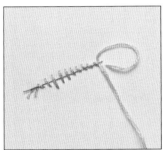

8 Pull through. Turn the work to the wrong side. Slide the needle under the straight stitches on the back of the work.

9 Turn work to the right side. Re-emerge at A. Work a second row of raised stem stitch in the same manner. The rows of stitches will touch each other.

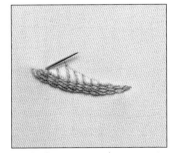

10 Continue working rows in the same manner. As the shape fills, start and finish rows away from the tips of the shape so they don't become too thick and bulky.

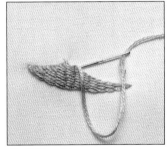

11 To achieve a clean, crisp look, ensure that the start and finish of each row is precisely on the pencil line. Pack down each row before beginning the next.

12 Continue working rows of stem stitch until the shape is filled and the straight stitches are completely covered. Take the thread to the back and end off. **Completed raised stem stitch.**

Stem Stitch – Padded Raised

This technique is particularly suited to stems as it gives a raised surface. Ensure that you have sufficient thread to finish each row of stem stitch.

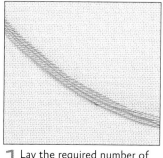

1 Lay the required number of threads along the line.

2 Starting at A, take a couching stitch over all of the laid threads.

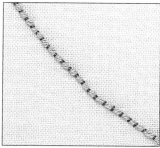

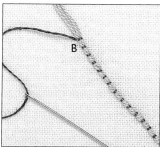

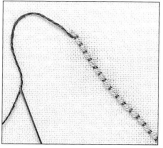

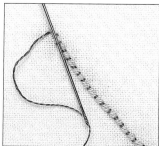

3 Continue couching at 3mm (1/8") intervals to the top of the stem.

4 With a new thread, bring the needle to the front at B, on the left of the stem and pull through.

5 Sink and secure the padding threads at both ends on the back of the work.

6 Keeping the thread below the needle, take it from right to left under the second couching stitch. The needle picks up only the couching stitches.

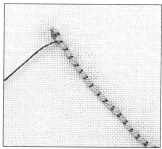

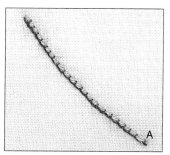

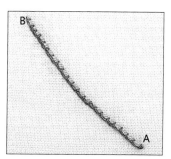

7 Pull the thread downwards so that the stem stitch wraps firmly around the couching stitch.

8 Continue to the end of the stem (A). Secure the thread on the back of the fabric.

9 Work a second row in the same manner, again working from B to A.

10 Work rows in the same manner until the laid threads are closely covered. **Completed padded raised stem stitch.**

Stem Stitch – Whipped

To create this stitch a foundation of stem stitch is worked first. The whipping stitches are worked over the foundation and do not go through the fabric. Use a tapestry needle for the whipping to prevent splitting the foundation stitches.

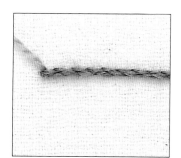

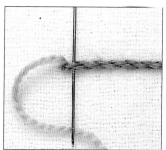

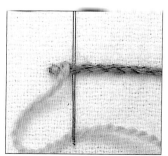

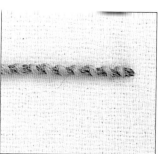

1 **Foundation.** Work a line of stem stitch. Whipping. Bring a new thread to the front just above the first stem stitch.

2 Slide the needle from bottom to top under the space shared by the first and second stem stitches. Do not go through the fabric.

3 Pull the thread through. Take the needle from bottom to top under the space shared by the second and third stem stitches.

4 Pull the thread through. Continue to the end in the same manner. To end off, take the needle to the back behind the last stem stitch and secure. **Completed whipped stem stitch.**

Stem Stitch–Ribbon Rose

The stitches are worked with a loose tension to keep the petals full.

We used a no. 24 chenille needle and 3 shades of 2mm (1/16") wide silk ribbon.

The arrow indicates the top of the fabric.

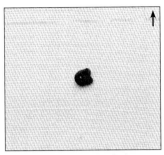

1 **Centre.** Using the darkest shade of ribbon, work a French knot for the centre.

2 **Inner petals.** Change to the medium shade. Bring the needle to the front at A alongside the knot.

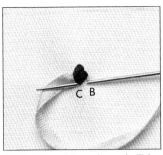

3 Pull the ribbon through. Take the needle to the back at B and re-emerge at C, keeping the ribbon below the needle.

4 Pull the ribbon through. **Completed first stem stitch.**

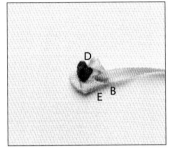

5 Take the needle to the back at D and re-emerge at E, close to B, and pull through.

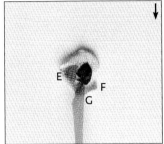

6 Work a third stitch from E to F emerging at G.

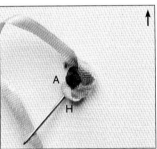

7 Take the needle to the back at H, just beyond A and on the outside of the first stitch.

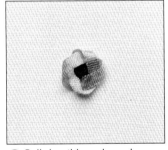

8 Pull the ribbon through. **Completed first round of petals.**

9 **Outer petals.** Change to the lightest shade. Bring the needle to the front at I, halfway along and on the outside of the first stitch.

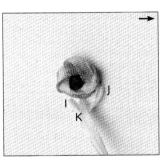

10 Pull the ribbon through. Work a stitch from I to J, re-emerging at K.

11 Work four more stitches with the last stitch overlapping the first stitch of this round. Rotate the fabric as you work.

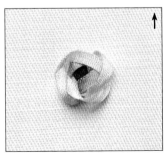

12 Pull the ribbon through and end off on the back. **Completed stem stitch ribbon rose.**

Straight Overcast Stitch

Also known as overcast stitch, straight overcast stitch is often featured in eyelets and cutwork.

Here it is used to create a beading eyelet. The eyelet is first outlined with running stitch to reinforce the cut edge.

The arrow indicates the top of the fabric.

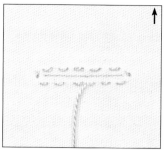

1 Mark a line on the fabric. Carefully outline the marked line for the eyelet with tiny running stitches starting on one side. Finish with the thread on the front of the fabric.

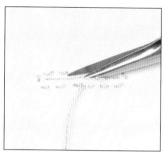

2 Leave the thread hanging free. Using small sharp-pointed scissors, carefully snip along the marked line.

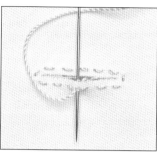

3 Take the needle to the back through the opening and re-emerge just beyond the running stitches to the right of the starting point.

4 Pull the thread through. Take the needle through the opening and re-emerge as close as possible to the first stitch on the right hand side.

5 Continue stitching in this manner along the side, keeping an even tension and ensuring the stitches are the same length

6 At the end, slightly fan the stitches until the corner is completely turned.

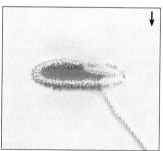

7 Turn the fabric and continue stitching along the second side.

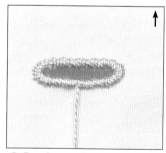

8 Fan the stitches at the second end in the same manner as before. Continue stitching until reaching the first stitch.

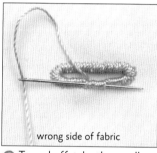

wrong side of fabric

9 To end off, take the needle through the opening to the back. Turn the fabric over to the wrong side. Slide the needle behind the stitches only.

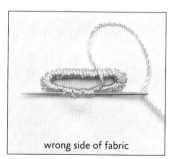

wrong side of fabric

10 Take the needle over 1–2 threads, then slide the needle behind the stitches in the opposite direction.

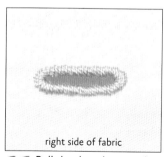

right side of fabric

11 Pull the thread taut and cut close to the stitches. **Completed straight overcast stitch eyelet.**

Ribbon threaded beading, created from straight overcast stitch eyelets.

Straight Stitch

Also known as stroke stitch, straight stitch is the most basic embroidery stitch. It can be stitched in any direction and to any length and it forms the basis of many other stitches.

HINTS

FOR LEFT-HANDED EMBROIDERERS

For most stitches, work from right to left (or the opposite direction to right handers' instructions).

Most stitches are worked as a mirror image to the way right handers work them. When following instructions imagine you are looking into a mirror rather than copying exactly what you see. If taking a class, sit in front of the teacher rather than alongside.

Some instructions are easier to follow if you turn them upside down.

Stitches that are worked from top to bottom for right handers are also worked from top to bottom for left handers.

1 Bring the thread to the front at the beginning of the stitch, A.

2 Take the needle to the back at the end of the stitch, B.

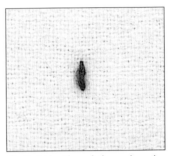

3 Pull the thread through and end off on the back of the fabric.

4 Straight stitches worked at different angles.

Straight Stitch – Flower

Straight stitch can be used in a variety of ways and is often combined with other stitches. Here, straight stitches worked in a circle are used to form the petals of a flower.

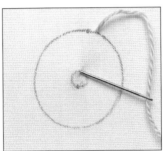

1 Draw two circles on the fabric. Bring the thread to the front on the outer edge of the circle. Take it to the back on the inner circle.

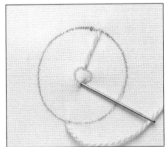

2 Pull the thread through. Re-emerge on the outer edge opposite the first stitch. Take the needle to the back on the inner circle.

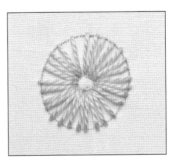

3 Continue working stitches, varying their length slightly and always working the stitches roughly opposite each other.

4 Continue until circles are filled. Add 3–7 colonial knots for the centre. **Completed straight stitch flower.**

Tassel

Tassels of all sizes can be used as trimmings on embroidered pieces. Cut two pieces of cardboard 10cm (4") wide and slightly longer than the finished length of your tassel.

1 Place the two pieces of cardboard together. Wind the thread around the card.

2 Thread a needle with a small length of thread. Take it under the wrapped threads at the top, between the pieces of card. Tie a double knot to secure. Do not trim.

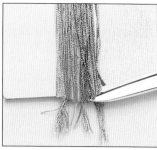

3 With small sharp scissors, cut the threads at the lower edge of the cardboard.

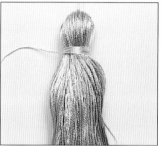

4 Remove the cardboard. Measure 2cm (¾") from the top of the tassel and wrap the neck of the tassel tightly.

5 Secure the thread, leaving a length extending at the top to attach the tassel.

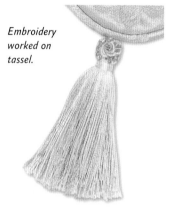

Embroidery worked on tassel.

Tent Stitch – Basket Weave

Tent stitch is also known as petit point, continental stitch or needlepoint stitch. It is a small diagonal stitch. Each stitch covers a single intersection of two canvas threads.

Worked diagonally the stitch is known as basket weave, creating a woven pattern of straight stitches on the reverse side of the canvas.

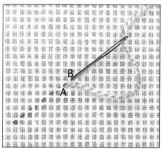

1 **First row.** Bring the needle to the front at A and take it to the back at B over one intersection of threads.

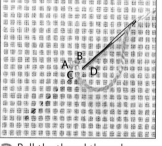

2 Pull the thread through. Re-emerge at C, two threads below B, forming a vertical stitch on the reverse side of the canvas. Insert the needle at D, two threads to the right of A.

3 Pull the thread through to complete the second stitch. Continue to work a diagonal row of stitches in this manner.

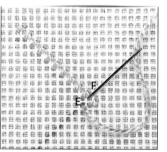

4 **Second row.** Bring the needle to the front at E, one thread to the left of the last stitch. Insert the needle at F, between the two last stitches of the first row.

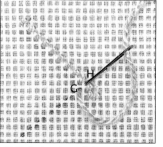

5 Pull the thread through. Re-emerge at G, forming a horizontal stitch on the reverse side of the canvas. Take the needle over one intersection and insert at H, between two stitches of the previous row.

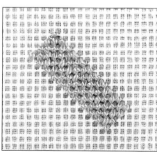

6 Continue working in this manner alternating the direction of the stitching. **Completed basket weave tent stitch.**

Tent Stitch – Continental

When worked in horizontal or vertical rows tent stitch is known as continental tent stitch.

The arrow indicates the top of the fabric.

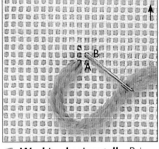

1 **Working horizontally.** Bring the thread to the front at A. Take the needle to the back at B, through the next hole above and to the right of A.

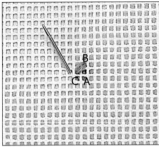

2 Pull the thread through. Re-emerge at C, one hole to the left of A.

3 Take the thread to the back at D, in the hole directly above A.

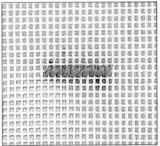

4 Pull the thread through to complete the second stitch. Continue working stitches along the row in the same manner.

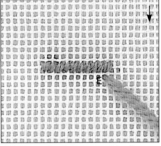

5 Turn the fabric upside down. Emerge at E.

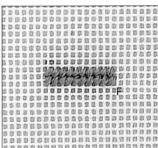

6 Take the thread to the back at F. Continue along the row in the same manner.

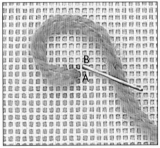

7 **Working vertically.** Bring the thread to the front at A. Take the needle to the back at B.

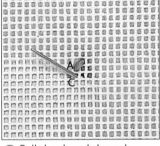

8 Pull the thread through. Re-emerge at C, directly below A.

9 Take the needle to the back at D, one hole to the right of A.

10 Pull the thread through to complete the second stitch. Continue working stitches downwards in the same manner.

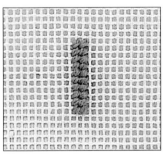

11 Work subsequent rows in the same manner, turning the fabric before beginning each one.

Tête de Boeuf Stitch (Bull's Head Stitch)

A filling stitch, tête de boeuf produces an attractive pattern and can be used on a variety of fabrics.
It can be worked with any type of thread, but the stitches stand out most effectively if a round thread such as perlé cotton is used.

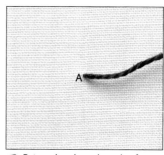

1 Bring the thread to the front at A.

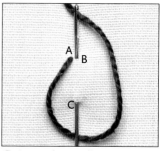

2 Insert the needle at B, as close as possible to A, and re-emerge at C. Loop the thread under the tip of the needle.

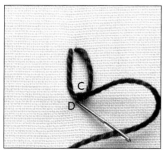

3 Pull the thread through to tighten the loop. Take the needle to the back at D, just below C, to anchor the loop.

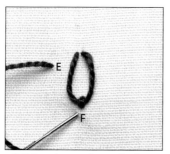

4 Bring the needle to the front at E. Pull the thread through. Take the needle to the back at F.

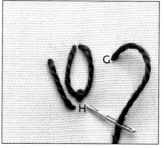

5 Pull the thread through. Re-emerge at G and take the needle to the back at H.

6 Pull the thread through. **Completed tête de boeuf stitch.**

Thread Painting– Peach

Thread painting or painting with thread, is a beautiful and challenging form of embroidery. Painting with thread allows you to incorporate the wonderful tactile qualities of embroidery with the art of image making.

To create natural looking objects 'painted' with thread, each row is worked with stitches of random length, unlike conventional long and short stitch.

See also long and short stitch, page 100 and soft shading, page 134.

1 The peach is worked in 5 shades, the leaves in 3 shades of green and the stem in 1 shade of light brown. Stitch the outlines in back stitch or split stitch.

2 **Peach.** Starting from an outlined edge, work long and short stitch in the darkest shade. Vary the length of the stitches and ensure that they just cover the outlines.

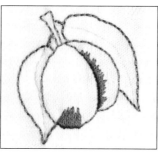

3 Graduating from the darker to the lighter shades, continue filling the shape in long and short stitch.

4 Complete the peach using the lightest shade for the highlights. **Leaves.** Using the palest green, work the centre vein in stem stitch.

5 Fill in the leaves with satin stitch, completing one side before stitching the next. The darkest green is used close to the peach.

6 **Stem.** Using the light brown thread and starting from the base, work the stem in satin stitch. **Completed peach.**

Trellis Couching

Trellis couching is also known as Jacobean couching and is a commonly used stitch in traditional crewel embroidery. It consists of a grid of long straight stitches which are couched in place with small crosses or straight stitches.

Traditional Jacobean crewel work

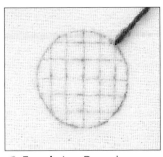

1 **Foundation.** Draw the outline of the shape and mark the grid lines. Bring the thread to the front where one grid line meets the outline.

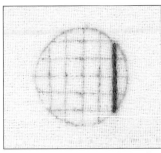

2 Take the thread to the back of the fabric at the opposite end of the grid line.

3 Re-emerge on the next line across. Pull the thread through.

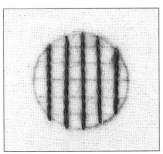

4 Take the thread to the back at the end of the grid line. Continue in the same manner until all the vertical grid lines are covered with stitches.

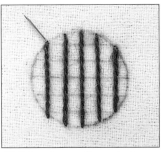

5 Bring the needle to the front on the left hand side of the outline where it meets one horizontal grid line.

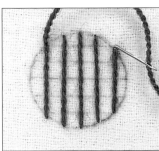

6 Pull the thread through. Take the needle over the previous straight stitches and to the back of the fabric at the opposite end of the grid line.

7 Continue working long straight stitches across the shape until all the grid lines are covered.

8 **Cross stitch couching.** Using a different thread, bring it to the front just below and to the left of one intersection of the foundation.

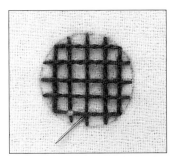

9 Take the needle to the back of the fabric just above and to the right of the intersection. Pull through. Re-emerge at the lower left of the next intersection.

10 Pull the thread through. Continue working stitches to the end of the row. Bring the needle to the front just below and to the right of the last intersection.

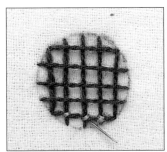

11 Pull the thread through. Take the thread to the back diagonally opposite, forming a cross. Re-emerge just below and to the right of the next intersection.

12 Continue to the end of the row. Work all other rows in the same manner. **Completed trellis couching.**

Twirled Ribbon Rose

The special effect of a twirled ribbon rose is achieved by twisting the ribbon tightly as the rose is formed. The result is a firmly wound, soft ribbon rose. We used 4mm (3/16") wide silk ribbon. Cut short lengths, no longer than 20cm (8") so the ribbon does not become worn. Prepare a needle threaded with matching sewing thread. In this illustration we used contrasting thread for photographic purposes only.

1 Bring the ribbon to the front at the position for the centre of the rose (A).

2 Hold the needle up so that the ribbon is vertical to the fabric. Begin to twist the needle in a counter-clockwise direction.

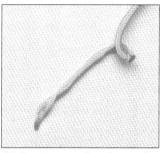

3 Continue twirling the needle until the ribbon is tightly twisted. Stop when the ribbon begins to buckle.

4 Using your thumb and forefinger, hold the coiled ribbon approx 3cm (1¼") from the fabric.

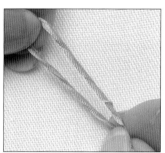

5 Keeping the ribbon taut, fold it over to form a loop.

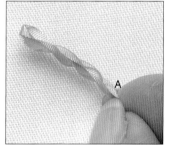

6 Hold the two parts of the ribbon close to A. Release the looped end. The ribbon will twist around itself forming a double coil.

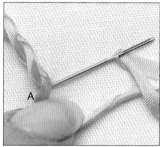

7 Still holding the double coil, take the needle to the back of the fabric just next to A.

8 Pull the ribbon through until reaching the doubled coil. Continue pulling gently until the rose is the desired size.

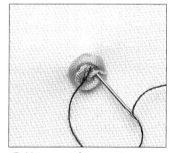

9 Using matching sewing thread, secure with two tiny stitches through the ribbon near the centre. Place stitches as invisibly as possible.

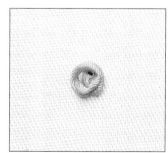

10 **Completed twirled ribbon rose.**

Twirled ribbon roses are part of this floral border

Vandyke Stitch

Vandyke stitch is an attractive filling stitch often used for leaf shapes. It can also be worked as a border.

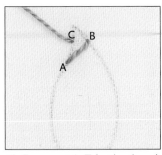

1 Emerge at A. Take the thread to the back at B and emerge at C.

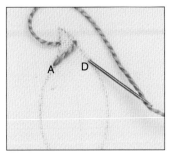

2 Take the needle to the back at D, aligned with A.

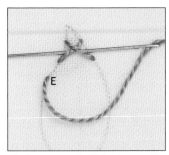

3 Emerge at E. Slide the needle under the crossed threads without piercing the fabric.

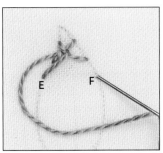

4 Pull the thread through. Take the needle to the back at F, aligned with E.

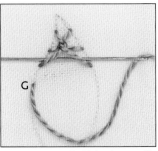

5 Emerge at G. Slide the needle under the crossed threads without piercing the fabric.

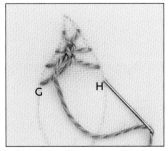

6 Pull the thread through. Take the needle to the back at H, aligned with G.

7 Continue the stitching sequence to the end of the shape, ending on the right-hand side.

Wheatear Stitch

This stitch is usually worked in straight lines and often in short segments. It is worked down a line towards you. The appearance of the stitch can be varied by altering the placement and length of the straight stitch 'ears'. Rule a vertical line on the fabric to help with stitch placement.

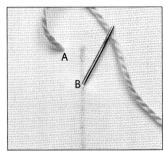

1 Bring the thread to the front at A to the left of the line. Take the needle to the back at B, on the line below and to the right of A.

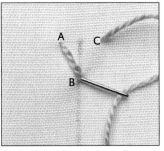

2 Pull the thread through. Re-emerge at C directly opposite A. Take the needle to the back at B.

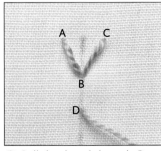

3 Pull the thread through. Re-emerge at D directly below B on the marked line.

4 Slide the needle from right to left behind the previous two stitches. Do not pierce the fabric.

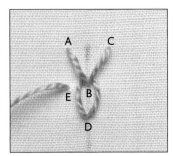

5 Take the needle to the back at D using the same hole in the fabric. Pull the thread through and re-emerge at E on the left hand side.

6 Continue working stitches down the line in the same manner. **Completed wheatear stitch.**

Wheatear Stitch – Detached

This is similar in appearance to wheatear stitch.

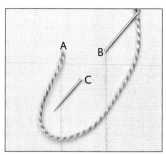

1 Mark two parallel lines down the fabric to keep stitches even. Bring the thread to the front at A. Take the needle from B to C, halfway between the lines.

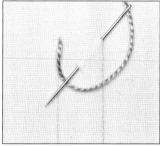

2 Loop the thread under the tip of the needle.

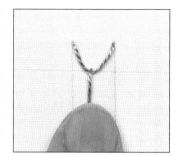

3 Pull the thread through in a downward movement. Hold the thread taut under your thumb.

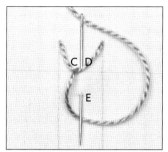

4 Take the needle to the back at D, very close to C. Re-emerge at E, directly below. Loop the thread under the needle tip.

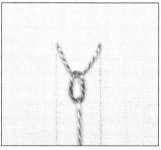

5 Pull the thread through in a downward movement until the loop rests snugly on the emerg-ing thread.

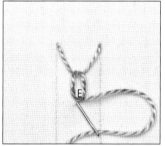

6 Take the needle to the back directly below E, just over the loop.

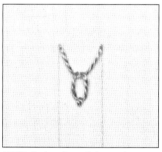

7 Pull the thread through. **Completed first detached wheatear stitch.**

8 Continue working stitches in the same manner, positioning them close together or further apart as required.

Whipping Stitch

Whipping is a combination stitch where a second thread is worked over a foundation line of another stitch. It can be worked over a multitude of stitches, but here it is worked over a couched thread.

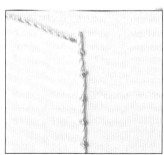

1 Work a line of couched thread to cover the design line. Secure a new thread on the back. Bring it to the front, just to the left of the foundation stitching.

2 Taking the needle from right to left, slide the eye under the second segment of laid thread. Do not pierce the fabric.

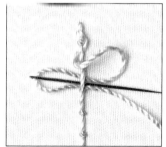

3 Pull the thread through gently. Slide the eye of the needle from right to left under the third segment.

4 Pull the thread through. Continue working in the same manner to the end of the line. **Completed whipping.**

Whipped Straight Stitch Rose

Keep the ribbon perfectly flat and smooth at all times. To achieve this, place the needle under the ribbon as it is being pulled through to smooth out any twists.

1 **Centre.** Using the darkest shade of ribbon, work three colonial knots close together.

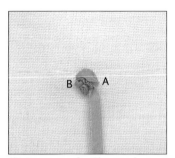

2 **Inner petals.** Change the ribbon. Work a straight stitch from A to B. Bring the ribbon to the front just below and to the left of A.

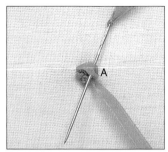

3 Take the needle over the straight stitch and then under it. The needle does not go through the fabric.

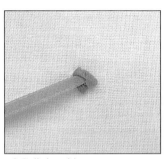

4 Pull the ribbon through.

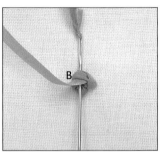

5 Again, take the needle under the straight stitch, positioning it near B.

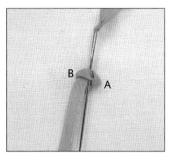

6 Pull through to form a second wrap. Take the needle under the straight stitch halfway between A and B.

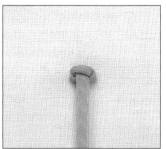

7 Pull the ribbon through. Work another wrap over the middle wrap in the same manner as before.

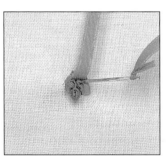

8 Take the ribbon to the back of the fabric inside the whipped stitch.

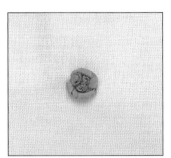

9 Pull the ribbon through. Work a second whipped straight stitch in the same manner, below the centre.

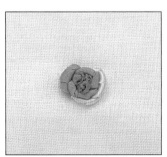

10 **Outer petals.** Changing ribbon as required, work three whipped straight stitches. Increase the number of wraps by two.

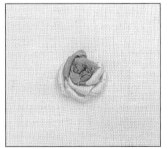

11 Work three more whipped straight stitches, increasing the number of wraps by two. **Completed whipped straight stitch rose.**

Whipped straight stitch rose incorporated into a design with rosebuds and forget-me-nots

Wool Rose

This quick and easy rose is created from a series of straight stitches. The size of the rose can be varied by changing the thickness of the yarn.

The arrow indicates the top of the fabric.

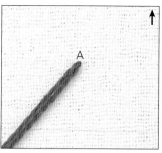

1 **Centre.** Bring the thread to the front at A.

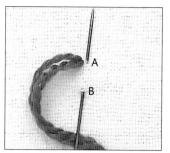

2 Take the needle to the back at B and re-emerge 1–2 fabric threads from A. The needle is slightly angled.

3 Pull the thread through. Take a second stitch the same length, angling the needle as shown.

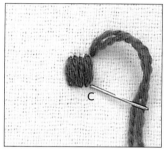

4 Pull the thread through. Work three more stitches in the same manner. Take the needle to the back at C to complete the last stitch, forming a square.

5 Bring the needle to the front at A, through the same hole in the fabric as the stitch in the first layer.

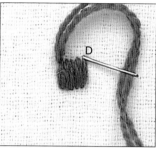

6 Pull the thread through. Take the needle to the back at D using the same hole in the fabric as the stitch in the first layer.

7 Pull the thread through. Bring the needle to the front just below A.

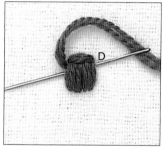

8 Pull the thread through. Take the needle to the back just below D and bring it to the front on the opposite side directly below the emerging thread.

9 Continue working stitches in the same manner until the first layer is completely covered. End off the thread on the back.

10 **First petal.** Using a lighter shade, bring the thread to the front at E.

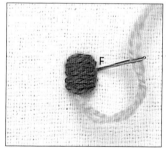

11 Take the needle to the back at F.

12 Pull the thread through. Re-emerge just to the right of E.

Wool Rose

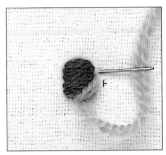

13 Take the needle to the back slightly higher and wider than F.

14 Pull the yarn through, positioning the stitch so it lies alongside the first stitch of the petal.

15 Bring the yarn to the front just to the right of where the previous stitch emerged.

16 Take the needle to the back slightly higher and wider than the previous stitch.

17 Pull the yarn through, positioning the stitch so it lies alongside the previous stitch.

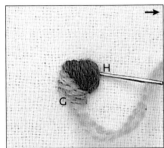

18 **Second petal.** Rotate the fabric a quarter turn. Bring the yarn to the front at G. Take the needle to the back at H.

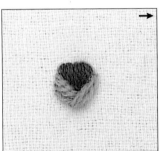

19 Pull the yarn through.

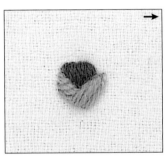

20 Following steps 12–17, work two more stitches to complete the petal.

21 **Third petal.** Rotate the fabric a quarter turn. Bring the yarn to the front at I and take the needle to the back at J.

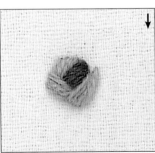

22 Pull the yarn through. Complete the petal following steps 12–17.

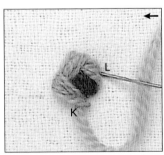

23 **Fourth petal.** Rotate the fabric a quarter turn. Bring the yarn to the front at K and take the needle to the back at L.

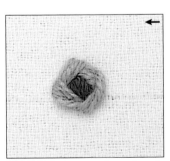

24 Pull the yarn through and complete the petal in the same manner as before. **Completed wool rose.**

Woven Filling Stitch

Also known as Queen Anne stitch, this is a darning stitch created from parallel straight stitches through which the thread is woven. The parallel vertical stitches covering the entire shape form the framework for the weaving.

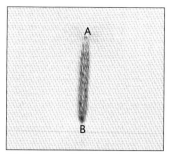

1 Framework. Bring the thread to the front at A. Take to the back at B to form a long straight stitch.

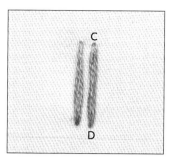

2 Re-emerge at C and take a second long straight stitch to D.

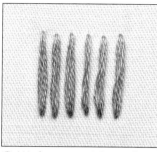

3 Work more straight stitches over the shape in the same manner to form the framework.

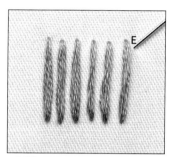

4 Weaving. Bring the needle to the front at E, just to the right of the last vertical stitch and very close to the top of it.

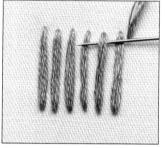

5 Weave the needle over the last vertical stitch and under the stitch next to it. You may find it easier to weave with the needle eye.

6 Continue weaving over and under the stitches.

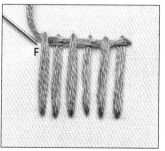

7 Take the needle to the back of the fabric at F, just to the left of the first vertical stitch and level with the line of weaving.

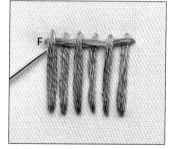

8 Pull the thread through. Bring the needle to the front just below F.

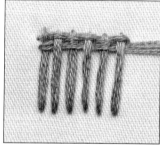

9 Pull the thread through. Weave to the other side – over, under, over, under, over, under.

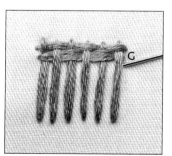

10 Take the needle to the back at G. Pull the thread through and re-emerge just below this point.

11 Continue weaving from side to side until the vertical stitches are completely covered. **Completed woven filling.**

Woven filling stitch is worked to form this flower basket

Zigzag Stitch

Zigzag stitch can be used as a counted thread or surface embroidery stitch. Pretty geometric patterns in zigzag are often used for outlines or borders.

Worked in multiple rows, it is effective for filling a shape. When used as a filling stitch, the vertical rows should touch. Ruling parallel lines will help to keep your stitches even when not working on evenweave fabric.

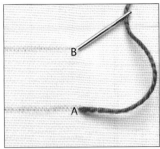

1 **First step.** Bring the thread to the front at A on the lower line. Take the needle to the back at B on the upper line directly above A.

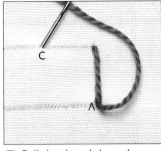

2 Pull the thread through to form a vertical straight stitch. Re-emerge at A, through the same hole. Take the needle to the back at C on the upper line.

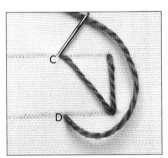

3 Pull the thread through to form a diagonal straight stitch. Re-emerge at D on the lower line directly below C. Insert the needle at C, through the same hole.

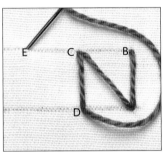

4 Pull the thread through. Re-emerge at D, through the same hole. Take the needle to the back at E on the upper line, same distance as B and C.

5 Pull the thread through. Bring the needle to the front at F directly below E. Work a straight stitch from F to E.

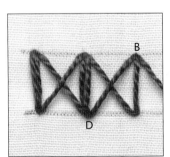

6 **Second step.** Re-emerge at F and insert the needle at E. This will form a second straight stitch between F and E.

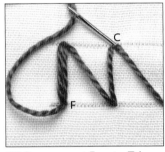

7 Re-emerge at F again. Take the needle to the back at C, through the same hole.

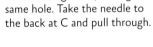

8 Pull the thread through. Re-emerge at D, through the same hole. Take the needle to the back at C and pull through.

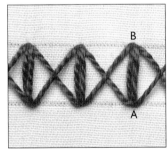

9 Re-emerge at D again. Take the needle to the back at B and pull through.

10 Re-emerge at A. Take the needle to the back at B to work a straight stitch from A to B. **Completed zigzag stitch.**

WOOL EMBROIDERY

Wool embroidery can be worked onto a large variety of fabrics. However, the weave of the fabric must be able to open up so the thread can easily pass through without wearing excessively.

Work with an even tension but one that is slightly looser than for other thread embroidery.

Ensure the fabric you are stitching on has similar care requirements as the thread you are stitching with.

To avoid the thread becoming worn, use short lengths no more than 40cm (16") long.

If the ply of the thread unravels, gently twist the thread with your fingers to re-ply it. If the thread appears to be over twisted, let the needle hang free for a few seconds and allow the thread to settle back to its twist.

Use a needle which will make a large enough hole in the fabric for the thread to pass through easily. This will help reduce wear on the thread. Tapestry and chenille needles are the most suitable.

Index

Algerian eye stitch, 10

Alternating chain stitch, 39

Antique hem stitch, 91

Arrowhead stitch, 11

Attaching beads, 11
Attaching with a second bead, 11
Individually sewn bead, 11

Back stitch, 12

Beaded stitch, see Coral stitch, 49

Beading
Back stitch, 12
Couching, 50
Edge, 13
Forget-me-not, 13
Hints, 13

Beads over cord, 11

Blanket stitch, 14
Detached filling, 15
Detached bar, 16
Detached twisted bar, 17
Double, 18
Joining a new thread, 14
Knotted, 19
Looped, 20
Pinwheel, 21
Long and short, 22
Scallops, 22

Blind knot, see Chinese knot, 46

Blind stitch, see Pekinese stitch, 111

Bokhara couching, 51

Braid stitch, 23

Brick stitch,
see Long and short stitch, 100

Bullions, 24
Bears, 29
Bullion knot, 25
Detached chain combination, 34
Hints, 24, 28, 32
Long, 26
Long couched, 26
Loop, 27
Rose, 30
Rose with satin stitch centre, 32
Rosebuds, 33
Starting, 24
Tapered, 28

Buttonhole stitch, 35

Candlewicking knot,
see Colonial knot, 47

Canvas work, *Hints* 56, 57, 58

Cast-on stitch rose, 36
Double sided, 38
Hints, 37

Catch stitch,
see Herringbone stitch, 93

Caterpillar stitch,
see Bullion knot, 25

Chain stitch, 39
Alternating, 39
Heavy, 40
Interlaced, 41
Open, 42
Rose, 43
Rosette, 44
Twisted, 45

Chequered chain,
see Alternating chain stitch, 39

Chinese knot, 46

Chinese stitch,
see Pekinese stitch, 111

Circular Rhodes stitch, 117

Cleaning embroidery, 103, 142, 154

Closed base needlewoven picot, 105

Closed feather stitch, 71

Clothing, embroidery on, 66, 120

Coil stitch, see Bullion knot, 25

Colonial knot, 47

Concertina rose, 48

Continental stitch, see Tent stitch, 145

Coral stitch, 49

Cordonnet stitch,
see Whipped running stitch, 122

Couched bullion knot, 26

Couching, 50
Beads, 50
Bokhara, 51
Puffy, 53
Ribbon, 52
Ribbon bow, 53
Roumanian, 54

Cretan stitch, 55

Crewel embroidery, 55

Crewel stitch, see Stem stitch, 138

Cross stitch, 56
Double, 57
Long-armed, 58
Straight stitch combination, 58

Crow's foot, 59

Cutwork, 60

Daisy stitch, see Detached chain, 63

Damask stitch, see Satin stitch, 124

Danish knot, 61

Detached back stitch, 62

Detached blanket stitch bar, 16

Detached blanket stitch filling, 15

Detached twisted blanket stitch bar, 17

Detached chain, 63
Flowers, 63
French knot combination flower, 64
Hints, 62
Twisted, 65

Detached herringbone stitch, 94

Diagonal gobelin stitch,
see Gobelin stitch, 86

Diagonal line stitch,
see Single faggoting, 70

Diagonal square stitch,
see Single faggoting, 70

Double blanket stitch, 18

Double cross stitch, 57

Double feather stitch, 71

Double herringbone stitch, 93

Double knot stitch,
see Palestrina stitch, 110

Double running stitch,
see Holbein stitch, 95

Double sided cast-on stitch, 38

Double whipped running stitch, 123

Drizzle stitch, 65

Embroidery on clothing, 66, 120

Embroidery stitch,
see Long and short stitch, 100

Encroaching stem stitch, 138

Ermine filling stitch, 67

Eyelet, 67
Flowers, 68
Shaped, 69

Faggot filling stitch,
see Sheaf filling stitch, 132

Faggotting, 69
Single, 70

Feather stitch, 71
Closed, 71
Double and triple, 71

Featherwork,
see Long and short stitch, 100

Fishbone stitch, 73
  Raised, 74
Fly stitch, 75
  Leaf, 76
  Twisted, 75
Folded ribbon rose, 77
Folded ribbon rosebud, 78
Folded ribbon stitch, 118
Forbidden knot,
  see Chinese knot, 46
Forbidden stitch,
  see Pekinese stitch, 111
Four-legged knot stitch, 79
Four sided open work stitch,
  see Four sided stitch, 79
Four sided stitch, 79
French knot, 80
  Colonial knot berry, 80
  Ribbon flower, 81

Gathered ribbon blossom, 82
Gathered ribbon rose, 83
German knot stitch,
  see Coral stitch, 49
Ghiordes knot, 84
  Hints, 84
Glove stitch, 85
Gobelin stitch, 86
  Straight, 87
Grab stitch, 85
Granitos, 88
  Blossom, 88
  Bud, 89
Gros point, see Gobelin stitch, 86
Grub stitch, see Bullion knot, 25

Hardanger embroidery, 96
Heavy chain stitch, 40
Hem stitch - *Antique,* 91
  Serpentine, 92
Herringbone stitch, 93
  Detached, 94
  Double, 93
  Shadow work, 94
Holbein stitch, 95
  Hint 95
Hoops, *Hint* 45

Indian herringbone stitch,
  see Herringbone stitch, 93

Interlaced chain stitch, 41
Irish stitch,
  see Long and short stitch, 100
Isolated back stitch, see Seed stitch, 128
Italian quilting,
  see Shadow trapunto, 130

Jacobean couching,
  see Trellis couching, 148

Kensington outline stitch,
  see Split stitch, 137
Kloster blocks, 96
  Cutting away fabric threads, 96
Knot stitch, see Bullion knot, 25
Knotted blanket stitch, 19
Knotted knot stitch,
  see Detached chain, 63
Knotted stitch, see Coral stitch, 49

Lacing embroidery, 97
Laid work, 98
Lattice couching, 99
Lazy daisy stitch,
  see Detached chain, 63
Lazy stitch, 101
Leaf stitch,
  see Long and short stitch, 100
Leviathan stitch,
  see Double cross stitch, 57
Link powdering stitch,
  see Detached chain, 63
Long-armed cross stitch, 58
Long-armed feather stitch,
  see Cretan stitch, 55
Long-legged cross stitch,
  see Long-armed cross stitch, 58
Long and short stitch, 100
Long bullion knot, 26
Loop stitch, 101
  Bow, 101
  Flower 1, 102
  Flower 2, 102
  Hint, 101
Looped blanket stitch, 20
Looped ribbon stitch, 118
Looped stitch, see Detached chain, 63
Long and short blanket stitch, 22

Magic chain,
  see Alternating chain stitch, 39
Moss stitch, 103

Needlelace - Woven bar, 104
Needlepoint, 87
Needlepoint stitch, see Tent stitch, 145
Needleweaving bar, 104
  Closed base picot, 105
  Heartsease, 107
  Open base picot, 106
Net stitch 108

Oblique gobelin stitch,
  see Gobelin stitch, 86
Old English knot,
  see Palestrina stitch, 110
Open base picot, 106
Opus Plumarium,
  see Long and short stitch, 100
Outline stitch, 109
Overcast stitch,
  see Straight overcast stitch, 143
Overlapping herringbone stitch,
  see Raised fishbone stitch, 74
Overlapping sequins, 109
Oyster stitch, 109

Padded raised stem stitch, 141
Padded satin stitch, 126
Palestrina stitch, 110
Pekinese stitch, 111
Peking knot, see Chinese knot, 46
Perlé cotton, *Hint,* 23
Petit point, see Tent stitch 145
Picot, *closed base* 105
  Heartsease 107
  Hint 105
  Open base, 106
Picot stitch,
  see Detached chain, 63
Pin stitch, 112
Pistil stitch, 113
Plaited Slav stitch,
  see Long-armed cross stitch, 58
Plaited stitch,
  see Herringbone stitch, 93
Plaiting, 113

Plumage stitch,
    see Long and short stitch, 100
Point de Paris, see Pin stitch, 112
Pompom, 114
Porto Rico rose, see Bullion knot, 25
Portuguese knot stem stitch, 139
Portuguese stitch,
    see Long-armed cross stitch, 58
Post stitch, see Bullion knot, 25
Pressing embroidery, 103
Puffy couching, 53

Queen Anne stitch,
    see Woven filling stitch, 155

Raised cup stitch, 115
Raised fishbone stitch, 74
Raised stem stitch, 140
Rayon embroidery threads, 38
Rhodes stitch, 116
    Circular, 117
Ribbon, *Hints,*
    48, 117, 118, 119, 149
Ribbon stitch 117
    Folded 118
    Looped 118
    Side 119
Roll stitch, see Bullion knot, 25
Rolled ribbon rose, 119
Roman chain, see Open chain stitch, 42
Roman stitch, see Roumanian stitch, 121
Rope stitch, 120
Rosette chain stitch, 44
Rosette stitch, 121
Roumanian couching, 54
Roumanian stitch, 121
Running stitch, 122
    Colonial knot
    combination rose, 123
    Double whipped, 123
    Whipped, 122

Satin stitch, 124
    Bow, 125
    Hints, 124
    Leaf, 126
    Padded, 126
    Padded spot, 127

Scottish stitch, 127
Scroll stitch, 128
Seed stitch, 128
Serpentine hem stitch, 92
Shading stitch,
    see Long and short stitch, 100
Shadow work,
    Closed herringbone stitch, 130
    Double back stitch, 129
    Hints, 131
Shadow trapunto, 130
Sheaf filling stitch, 132
Shisha stitch, 132
Side ribbon stitch, 119
Single faggoting, 70
Single knotted line stitch,
    see Scroll stitch, 128
Single knot tufting,
    see Ghiordes knot, 84
Smocker's knot, 134
Smyrna cross stitch,
    see Double cross stitch, 57
Snail trail, see Coral stitch, 49
Soft shading, 134
South Kensington stitch,
    see Stem stitch, 138
Speckling stitch, see Seed stitch, 128
Spider web rose, 135
Spider's web stitch,
    see Detached back stitch, 62
Split back stitch, 136
Split stitch, 137
Square chain, see Open chain stitch, 42
Square open work stitch,
    see Four sided stitch, 79
Star eyelet,
    see Algerian eye stitch, 10
Star stitch, 137
Stem stitch, 138
    Encroaching, 138
    Padded raised, 141
    Portuguese knotted, 139
    Raised, 140
    Ribbon rose, 142
    Whipped, 141
Straight overcast stitch, 143
Straight stitch, 144
    Flower, 144
Stroke stitch, see Straight stitch, 144

Tail stitch, see Detached chain, 63
Tapered bullion knot, 28
Tapestry shading stitch,
    see Long and short stitch, 100
Tassel, 145
Tent stitch - *Basket weave* 145
    Continental, 146
    Hints, 146
Tête de Boeuf stitch, 147
Threading needles,
    Hints, 64, 65
Thread painting, 147
    see Soft shading, 134
    see Long and short stitch, 100
    Hints, 135
Tied coral stitch,
    see Palestrina stitch, 110
Tied loop stitch,
    see Detached chain, 63
Trellis couching, 148
Triple feather stitch, 72
Turkey work, see Ghiordes knot, 84
Twirled ribbon rose, 149
Twist stitch,
    see Long-armed cross stitch, 58
Twisted chain stitch, 45
Twisted fly stitch, 75
Twisted insertion stitch,
    see Faggoting, 69

Vandyke stitch, 150

Wheatear stitch, 150
    Detached, 151
Whipped running stitch, 122
Whipped stem stitch, 141
Whipped straight stitch rose, 152
Whipping stitch, 151
Wool rose, 153
Worm stitch, see Bullion knot, 25
Woven filling stitch, 155

Zigzag stitch, 156